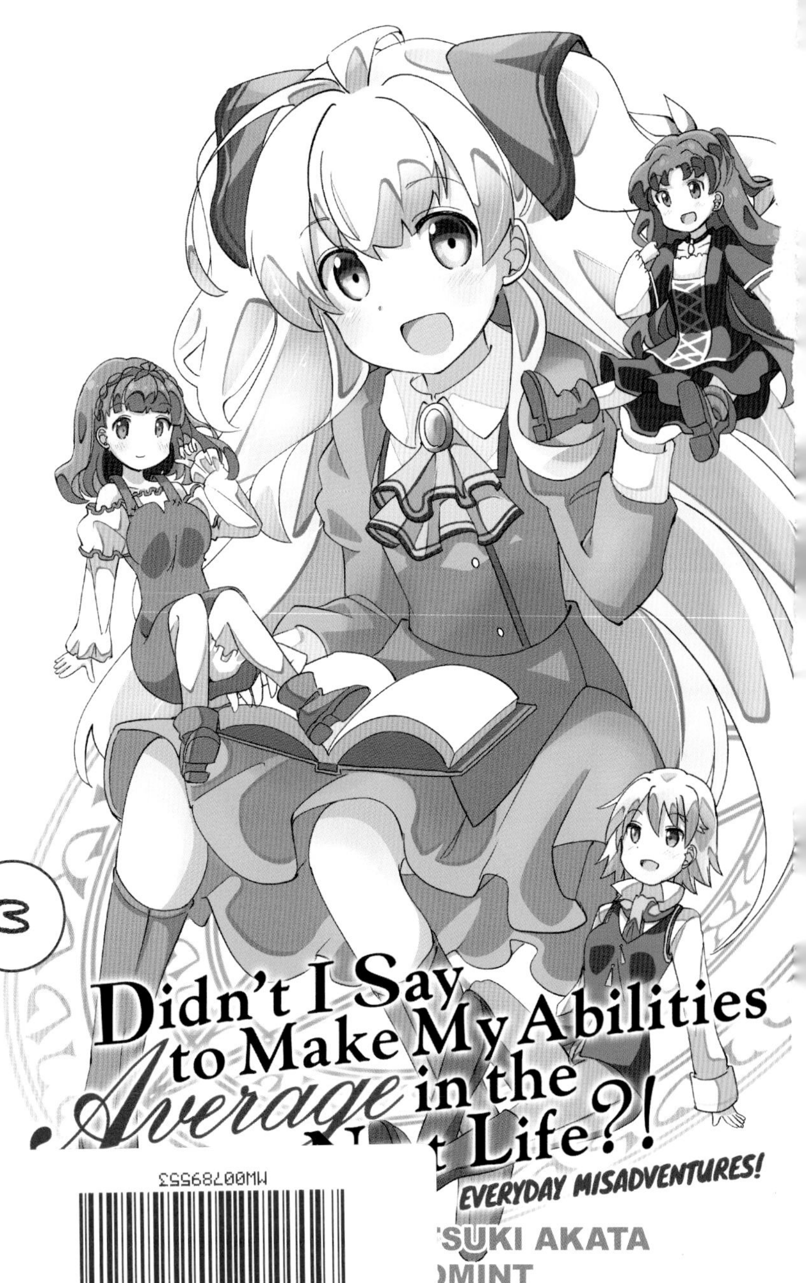
3
Didn't I Say to Make My Abilities Average in the
t Life?!
EVERYDAY MISADVENTURES!
SUKI AKATA
MINT

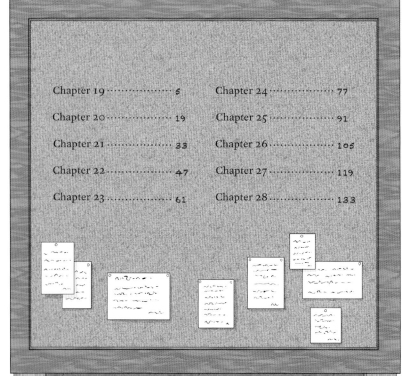

Contents

Characters

MILE (ADELE)

THE MAIN CHARACTER. SHE WISHED TO BE REBORN WITH AVERAGE ABILITIES, BUT INSTEAD WAS GIFTED WITH EXTRAORDINARY ONES. OBSESSED WITH LITTLE BEASTGIRLS.

REINA

A COMBAT MAGIC SPECIALIST KNOWN AS "CRIMSON REINA." FORCEFUL IN PERSONALITY, BUT ALWAYS LOOKS AFTER MILE.

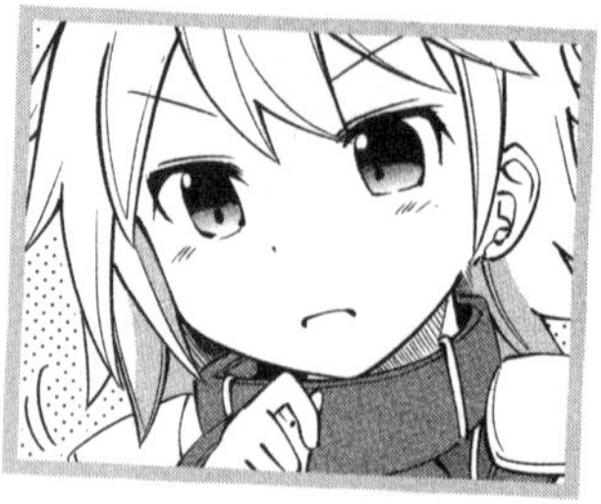

MAVIS

BORN FROM A LONG LINE OF KNIGHTS, HER FAMILY DISAPPROVED WHEN SHE WANTED TO BE A KNIGHT HERSELF, SO SHE RAN AWAY FROM HOME. OSTENSIBLY THE LEADER OF THE CRIMSON VOW.

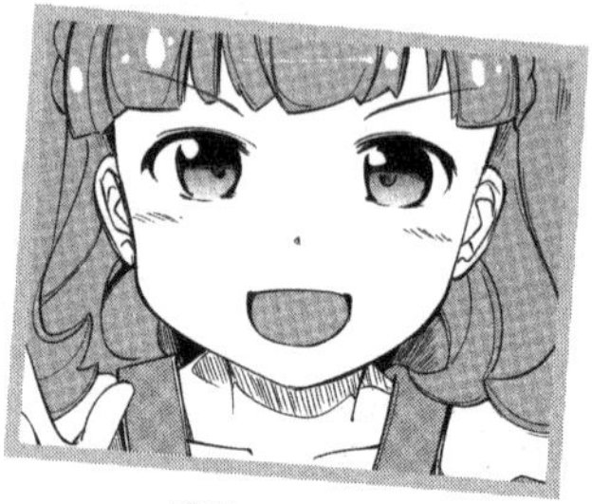

PAULINE

A SPECIALIST IN HEALING MAGIC. ALWAYS SOOTHES THE OTHERS WITH HER CALMING NATURE, BUT AT TIMES CAN BE QUITE TERRIFYING!!

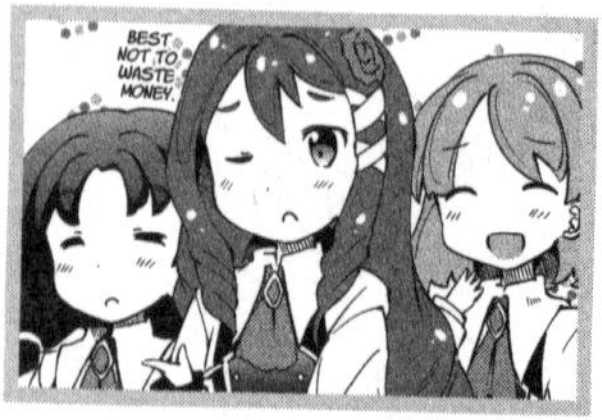
BEST NOT TO WASTE MONEY.

MARCELLA (CENTER), MONIKA (RIGHT), AUREANA (LEFT)

MILE'S FRIENDS AND CLASSMATES FROM HER TIME AT ECKLAND ACADEMY (WHEN SHE WAS CALLED ADELE). MARCELLA IS A LOWER-RANKING NOBLE, WHILE THE OTHER TWO ARE COMMONERS.

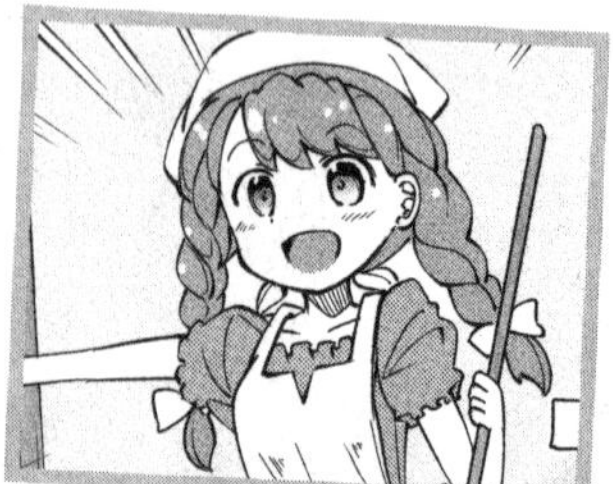

LENNY

INNKEEPERS' DAUGHTER AT THE INN WHERE THE CRIMSON VOW ARE REGULARS. YOUNG, BUT TAKES GREAT PRIDE IN THE INN'S BUSINESS AFFAIRS.

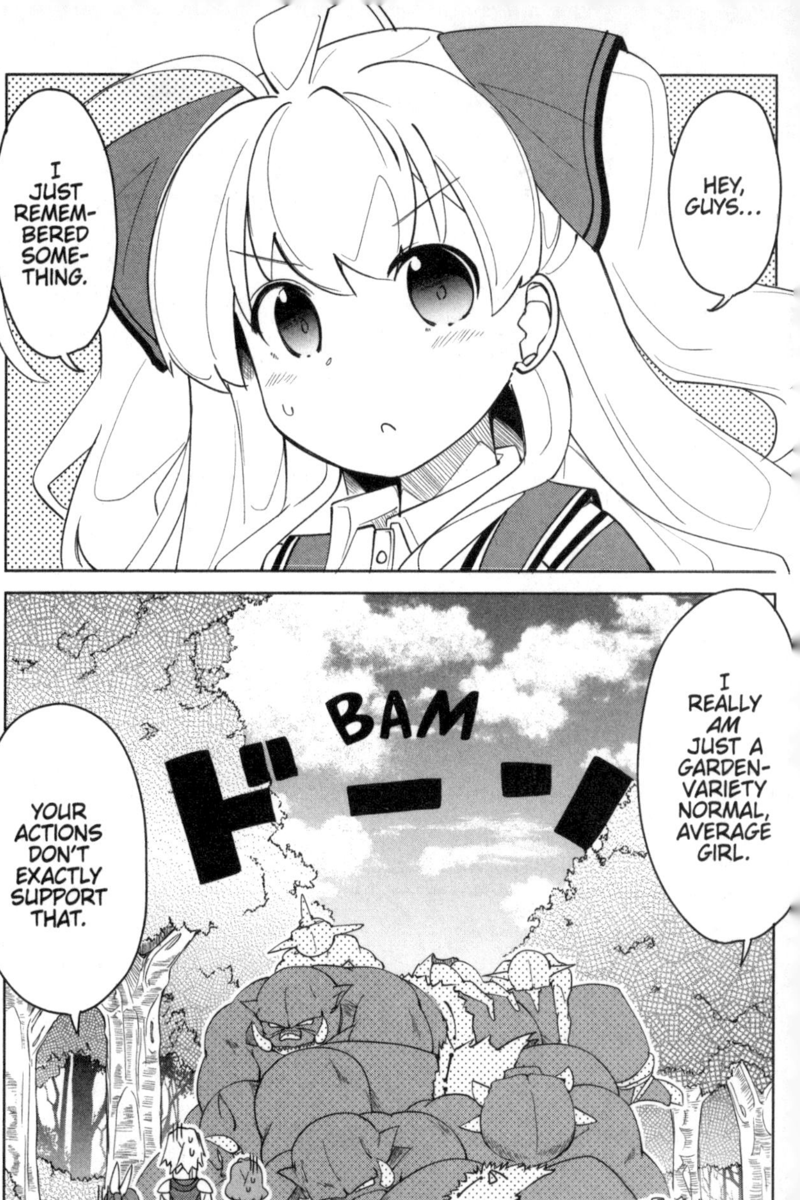
HEY, GUYS…
I JUST REMEMBERED SOMETHING.
I REALLY *AM* JUST A GARDEN-VARIETY NORMAL, AVERAGE GIRL.
BAM
ドーン
YOUR ACTIONS DON'T EXACTLY SUPPORT THAT.

Chapter 19

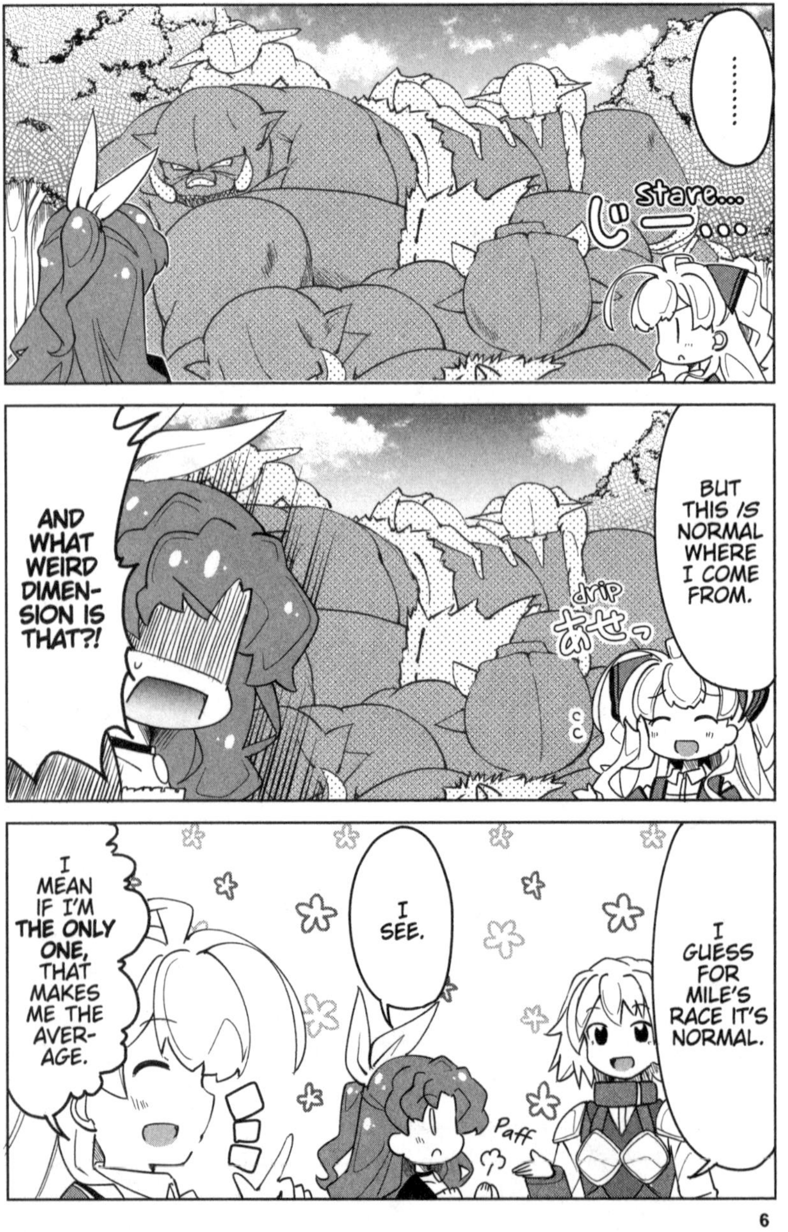
....
stare...
じー...
BUT THIS *IS* NORMAL WHERE I COME FROM.
drip
あせっ
AND WHAT WEIRD DIMENSION IS THAT?!
I GUESS FOR MILE'S RACE IT'S NORMAL.
I SEE.
Paff
I MEAN IF I'M THE ONLY ONE, THAT MAKES ME THE AVERAGE.

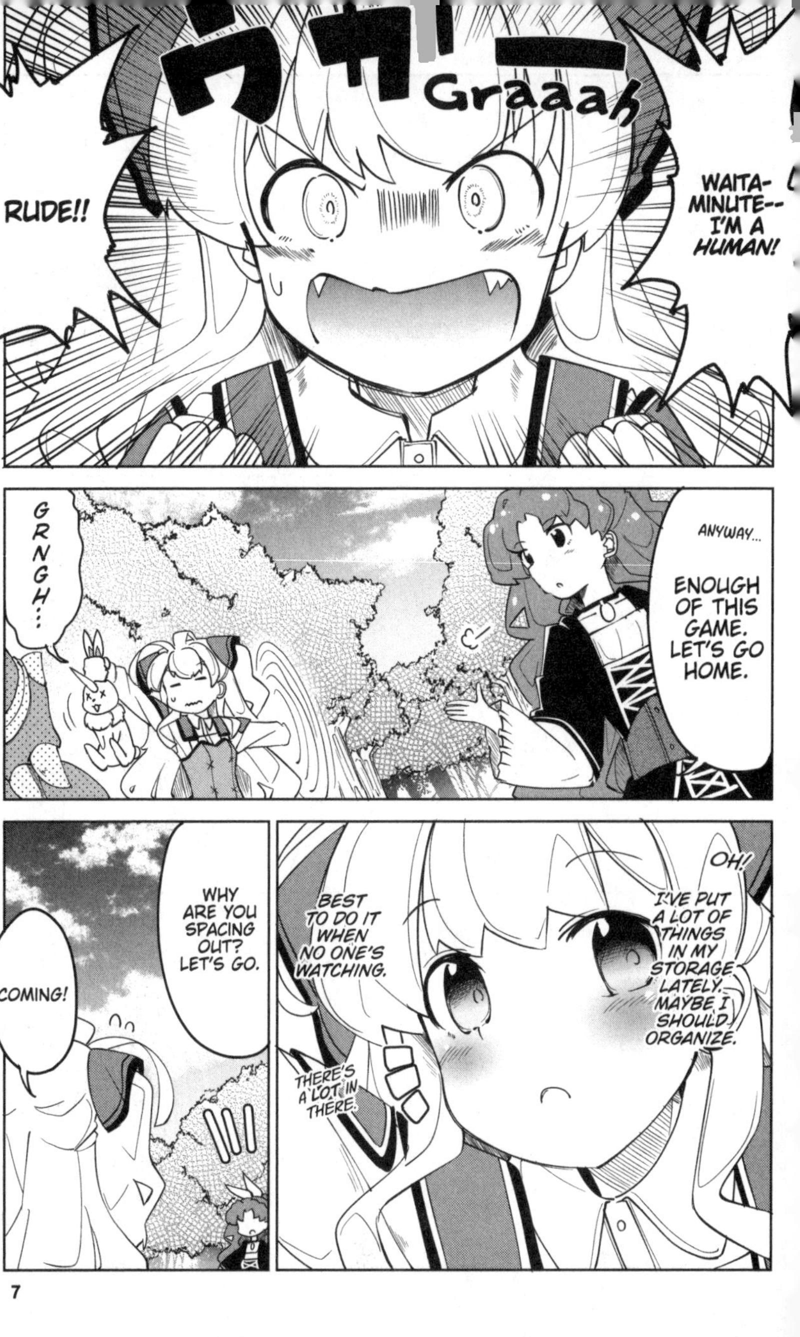
ウガー
Graaah
WAITA-MINUTE-- I'M A HUMAN!
RUDE!!
ANYWAY...
ENOUGH OF THIS GAME. LET'S GO HOME.
GRNGH...
OH!
I'VE PUT A LOT OF THINGS IN MY STORAGE LATELY. MAYBE I SHOULD ORGANIZE.
BEST TO DO IT WHEN NO ONE'S WATCHING.
THERE'S A LOT IN THERE.
WHY ARE YOU SPACING OUT? LET'S GO.
COMING!

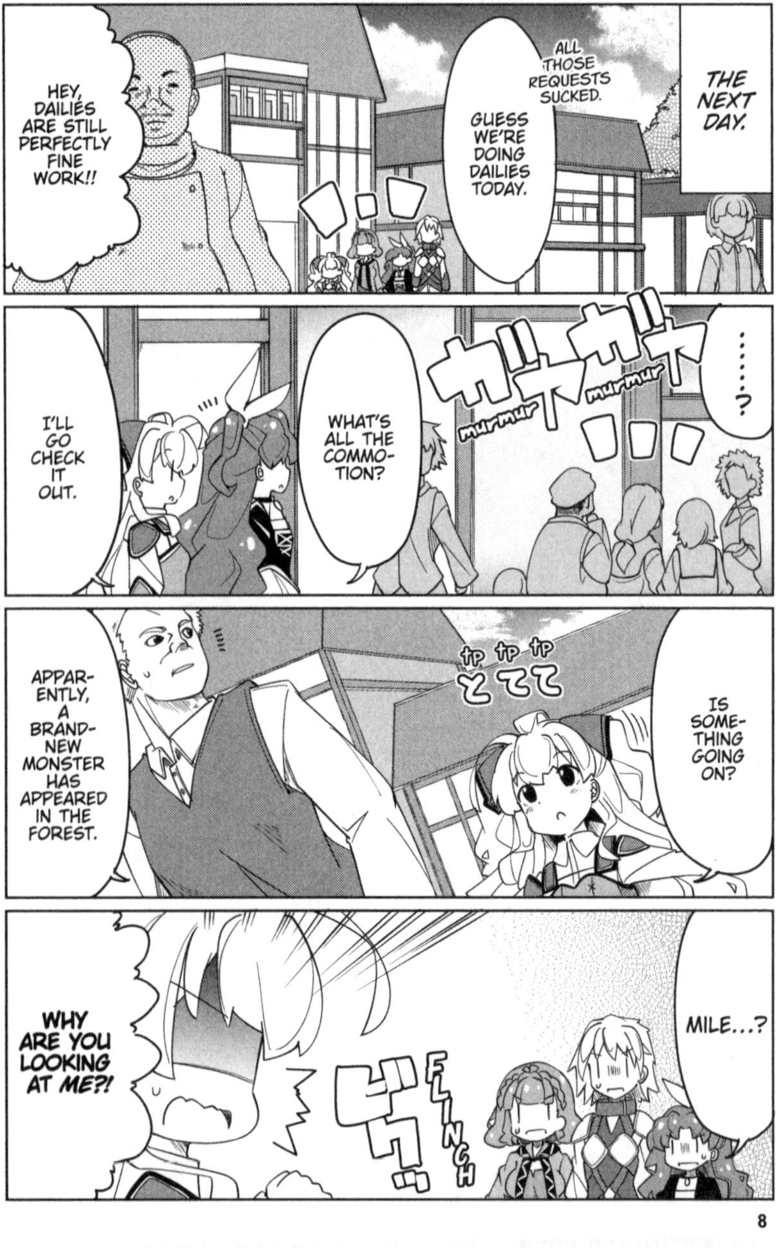
THE NEXT DAY.
ALL THOSE REQUESTS SUCKED.
GUESS WE'RE DOING DAILIES TODAY.
HEY, DAILIES ARE STILL PERFECTLY FINE WORK!!
......?
ガヤガヤ
murmur murmur
WHAT'S ALL THE COMMO-TION?
I'LL GO CHECK IT OUT.
IS SOMETHING GOING ON?
とてて
tp tp tp
APPAR-ENTLY, A BRAND-NEW MONSTER HAS APPEARED IN THE FOREST.
MILE...?
ビクッ
FLINCH
WHY ARE YOU LOOKING AT ME?!

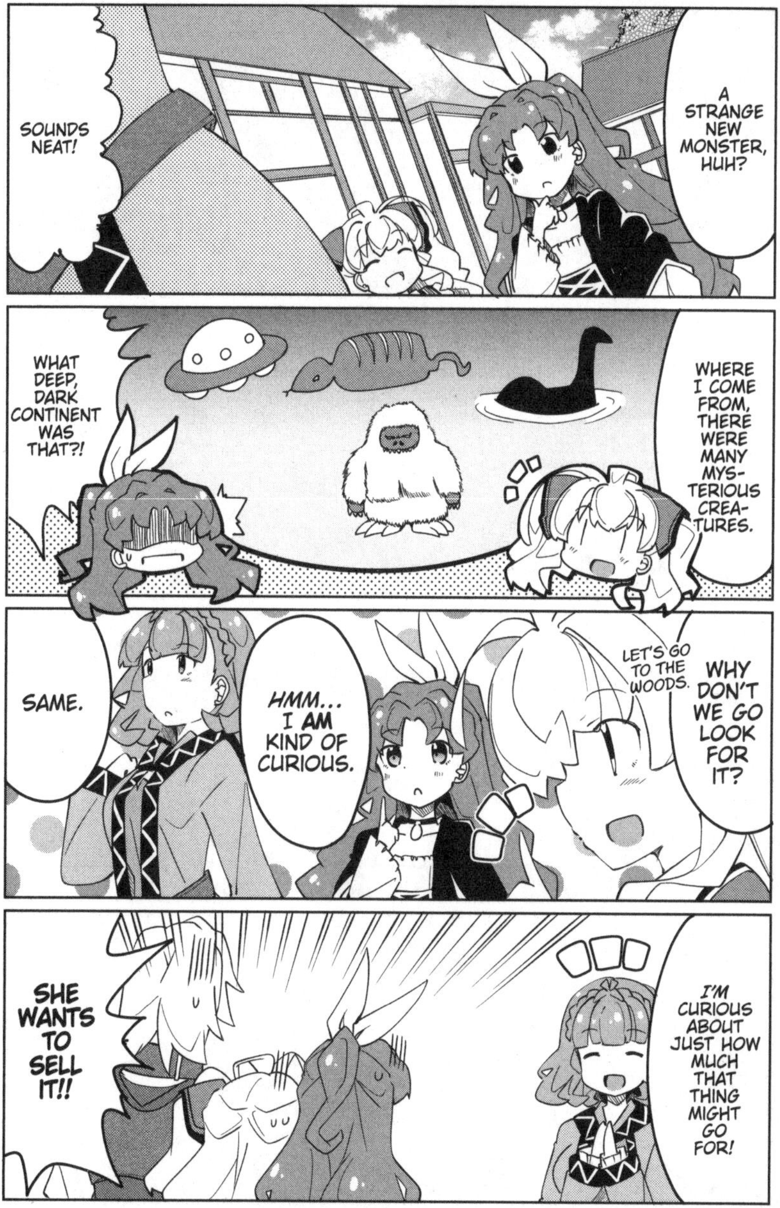
A STRANGE NEW MONSTER, HUH?
SOUNDS NEAT!
WHERE I COME FROM, THERE WERE MANY MYS-TERIOUS CREA-TURES.
WHAT DEEP, DARK CONTINENT WAS THAT?!
WHY DON'T WE GO LOOK FOR IT?
LET'S GO TO THE WOODS.
HMM... I AM KIND OF CURIOUS.
SAME.
I'M CURIOUS ABOUT JUST HOW MUCH THAT THING MIGHT GO FOR!
SHE WANTS TO SELL IT!!

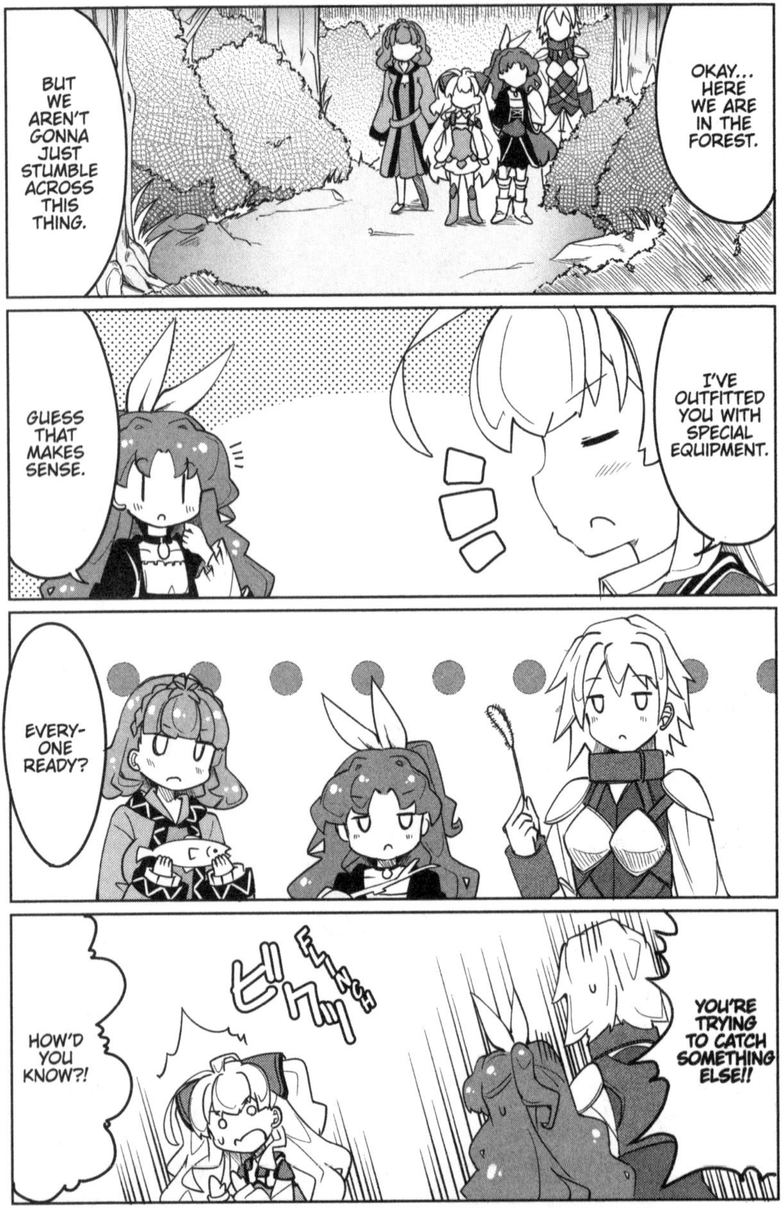

OKAY... HERE WE ARE IN THE FOREST.
BUT WE AREN'T GONNA JUST STUMBLE ACROSS THIS THING.
I'VE OUTFITTED YOU WITH SPECIAL EQUIPMENT.
GUESS THAT MAKES SENSE.
EVERY-ONE READY?
YOU'RE TRYING TO CATCH SOMETHING ELSE!!
ビクッ
FLINCH
HOW'D YOU KNOW?!

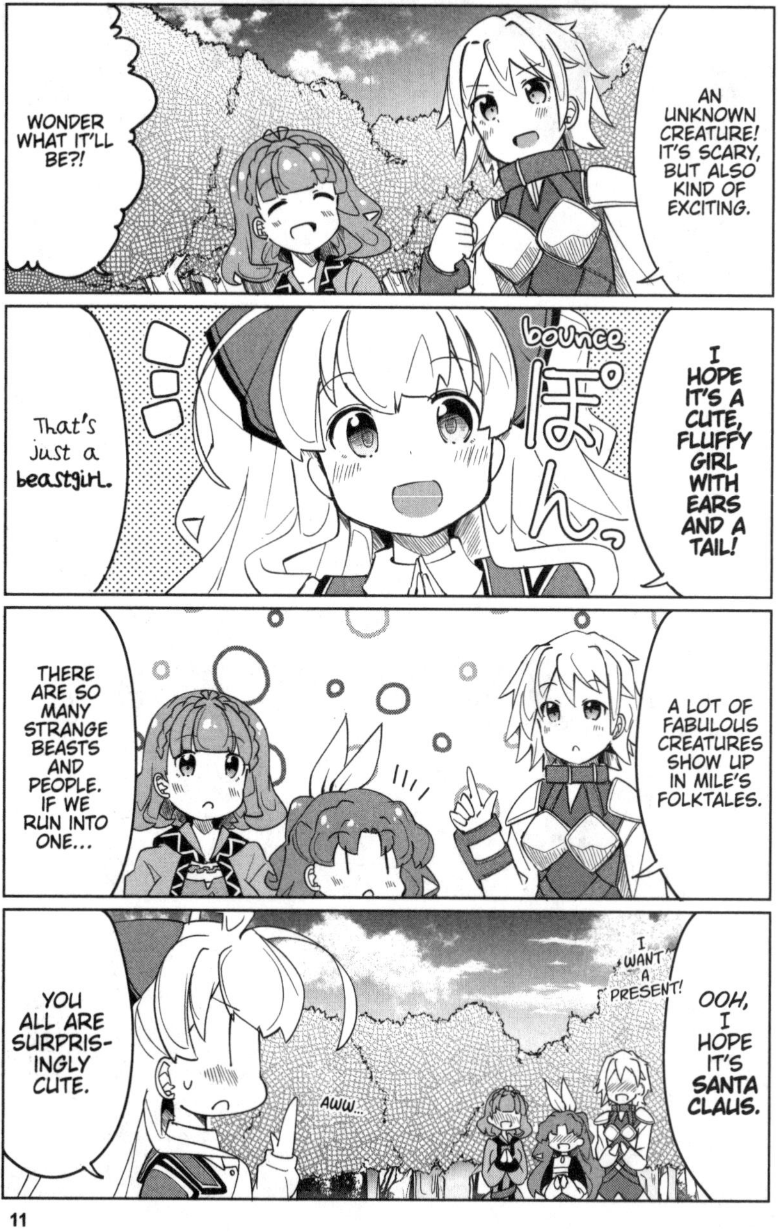
AN UNKNOWN CREATURE! IT'S SCARY, BUT ALSO KIND OF EXCITING.
WONDER WHAT IT'LL BE?!
I HOPE IT'S A CUTE, FLUFFY GIRL WITH EARS AND A TAIL!
bounce
ぽんっ
That's just a beastgirl.
A LOT OF FABULOUS CREATURES SHOW UP IN MILE'S FOLKTALES.
THERE ARE SO MANY STRANGE BEASTS AND PEOPLE. IF WE RUN INTO ONE...
OOH, I HOPE IT'S SANTA CLAUS.
I WANT A PRESENT!
AWW...
YOU ALL ARE SURPRISINGLY CUTE.

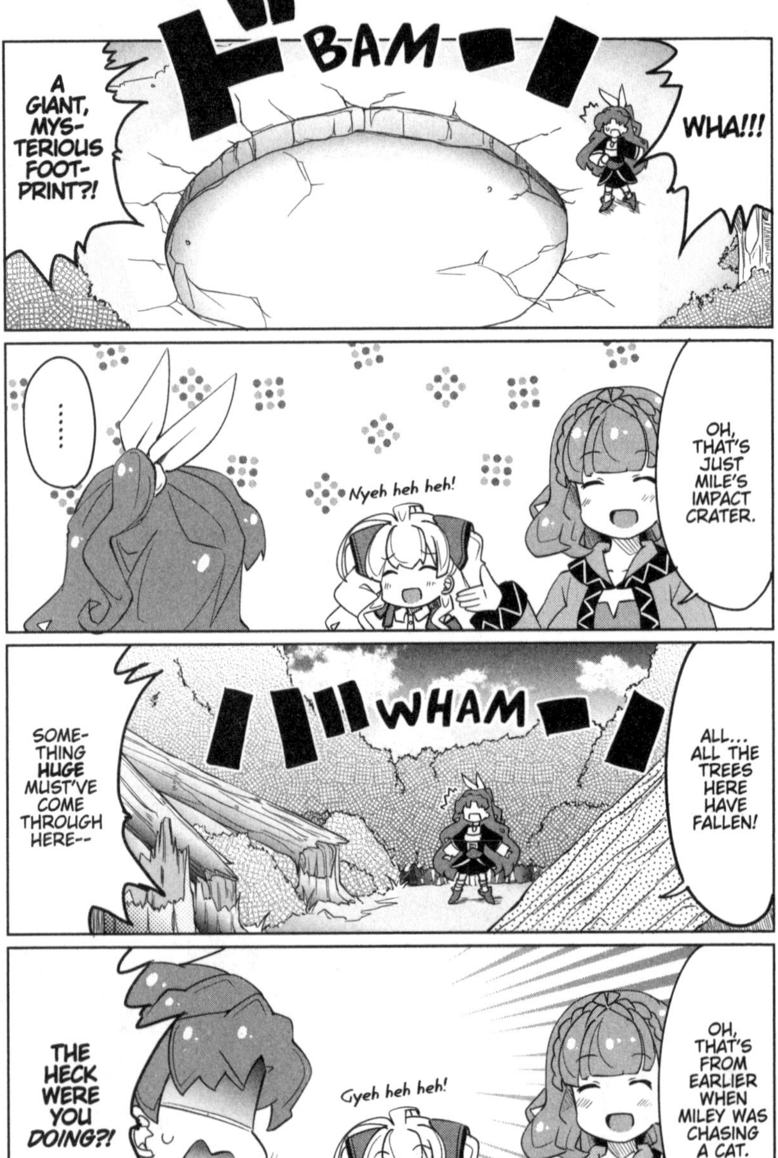
ドBAM
WHA!!!
A GIANT, MYS-TERIOUS FOOT-PRINT?!
OH, THAT'S JUST MILE'S IMPACT CRATER.
Nyeh heh heh!
......
WHAM
ALL... ALL THE TREES HERE HAVE FALLEN!
SOME-THING HUGE MUST'VE COME THROUGH HERE--
OH, THAT'S FROM EARLIER WHEN MILEY WAS CHASING A CAT.
Gyeh heh heh!
THE HECK WERE YOU DOING?!

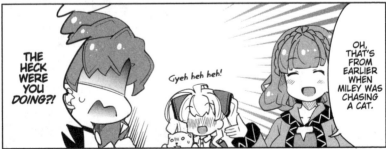

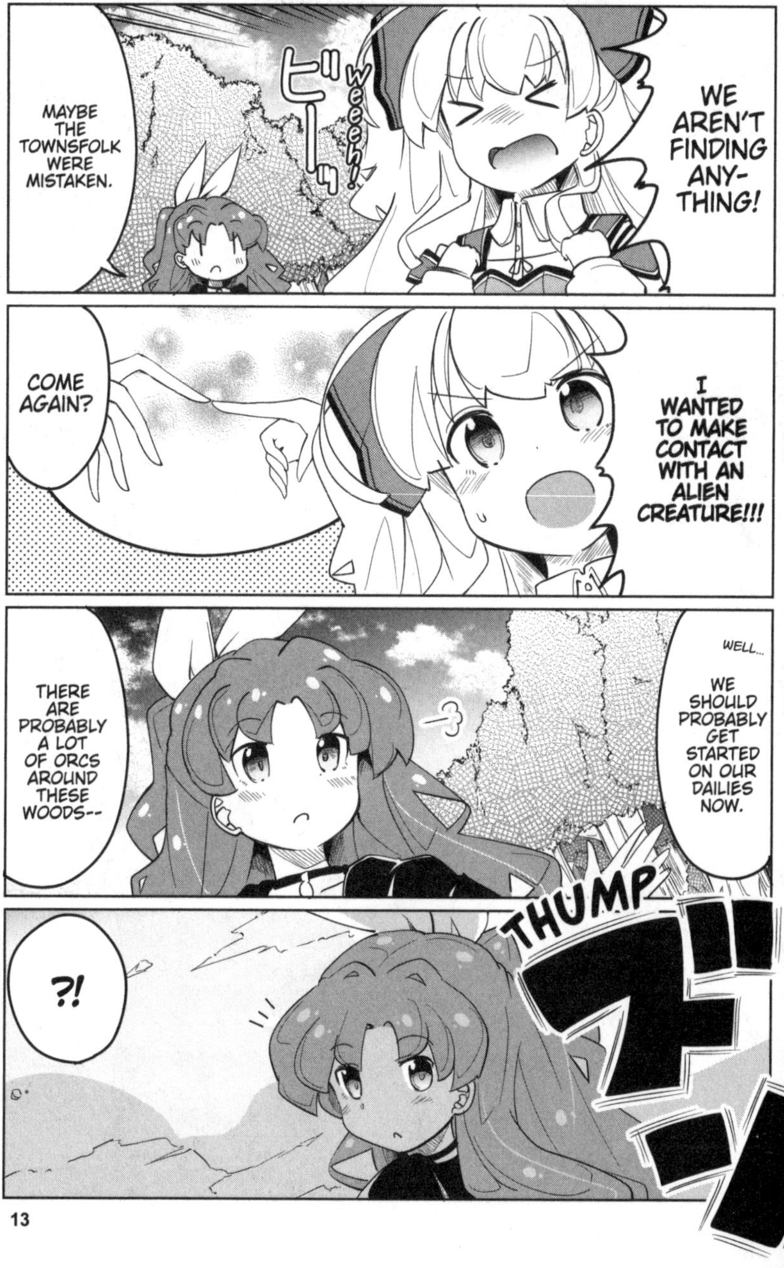
WE AREN'T FINDING ANY-THING!
Weeeh!
MAYBE THE TOWNSFOLK WERE MISTAKEN.
I WANTED TO MAKE CONTACT WITH AN ALIEN CREATURE!!!
COME AGAIN?
WELL...
WE SHOULD PROBABLY GET STARTED ON OUR DAILIES NOW.
THERE ARE PROBABLY A LOT OF ORCS AROUND THESE WOODS--
THUMP
?!

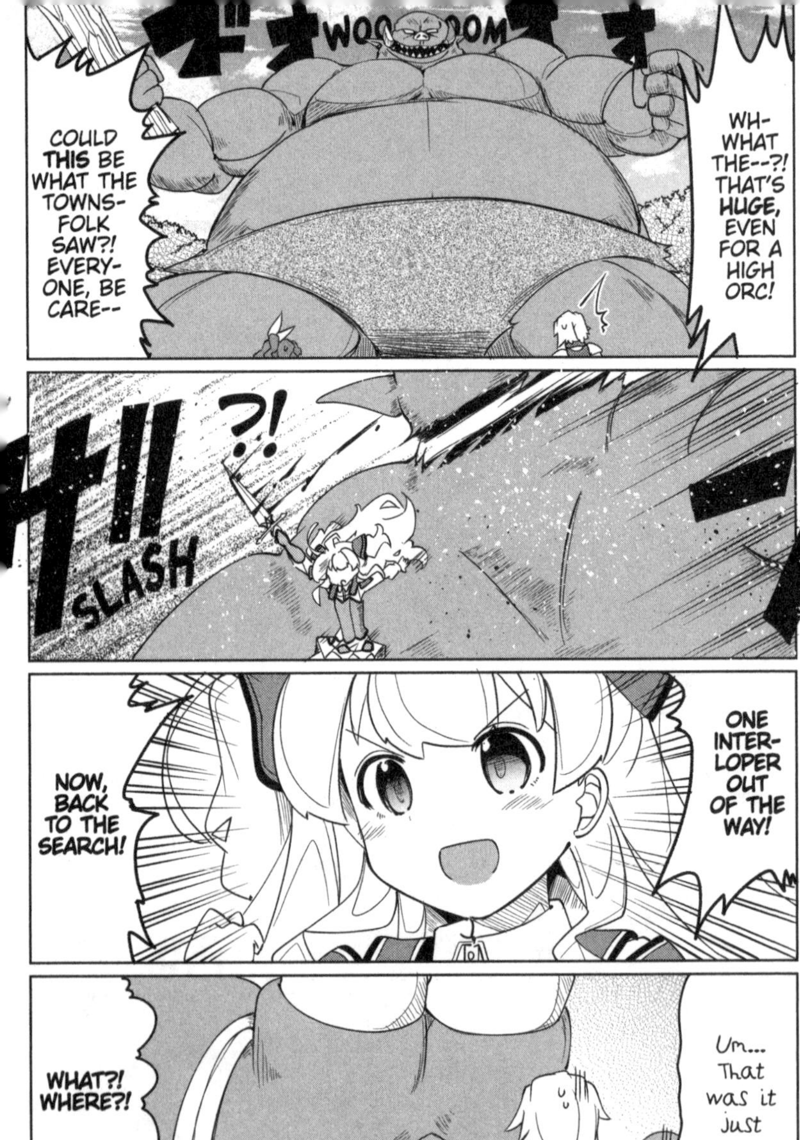
WOOOOOM
WH-WHAT THE--?! THAT'S HUGE, EVEN FOR A HIGH ORC!
COULD THIS BE WHAT THE TOWNS-FOLK SAW?! EVERY-ONE, BE CARE--
?!
SLASH
ONE INTER-LOPER OUT OF THE WAY!
NOW, BACK TO THE SEARCH!
Um... That was it just now.
WHAT?! WHERE?!

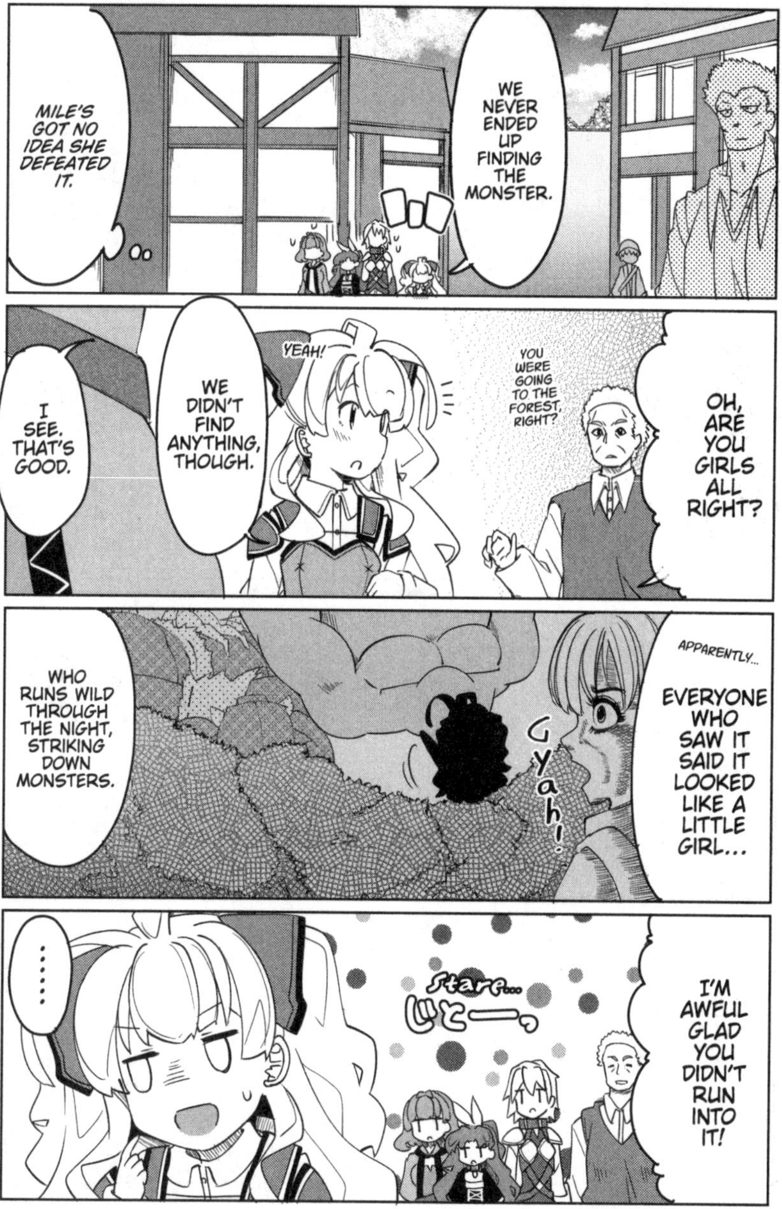
WE NEVER ENDED UP FINDING THE MONSTER.
MILE'S GOT NO IDEA SHE DEFEATED IT.
OH, ARE YOU GIRLS ALL RIGHT?
YOU WERE GOING TO THE FOREST, RIGHT?
YEAH!
WE DIDN'T FIND ANYTHING, THOUGH.
I SEE. THAT'S GOOD.
APPARENTLY...
EVERYONE WHO SAW IT SAID IT LOOKED LIKE A LITTLE GIRL...
Gyah!
WHO RUNS WILD THROUGH THE NIGHT, STRIKING DOWN MONSTERS.
I'M AWFUL GLAD YOU DIDN'T RUN INTO IT!
Stare...
じとーっ
......

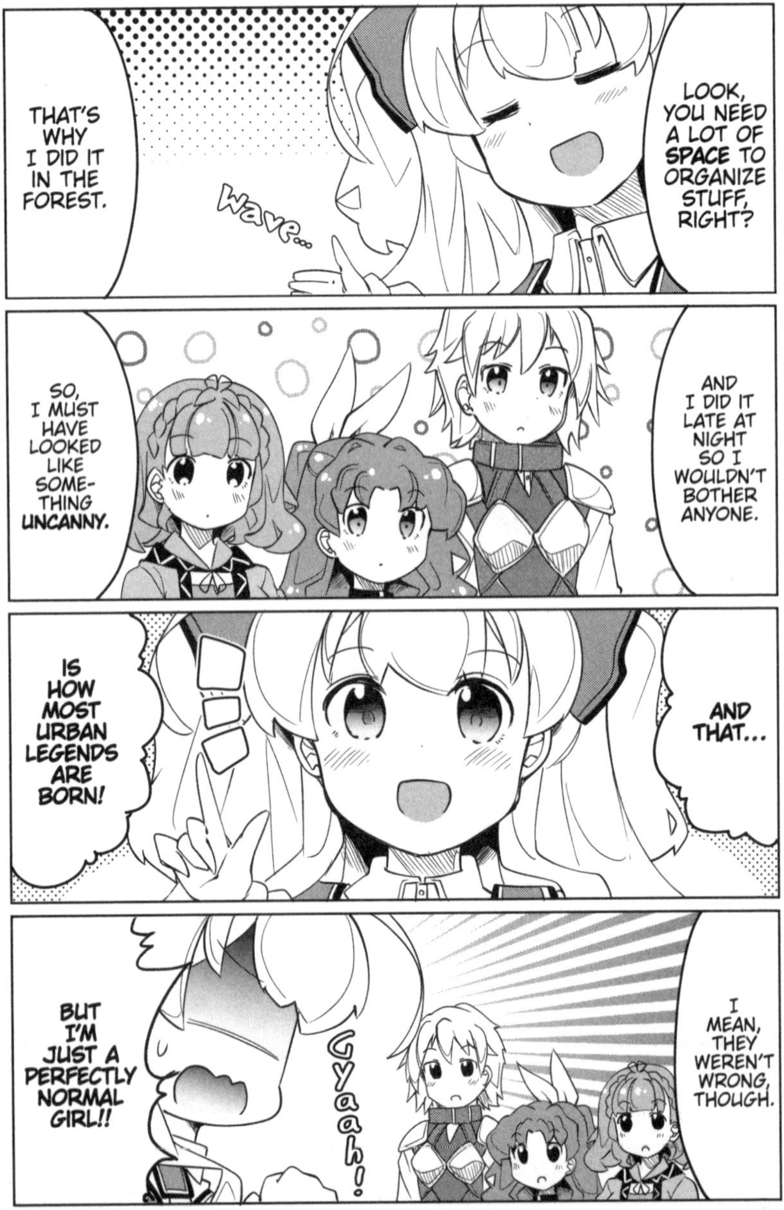
LOOK, YOU NEED A LOT OF SPACE TO ORGANIZE STUFF, RIGHT?
Wave...
THAT'S WHY I DID IT IN THE FOREST.
AND I DID IT LATE AT NIGHT SO I WOULDN'T BOTHER ANYONE.
SO, I MUST HAVE LOOKED LIKE SOME-THING UNCANNY.
AND THAT...
IS HOW MOST URBAN LEGENDS ARE BORN!
I MEAN, THEY WEREN'T WRONG, THOUGH.
Gyaah!
BUT I'M JUST A PERFECTLY NORMAL GIRL!!

Didn't I Say
to Make My
Abilities
Average in the
Next Life?!
EVERYDAY MISADVENTURES!

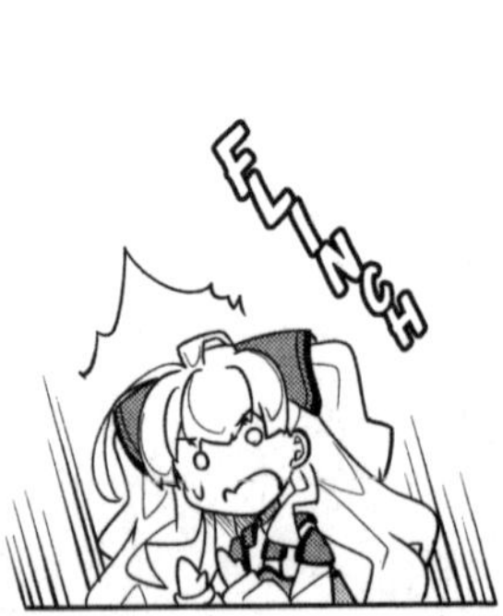
FLINCH

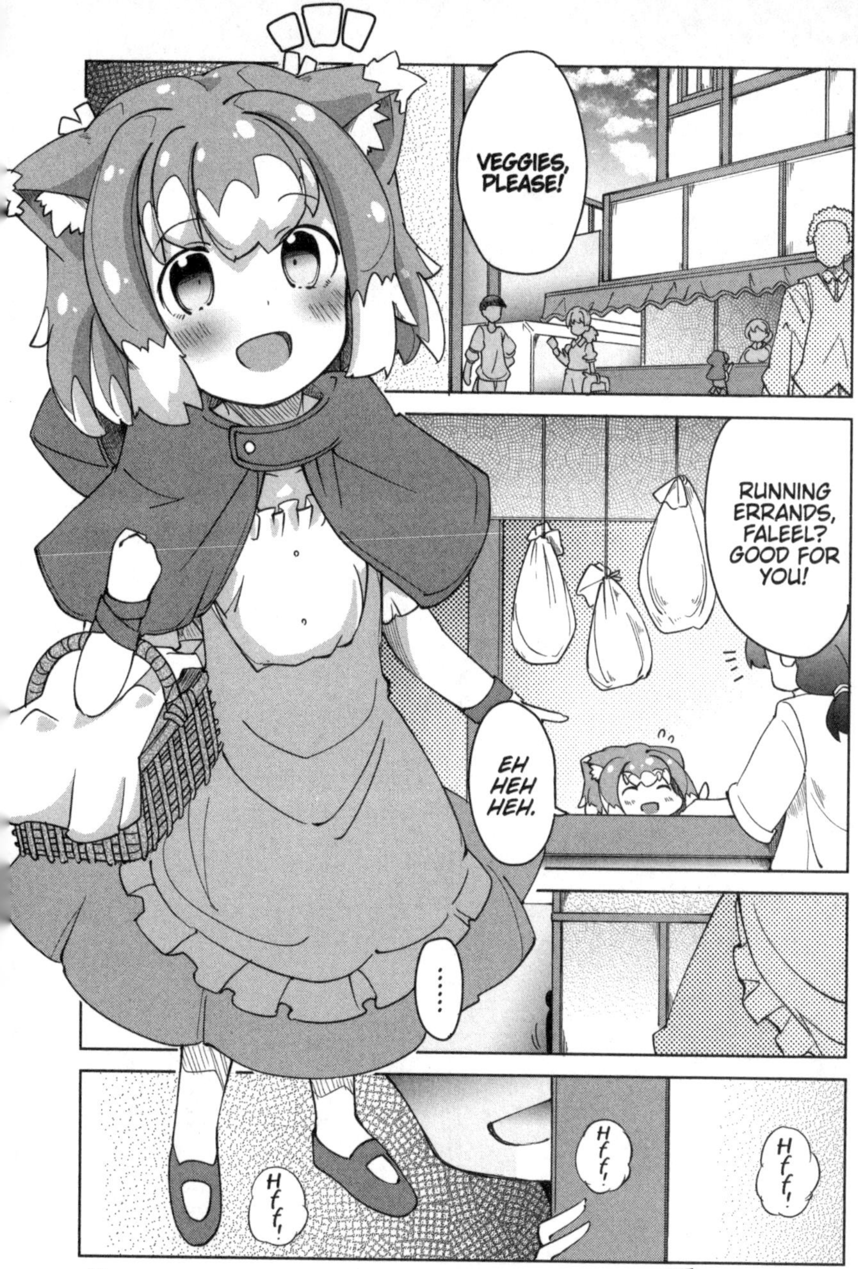

VEGGIES, PLEASE!
RUNNING ERRANDS, FALEEL? GOOD FOR YOU!
EH HEH HEH.
......
Hff!
Hff!
Hff!

Chapter 20

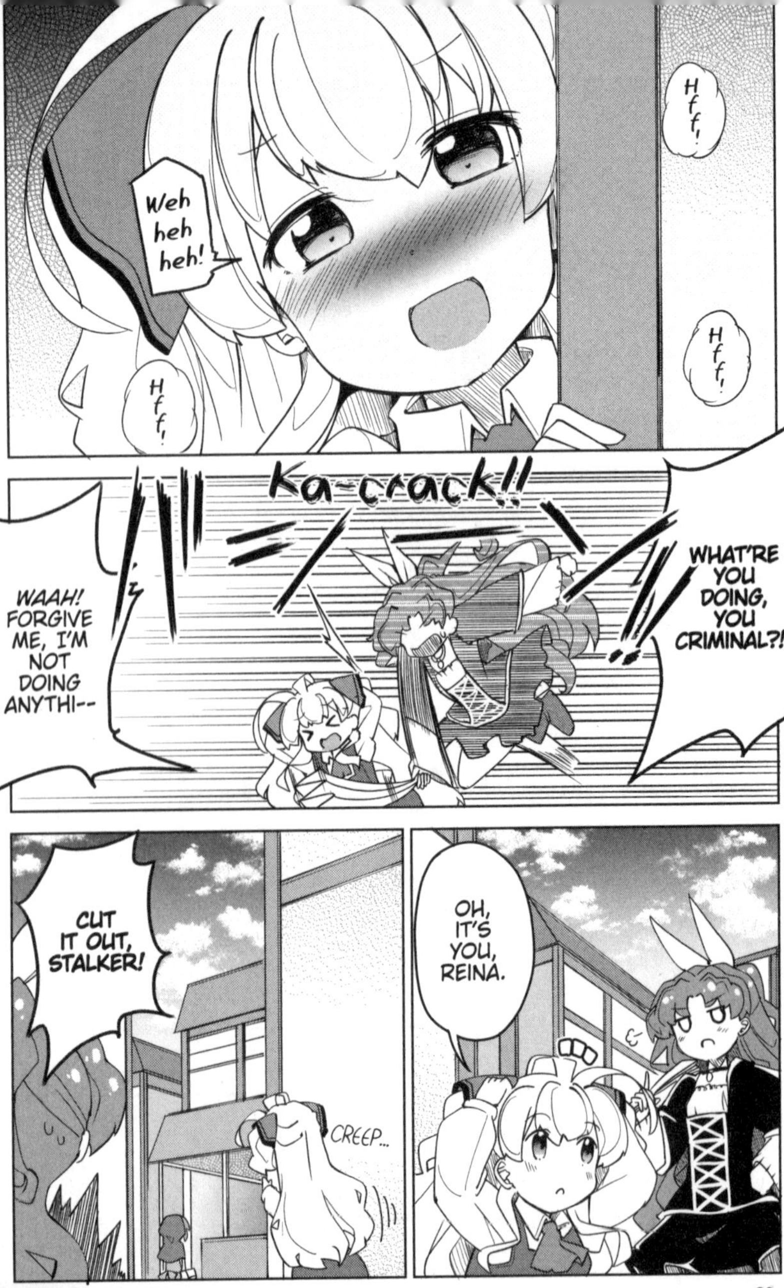
Hff!
Weh heh heh!
Hff!
Hff!
Ka-crack!!
WHAT'RE YOU DOING, YOU CRIMINAL?!!
WAAH! FORGIVE ME, I'M NOT DOING ANYTHI--
OH, IT'S YOU, REINA.
CUT IT OUT, STALKER!
CREEP...

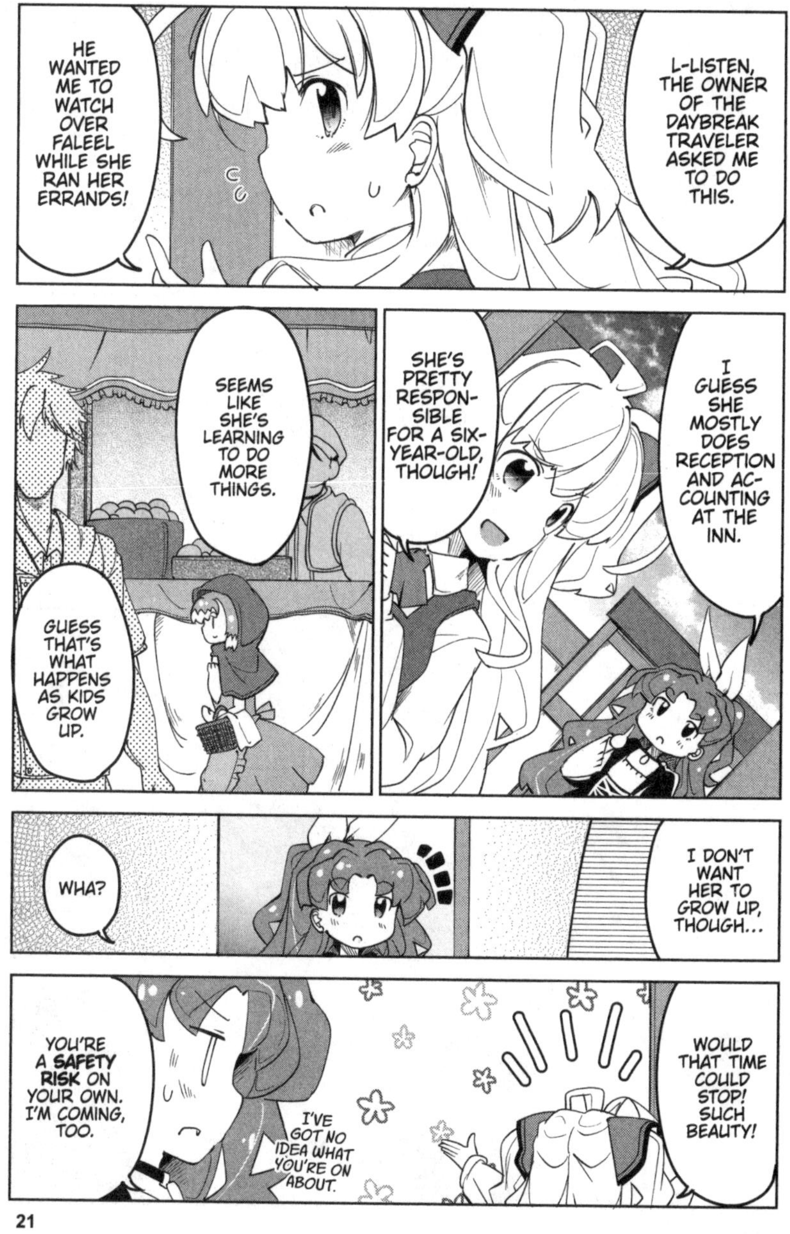
L-LISTEN, THE OWNER OF THE DAYBREAK TRAVELER ASKED ME TO DO THIS.
HE WANTED ME TO WATCH OVER FALEEL WHILE SHE RAN HER ERRANDS!
I GUESS SHE MOSTLY DOES RECEPTION AND AC-COUNTING AT THE INN.
SHE'S PRETTY RESPON-SIBLE FOR A SIX-YEAR-OLD, THOUGH!
SEEMS LIKE SHE'S LEARNING TO DO MORE THINGS.
GUESS THAT'S WHAT HAPPENS AS KIDS GROW UP.
I DON'T WANT HER TO GROW UP, THOUGH...
WHA?
WOULD THAT TIME COULD STOP! SUCH BEAUTY!
I'VE GOT NO IDEA WHAT YOU'RE ON ABOUT.
YOU'RE A **SAFETY RISK** ON YOUR OWN. I'M COMING, TOO.

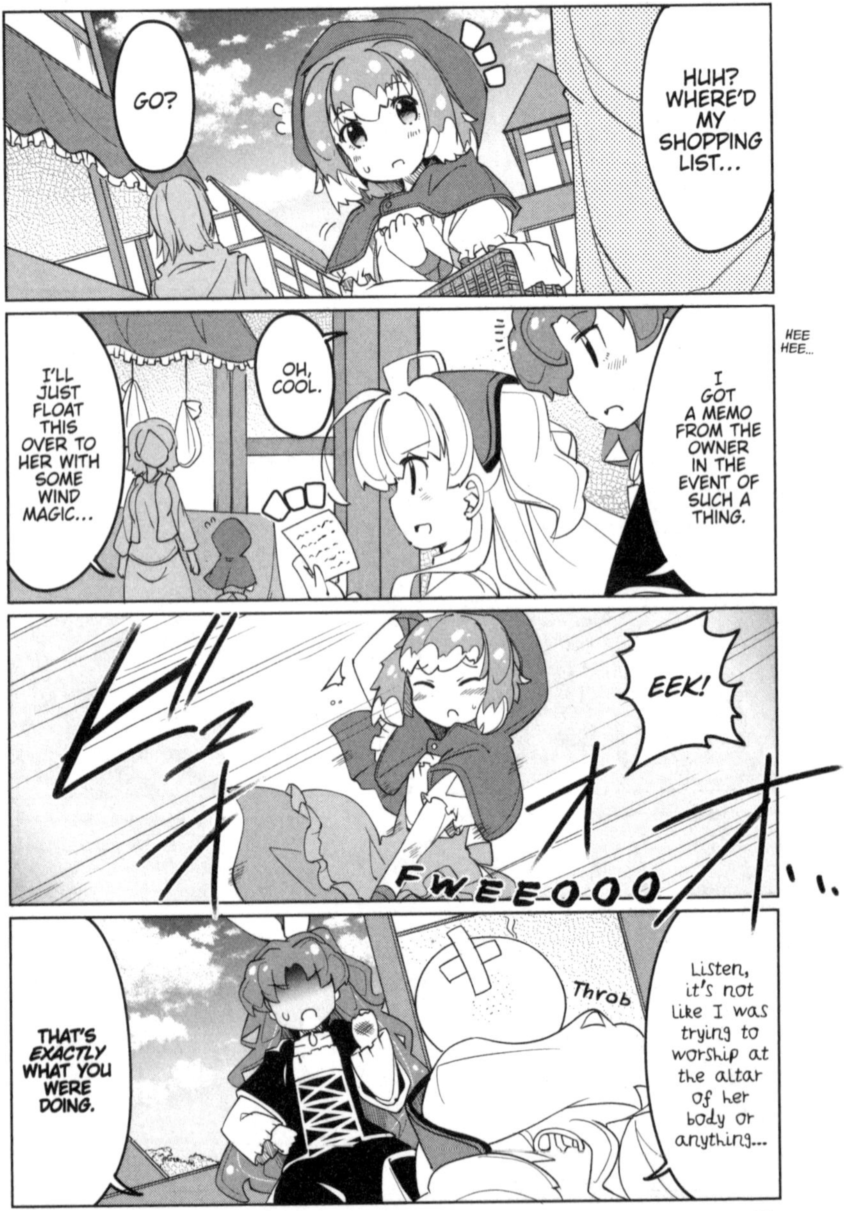
HUH? WHERE'D MY SHOPPING LIST...
GO?
HEE HEE...
I GOT A MEMO FROM THE OWNER IN THE EVENT OF SUCH A THING.
OH, COOL.
I'LL JUST FLOAT THIS OVER TO HER WITH SOME WIND MAGIC...
EEK!
FWEEOOO
Listen, it's not like I was trying to worship at the altar of her body or anything...
Throb
THAT'S *EXACTLY* WHAT YOU WERE DOING.

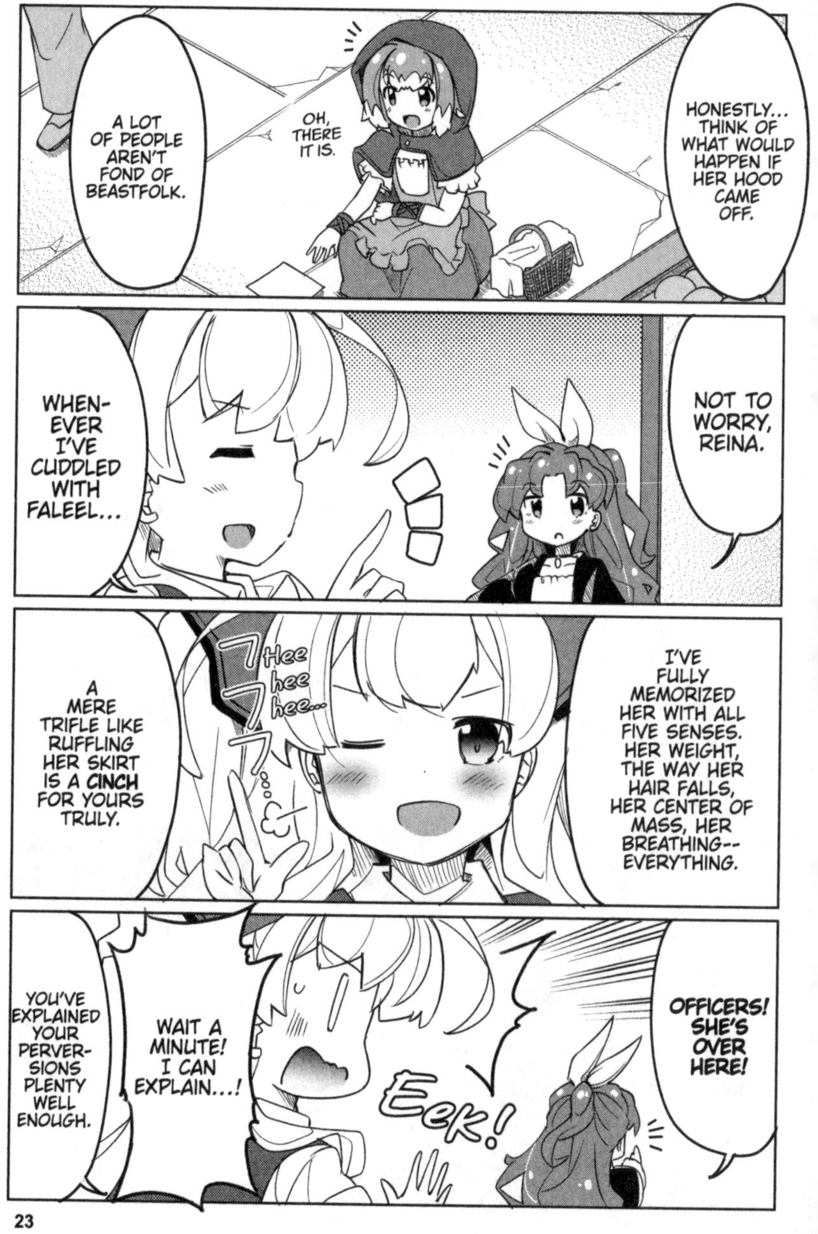

HONESTLY... THINK OF WHAT WOULD HAPPEN IF HER HOOD CAME OFF.
OH, THERE IT IS.
A LOT OF PEOPLE AREN'T FOND OF BEASTFOLK.
NOT TO WORRY, REINA.
WHEN-EVER I'VE CUDDLED WITH FALEEL...
I'VE FULLY MEMORIZED HER WITH ALL FIVE SENSES. HER WEIGHT, THE WAY HER HAIR FALLS, HER CENTER OF MASS, HER BREATHING--EVERYTHING.
Hee hee hee...
A MERE TRIFLE LIKE RUFFLING HER SKIRT IS A **CINCH** FOR YOURS TRULY.
OFFICERS! SHE'S OVER HERE!
Eek!
WAIT A MINUTE! I CAN EXPLAIN...!
YOU'VE EXPLAINED YOUR PERVER-SIONS PLENTY WELL ENOUGH.

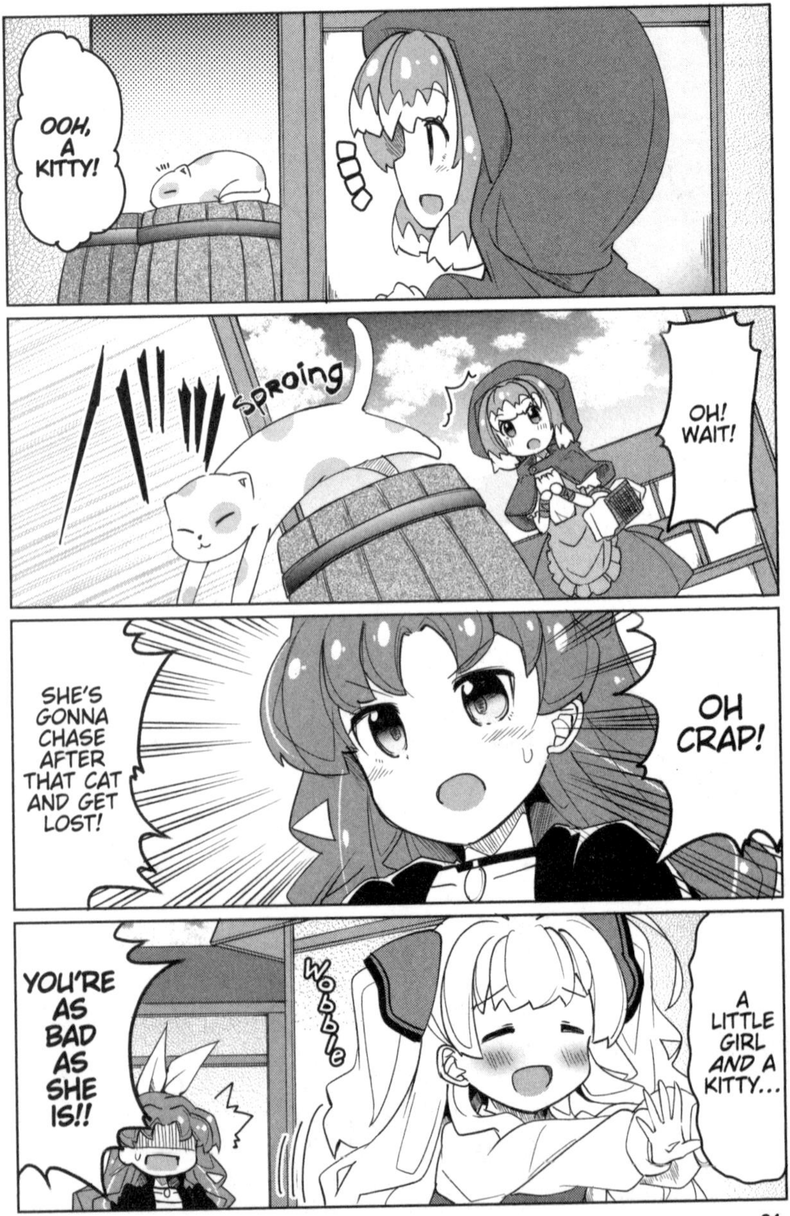
OOH, A KITTY!
sproing
OH! WAIT!
SHE'S GONNA CHASE AFTER THAT CAT AND GET LOST!
OH CRAP!
A LITTLE GIRL AND A KITTY...
Wobble
YOU'RE AS BAD AS SHE IS!!

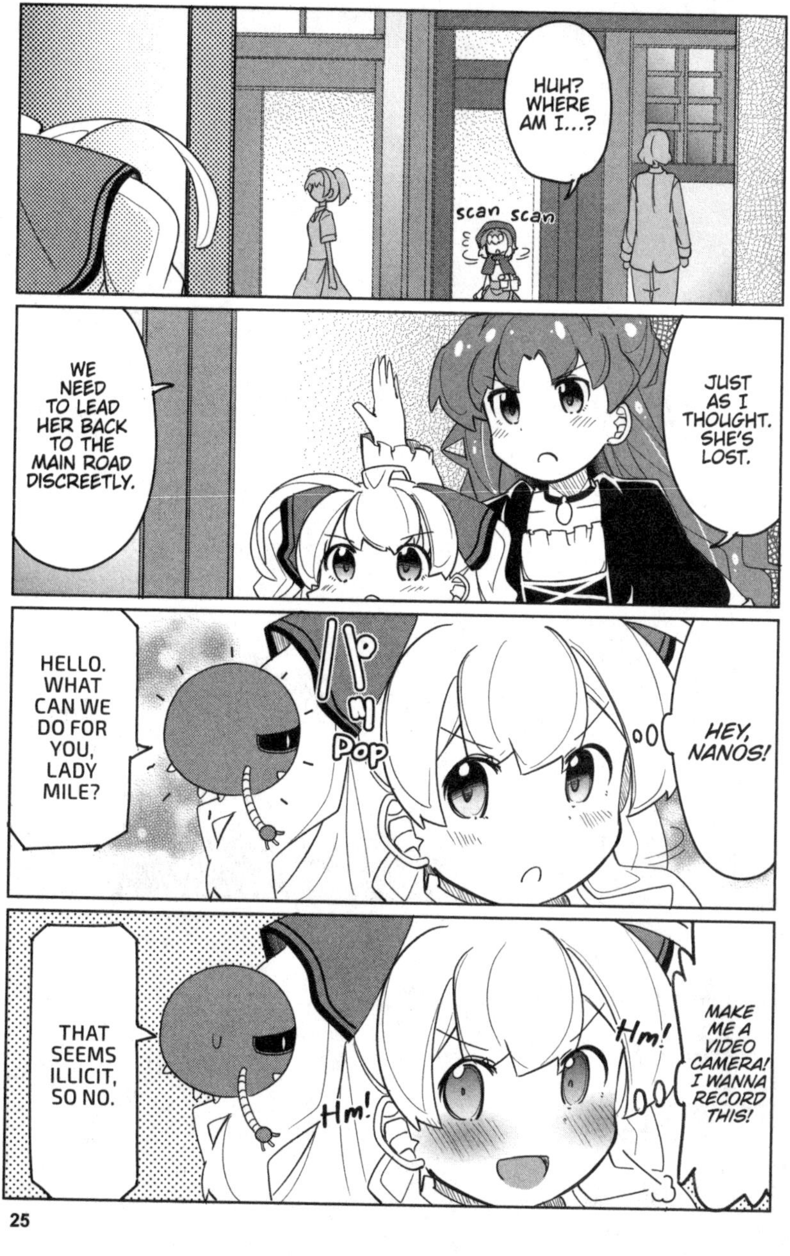
HUH? WHERE AM I...?
scan scan
JUST AS I THOUGHT. SHE'S LOST.
WE NEED TO LEAD HER BACK TO THE MAIN ROAD DISCREETLY.
HEY, NANOS!
Pop
HELLO. WHAT CAN WE DO FOR YOU, LADY MILE?
MAKE ME A VIDEO CAMERA! I WANNA RECORD THIS!
Hm!
Hm!
THAT SEEMS ILLICIT, SO NO.

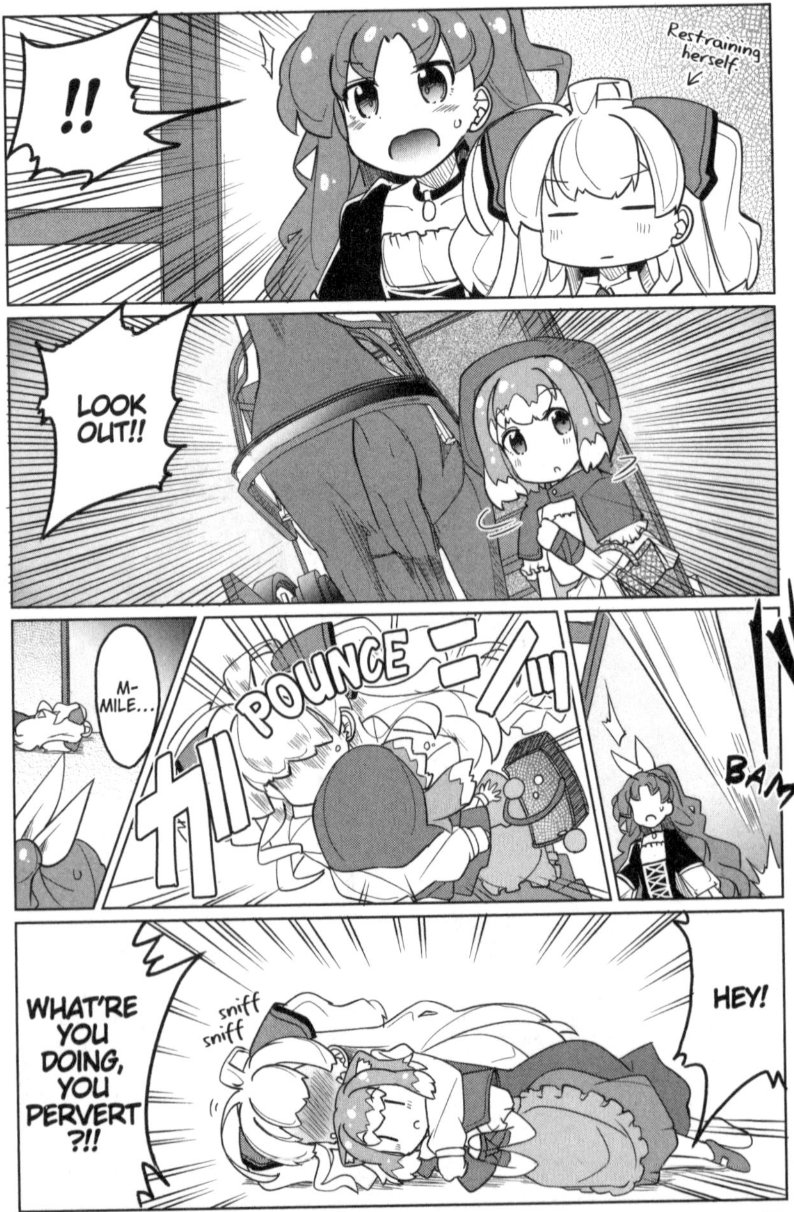
!!
Restraining herself.
LOOK OUT!!
BAM
POUNCE
M-MILE...
WHAT'RE YOU DOING, YOU PERVERT?!!
HEY!
sniff sniff

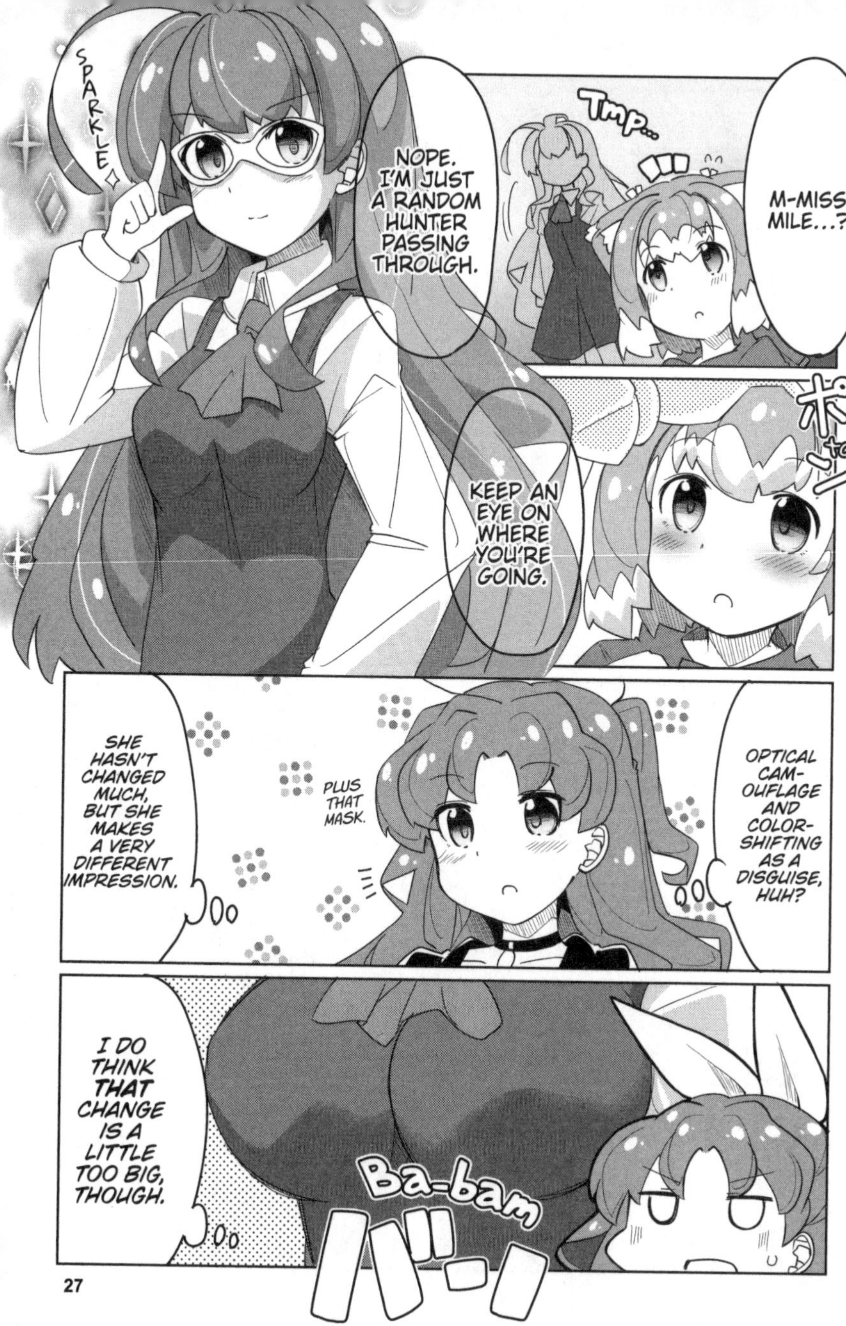
M-MISS MILE...?
Tmp...
NOPE. I'M JUST A RANDOM HUNTER PASSING THROUGH.
SPARKLE
tap
KEEP AN EYE ON WHERE YOU'RE GOING.
OPTICAL CAM-OUFLAGE AND COLOR-SHIFTING AS A DISGUISE, HUH?
PLUS THAT MASK.
SHE HASN'T CHANGED MUCH, BUT SHE MAKES A VERY DIFFERENT IMPRESSION.
I DO THINK **THAT** CHANGE IS A LITTLE TOO BIG, THOUGH.
Ba-bam

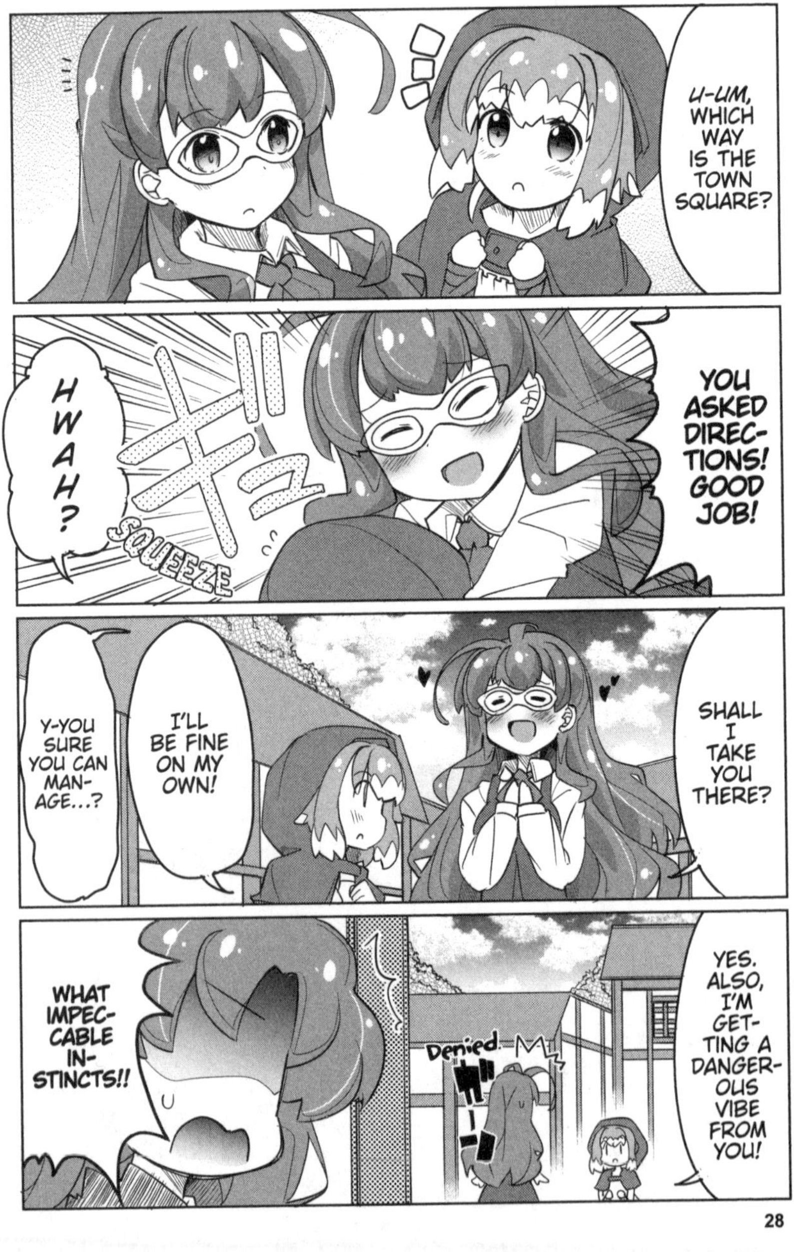
U-UM, WHICH WAY IS THE TOWN SQUARE?
YOU ASKED DIRECTIONS! GOOD JOB!
SQUEEZE
HWAH?
SHALL I TAKE YOU THERE?
I'LL BE FINE ON MY OWN!
Y-YOU SURE YOU CAN MAN-AGE...?
YES. ALSO, I'M GETTING A DANGEROUS VIBE FROM YOU!
Denied
WHAT IMPECCABLE INSTINCTS!!

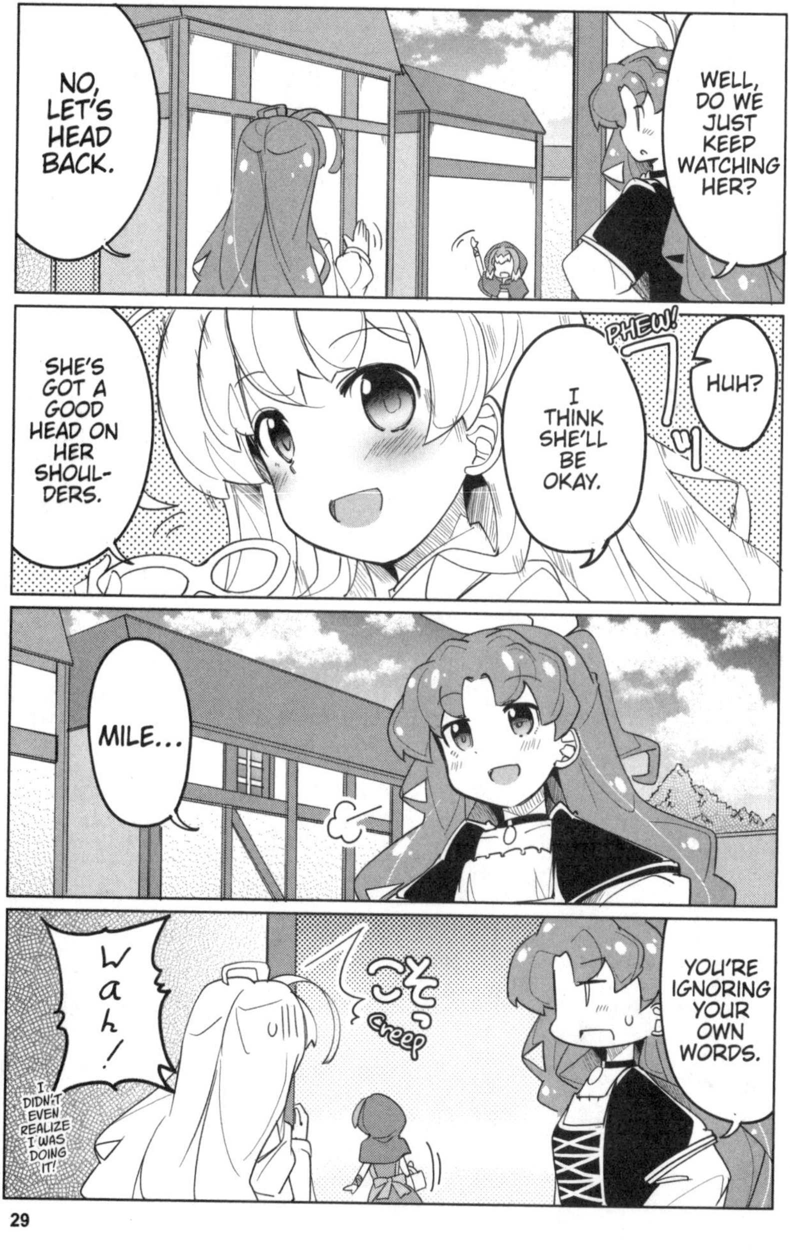

WELL, DO WE JUST KEEP WATCHING HER?
NO, LET'S HEAD BACK.
HUH?
PHEW!
I THINK SHE'LL BE OKAY.
SHE'S GOT A GOOD HEAD ON HER SHOUL-DERS.
MILE...
YOU'RE IGNORING YOUR OWN WORDS.
こそっ
Creep
Wah!
I DIDN'T EVEN REALIZE I WAS DOING IT!

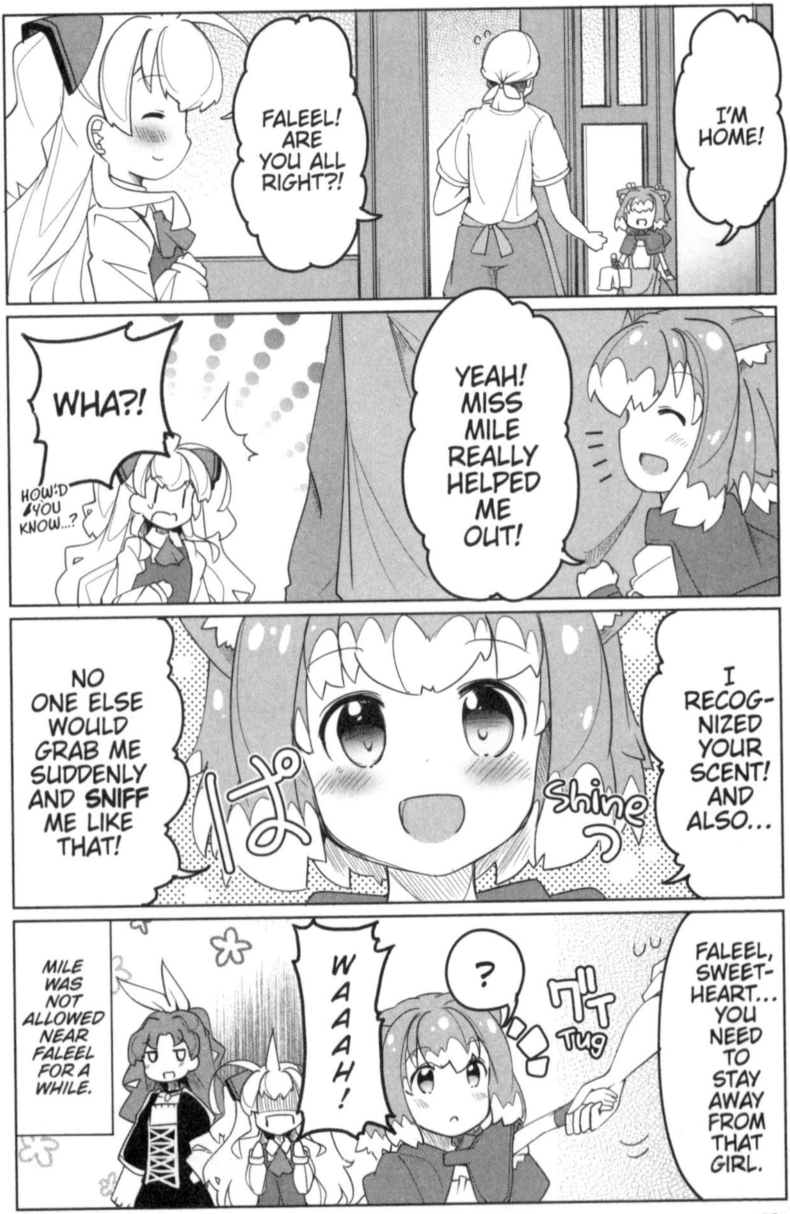
I'M HOME!
FALEEL! ARE YOU ALL RIGHT?!
YEAH! MISS MILE REALLY HELPED ME OUT!
WHA?!
HOW'D YOU KNOW...?
I RECOGNIZED YOUR SCENT! AND ALSO...
Shine
ぱ
NO ONE ELSE WOULD GRAB ME SUDDENLY AND SNIFF ME LIKE THAT!
FALEEL, SWEETHEART... YOU NEED TO STAY AWAY FROM THAT GIRL.
Tug
?
WAAAAH!
MILE WAS NOT ALLOWED NEAR FALEEL FOR A WHILE.

Didn't I Say to Make My Abilities Average in the Next Life?! EVERYDAY MISADVENTURES!

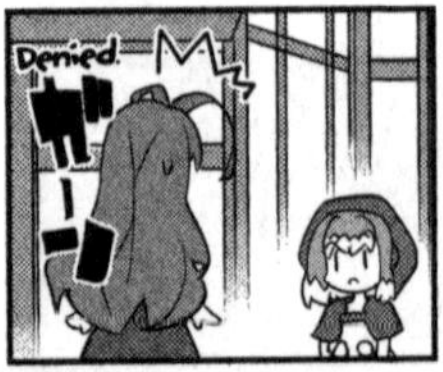
Denied.

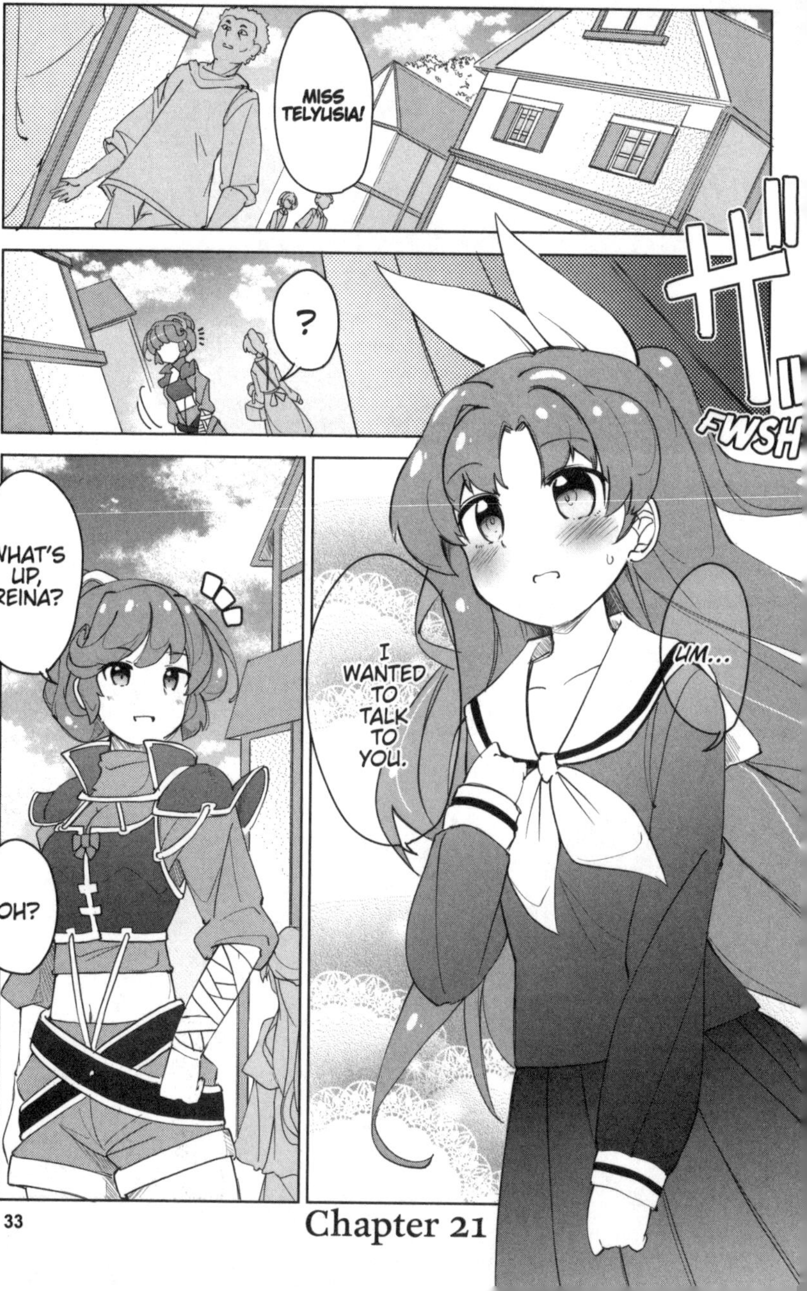
MISS TELYUSIA!
?
FWSH
WHAT'S UP, REINA?
THAT'S A NEW LOOK FOR YOU.
OH?
UM...
I WANTED TO TALK TO YOU.

Chapter 21

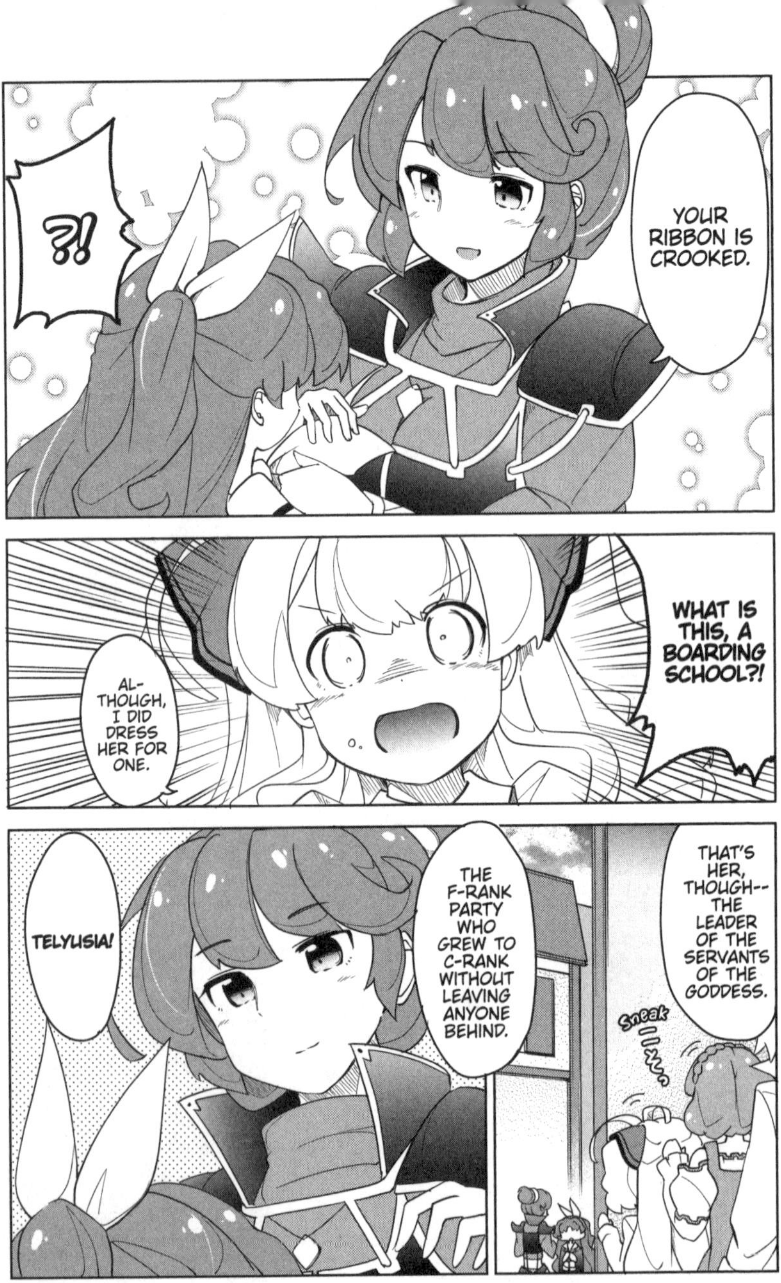
?!
YOUR RIBBON IS CROOKED.
WHAT IS THIS, A BOARDING SCHOOL?!
ALTHOUGH, I DID DRESS HER FOR ONE.
THAT'S HER, THOUGH-- THE LEADER OF THE SERVANTS OF THE GODDESS.
THE F-RANK PARTY WHO GREW TO C-RANK WITHOUT LEAVING ANYONE BEHIND.
TELYUSIA!
Sneak

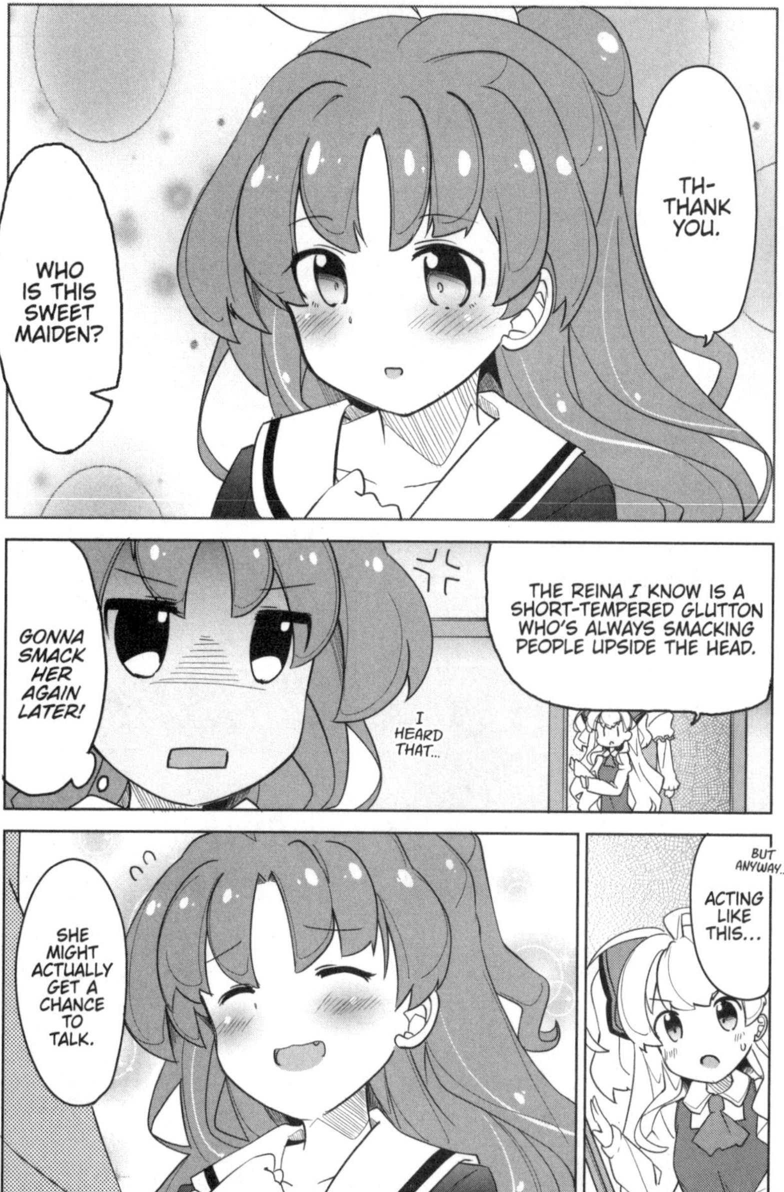
TH- THANK YOU.
WHO IS THIS SWEET MAIDEN?
THE REINA *I* KNOW IS A SHORT-TEMPERED GLUTTON WHO'S ALWAYS SMACKING PEOPLE UPSIDE THE HEAD.
I HEARD THAT...
GONNA SMACK HER AGAIN LATER!
BUT ANYWAY...
ACTING LIKE THIS...
SHE MIGHT ACTUALLY GET A CHANCE TO TALK.

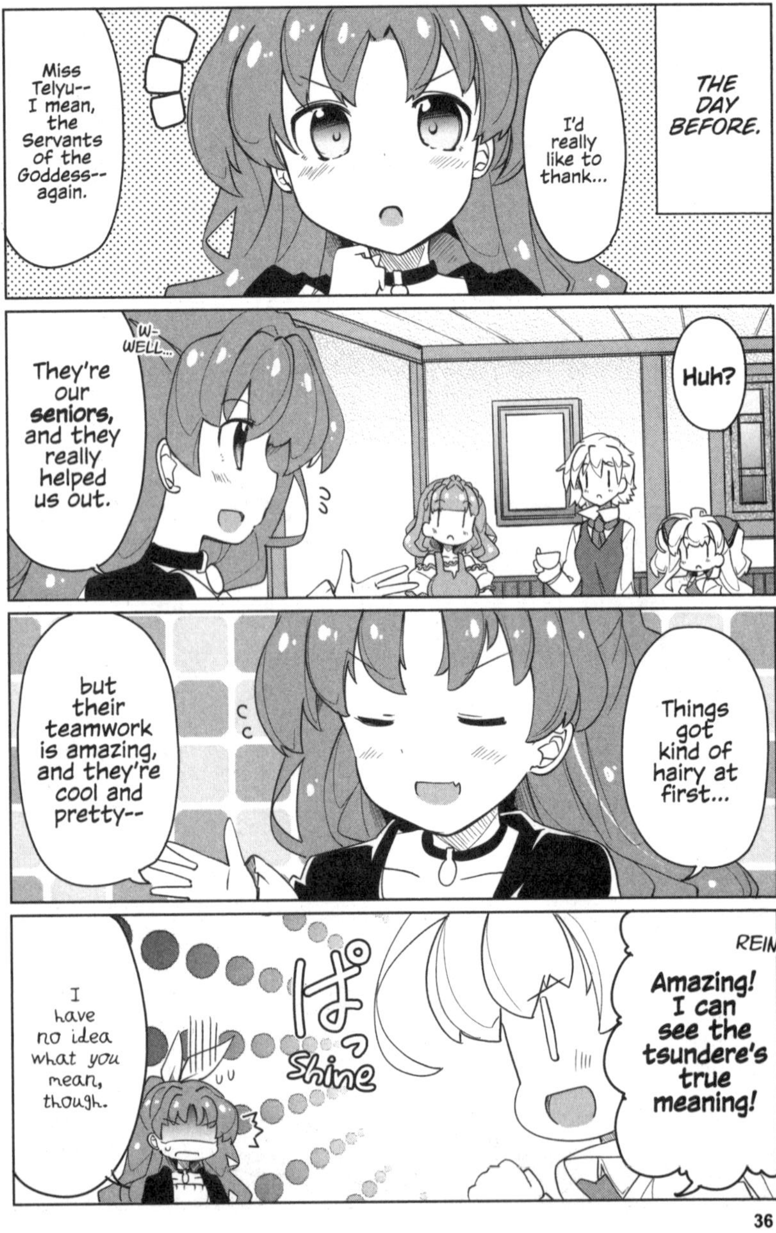
THE DAY BEFORE.
I'd really like to thank...
Miss Telyu-- I mean, the Servants of the Goddess-- again.
Huh?
W-WELL...
They're our seniors, and they really helped us out.
Things got kind of hairy at first...
but their teamwork is amazing, and they're cool and pretty--
REINA!
Amazing! I can see the tsundere's true meaning!
ぱっ
Shine
I have no idea what you mean, though.

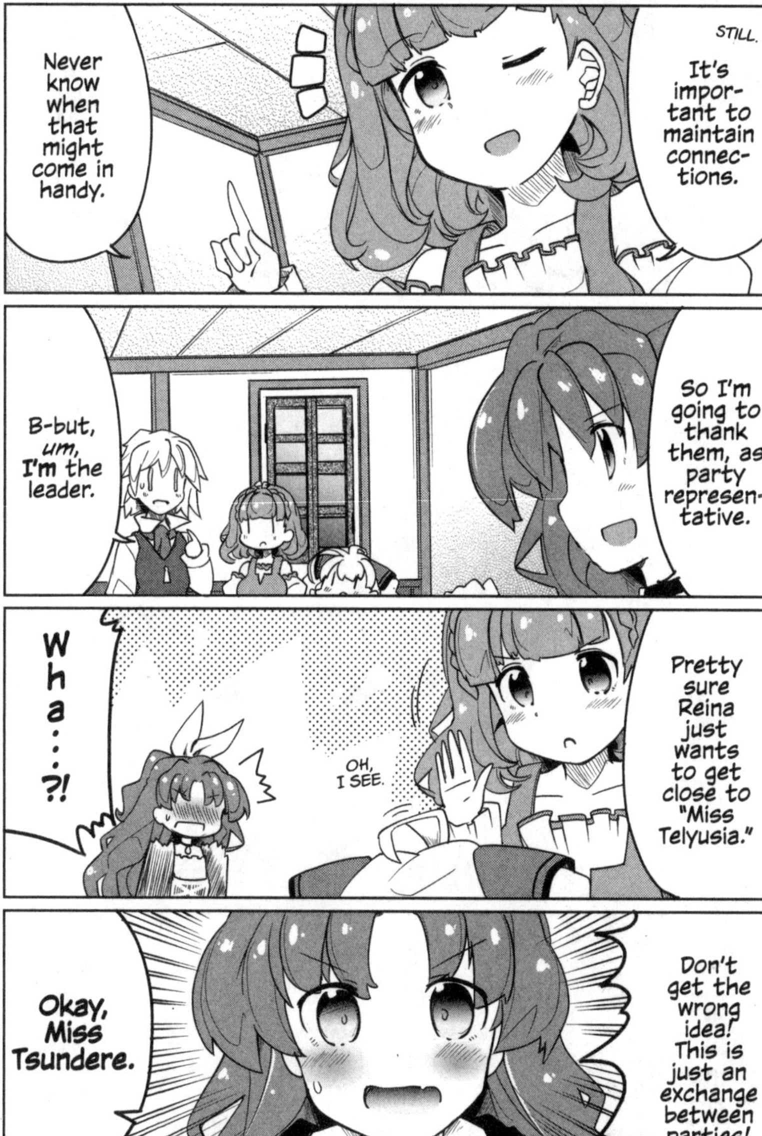
STILL.
It's important to maintain connections.
Never know when that might come in handy.
So I'm going to thank them, as party representative.
B-but, *um*, **I'm** the leader.
Pretty sure Reina just wants to get close to "Miss Telyusia."
OH, I SEE.
Wha...?!
Don't get the wrong idea! This is just an exchange between parties!
Okay, Miss Tsundere.

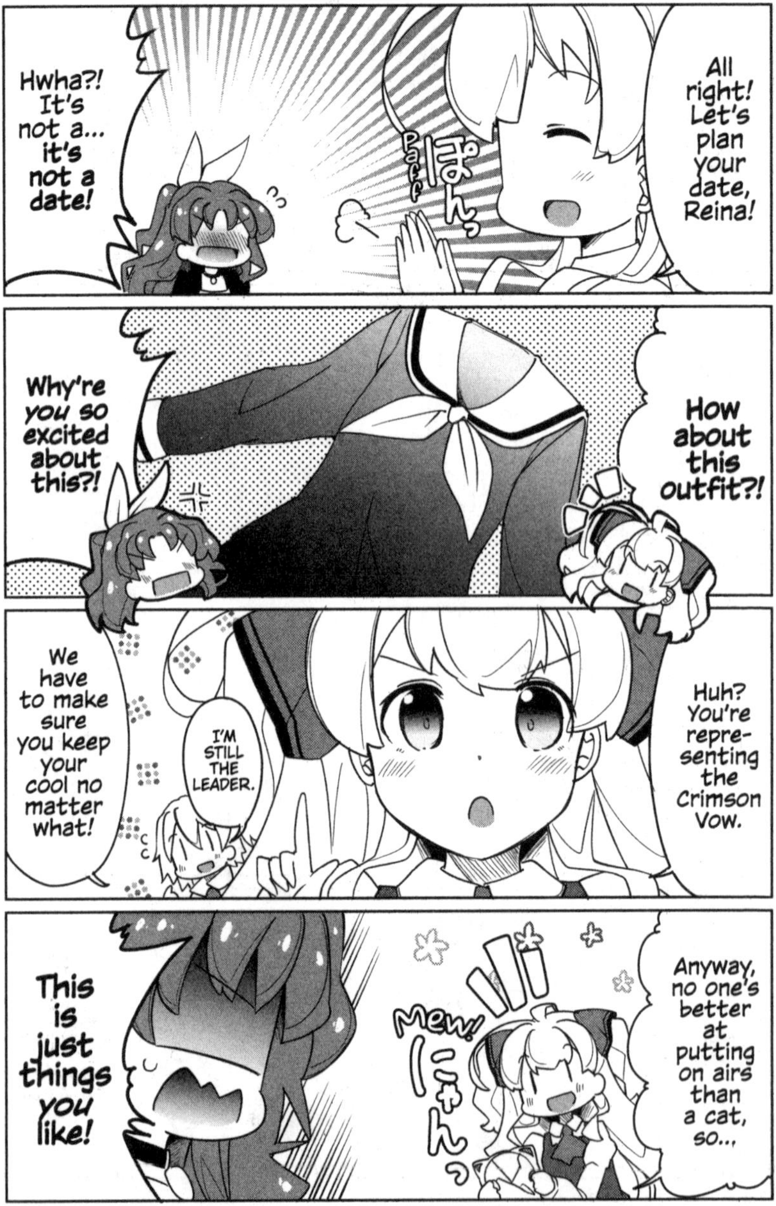
All right! Let's plan your date, Reina!
ぽんっ
Paff
Hwha?! It's not a... it's not a date!
How about this outfit?!
Why're you so excited about this?!
Huh? You're repre-senting the Crimson Vow.
I'M STILL THE LEADER.
We have to make sure you keep your cool no matter what!
Anyway, no one's better at putting on airs than a cat, so...
にゃんっ
Mew!
This is just things you like!

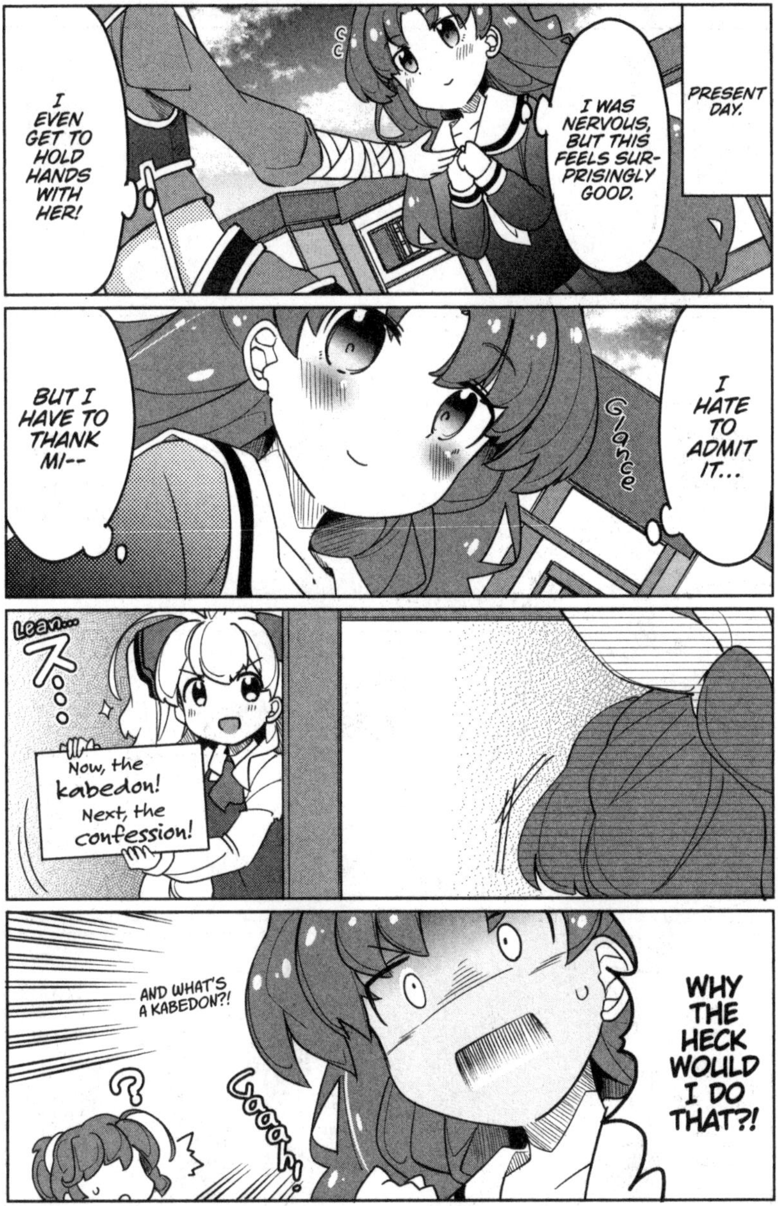
PRESENT DAY.
I WAS NERVOUS, BUT THIS FEELS SURPRISINGLY GOOD.
I EVEN GET TO HOLD HANDS WITH HER!
I HATE TO ADMIT IT...
Glance
BUT I HAVE TO THANK MI--
Lean...
Now, the kabedon! Next, the confession!
WHY THE HECK WOULD I DO THAT?!
AND WHAT'S A KABEDON?!
Gaaah!
?

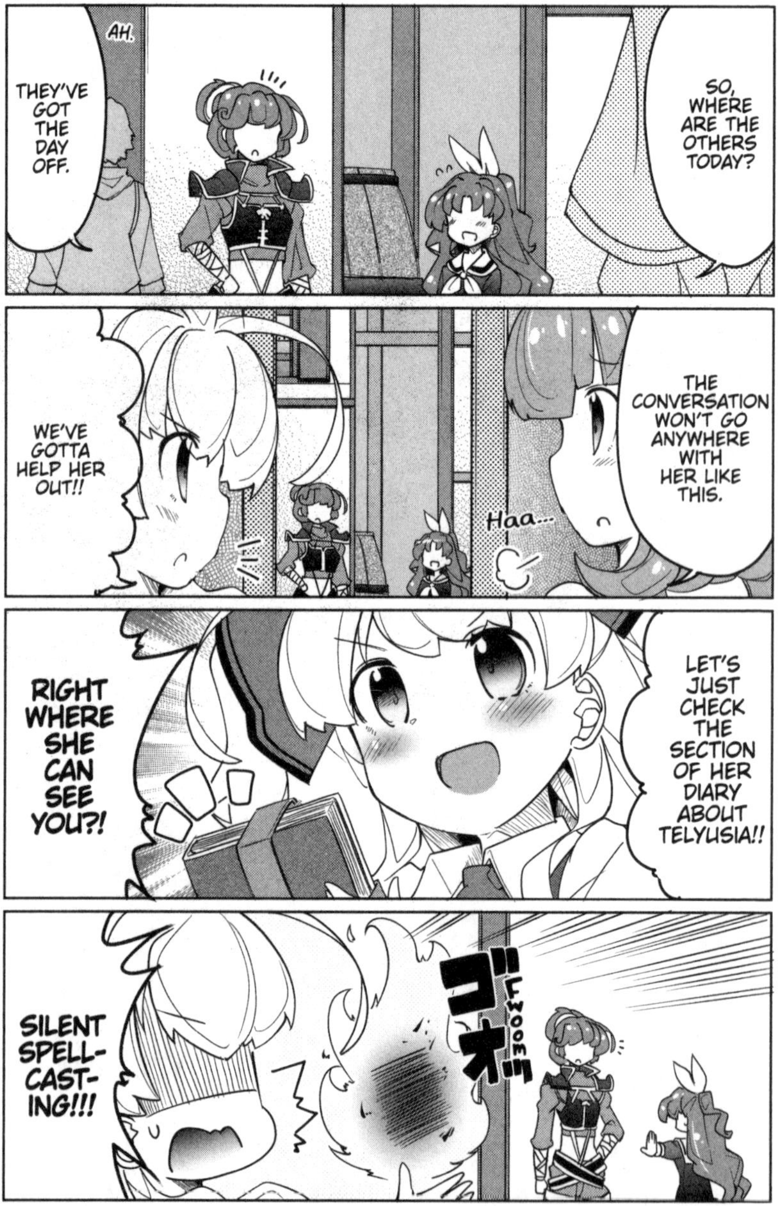
SO, WHERE ARE THE OTHERS TODAY?
AH.
THEY'VE GOT THE DAY OFF.
THE CONVERSATION WON'T GO ANYWHERE WITH HER LIKE THIS.
Haa...
WE'VE GOTTA HELP HER OUT!!
LET'S JUST CHECK THE SECTION OF HER DIARY ABOUT TELYUSIA!!
RIGHT WHERE SHE CAN SEE YOU?!
ゴオ
FWOOM
SILENT SPELL-CASTING!!!

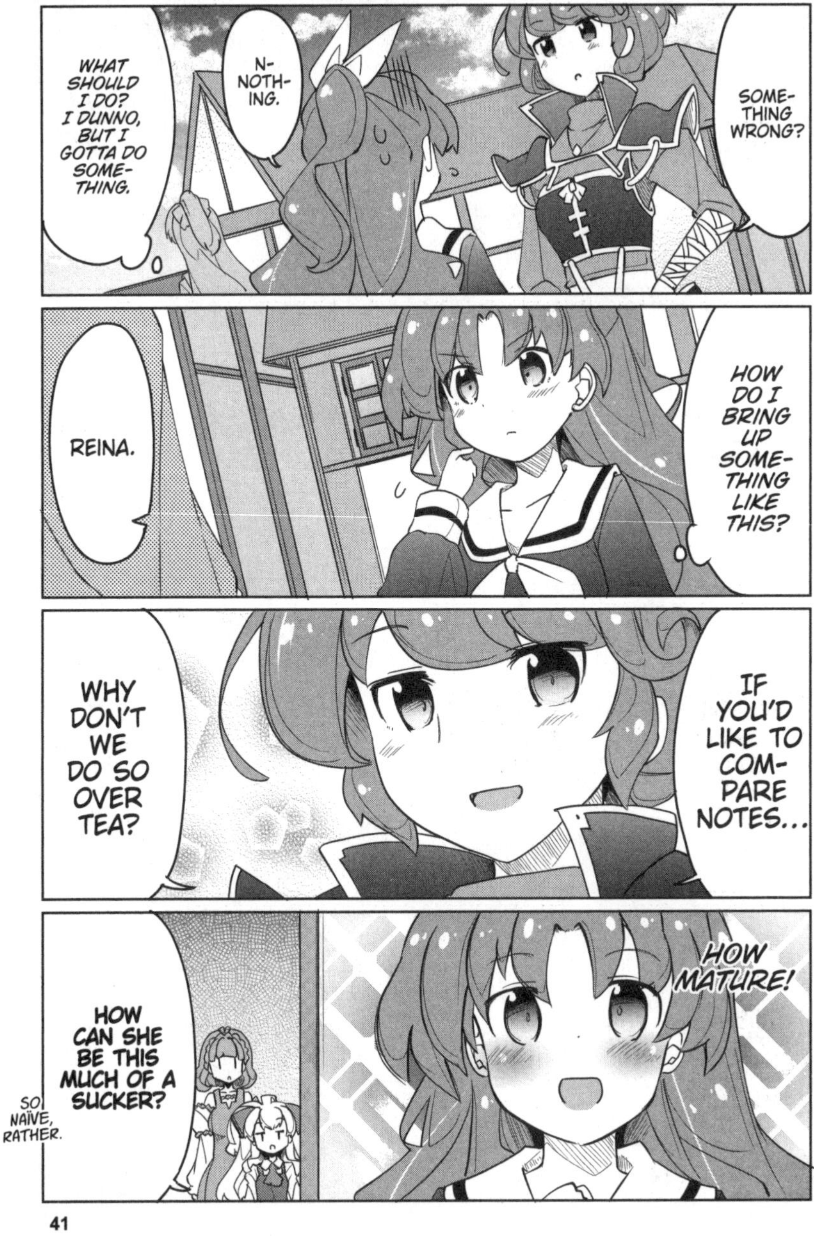
SOME-THING WRONG?
N-NOTH-ING.
WHAT SHOULD I DO? I DUNNO, BUT I GOTTA DO SOME-THING.
HOW DO I BRING UP SOME-THING LIKE THIS?
REINA.
IF YOU'D LIKE TO COM-PARE NOTES...
WHY DON'T WE DO SO OVER TEA?
HOW MATURE!
HOW CAN SHE BE THIS MUCH OF A SUCKER?
SO NAÏVE, RATHER.

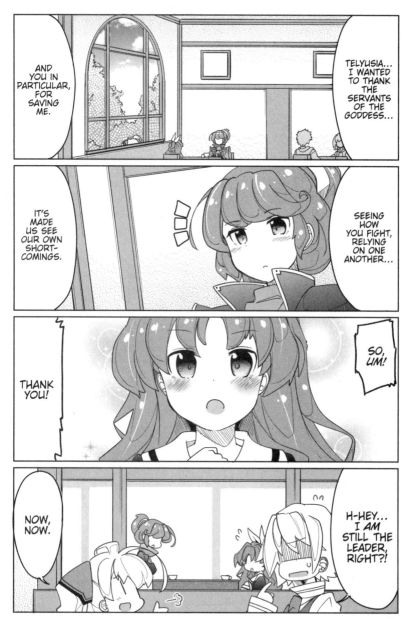

TELYUSIA... I WANTED TO THANK THE SERVANTS OF THE GODDESS...

AND YOU IN PARTICULAR, FOR SAVING ME.

SEEING HOW YOU FIGHT, RELYING ON ONE ANOTHER...

IT'S MADE US SEE OUR OWN SHORT-COMINGS.

SO, UM!

THANK YOU!

NOW, NOW.

H-HEY... I *AM* STILL THE LEADER, RIGHT?!

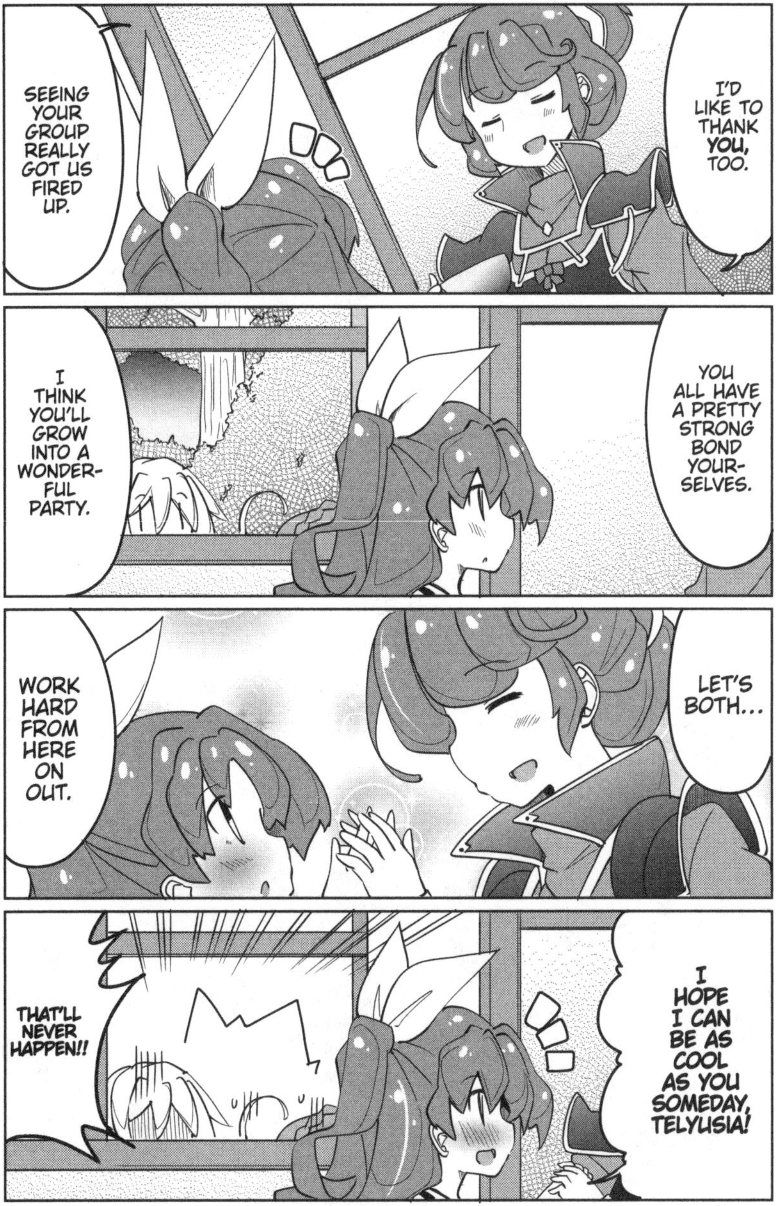
I'D LIKE TO THANK YOU, TOO.
SEEING YOUR GROUP REALLY GOT US FIRED UP.
YOU ALL HAVE A PRETTY STRONG BOND YOUR-SELVES.
I THINK YOU'LL GROW INTO A WONDER-FUL PARTY.
LET'S BOTH...
WORK HARD FROM HERE ON OUT.
I HOPE I CAN BE AS COOL AS YOU SOMEDAY, TELYUSIA!
THAT'LL NEVER HAPPEN!!

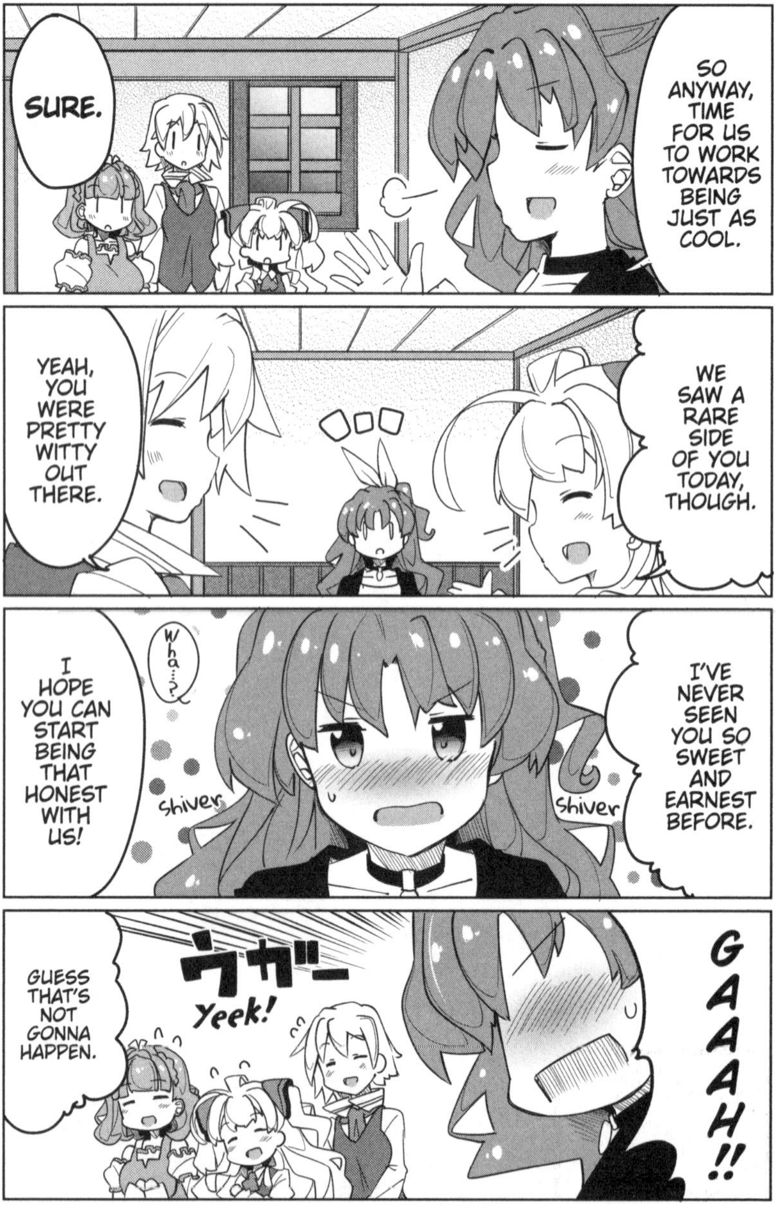
SO ANYWAY, TIME FOR US TO WORK TOWARDS BEING JUST AS COOL.
SURE.
WE SAW A RARE SIDE OF YOU TODAY, THOUGH.
YEAH, YOU WERE PRETTY WITTY OUT THERE.
I'VE NEVER SEEN YOU SO SWEET AND EARNEST BEFORE.
Shiver
Shiver
Wha...?
I HOPE YOU CAN START BEING THAT HONEST WITH US!
GAAAAH!!
ウガー
Yeek!
GUESS THAT'S NOT GONNA HAPPEN.

Didn't I Say to Make My Abilities Average in the Next Life?!
EVERYDAY MISADVENTURES!

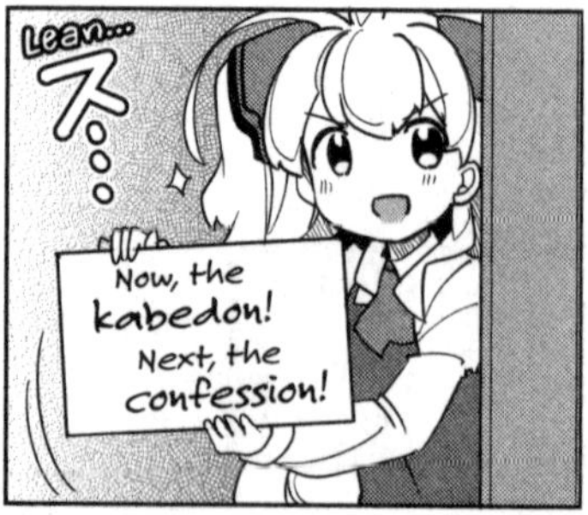
Lean...
ス...
Now, the kabedon! Next, the confession!

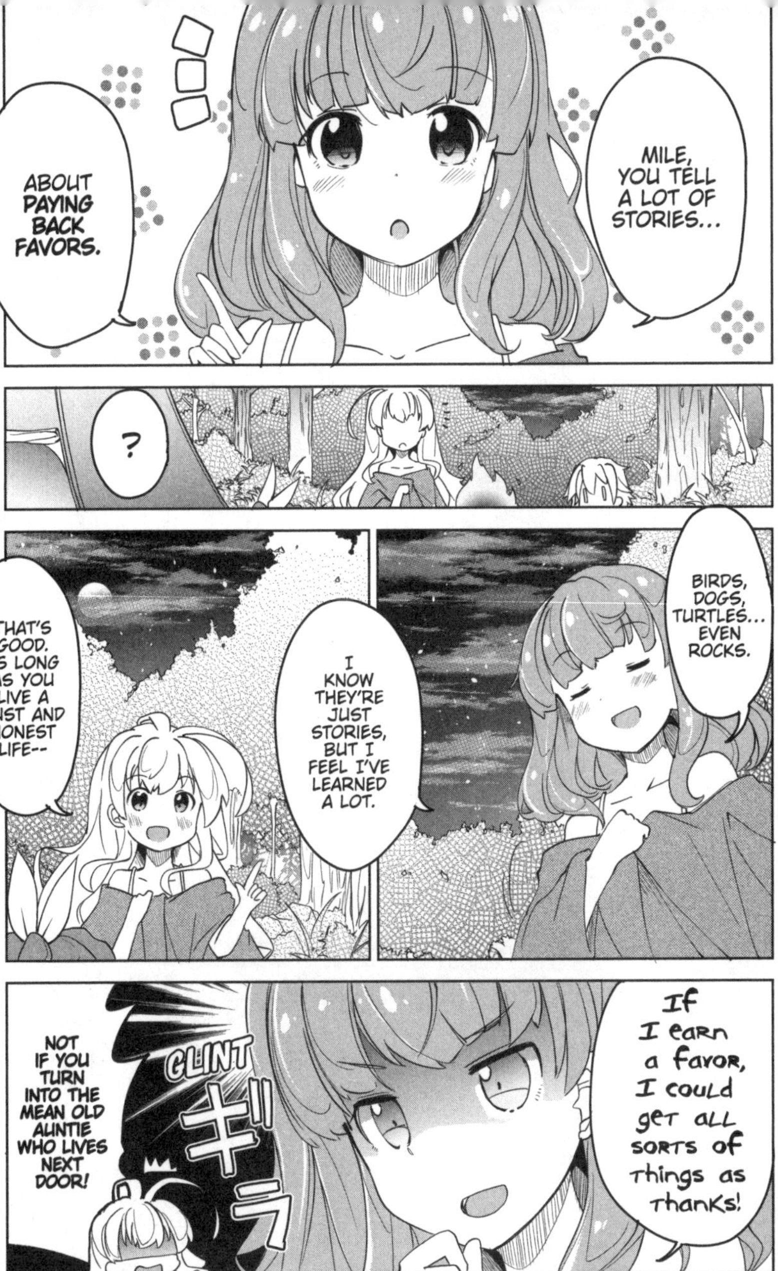
MILE, YOU TELL A LOT OF STORIES...
ABOUT PAYING BACK FAVORS.
?
BIRDS, DOGS, TURTLES... EVEN ROCKS.
I KNOW THEY'RE JUST STORIES, BUT I FEEL I'VE LEARNED A LOT.
THAT'S GOOD. AS LONG AS YOU LIVE A JUST AND HONEST LIFE--
If I earn a favor, I could get all sorts of things as thanks!
GLINT
ギラ
NOT IF YOU TURN INTO THE MEAN OLD AUNTIE WHO LIVES NEXT DOOR!

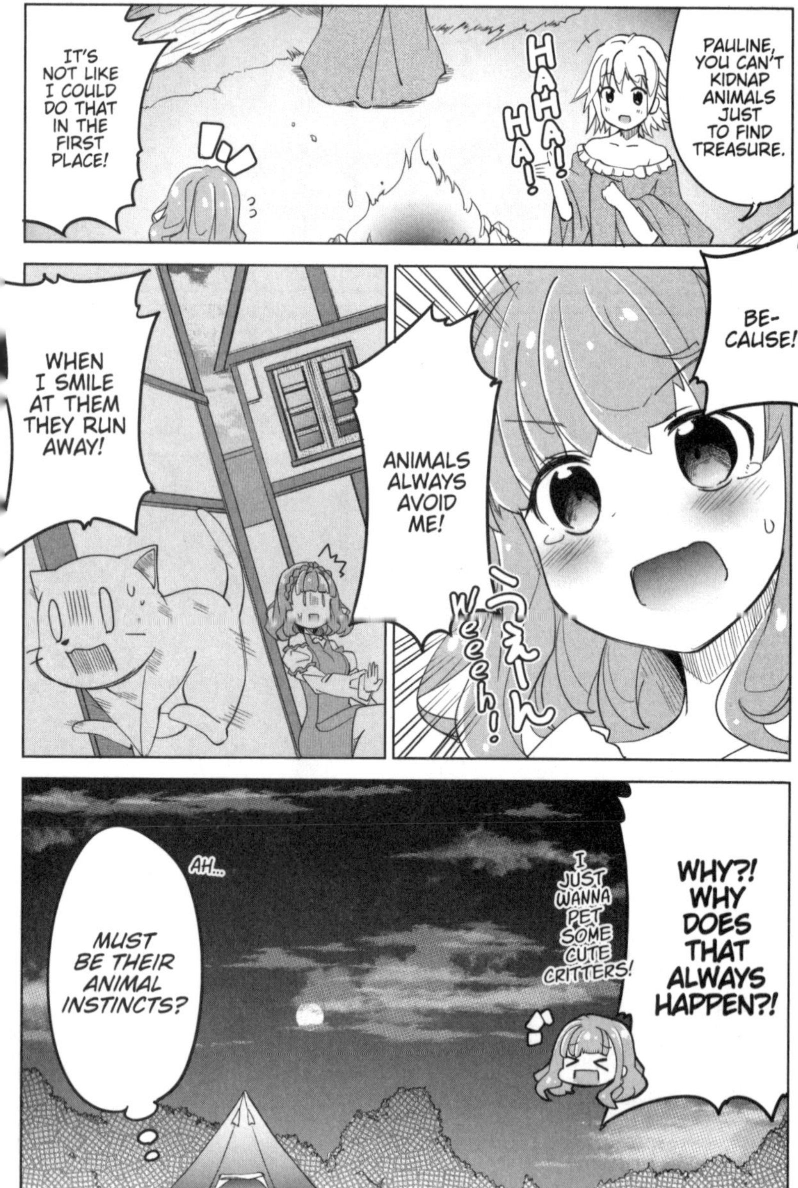
PAULINE, YOU CAN'T KIDNAP ANIMALS JUST TO FIND TREASURE.
HAHAHA!
IT'S NOT LIKE I COULD DO THAT IN THE FIRST PLACE!
BE-CAUSE!
ANIMALS ALWAYS AVOID ME!
うえーん
Weeeh!
WHEN I SMILE AT THEM THEY RUN AWAY!
WHY?! WHY DOES THAT ALWAYS HAPPEN?!
I JUST WANNA PET SOME CUTE CRITTERS!
AH...
MUST BE THEIR ANIMAL INSTINCTS?

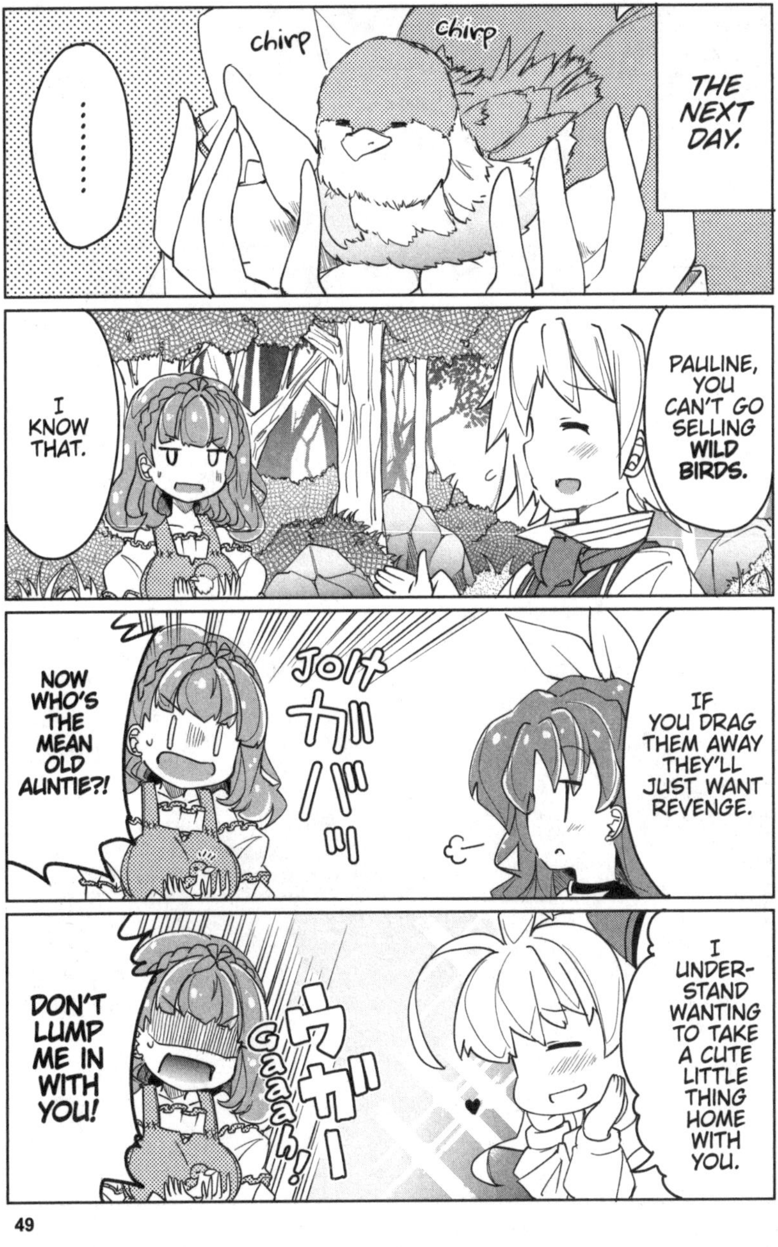
THE NEXT DAY.
chirp
chirp
....
PAULINE, YOU CAN'T GO SELLING **WILD BIRDS.**
I KNOW THAT.
IF YOU DRAG THEM AWAY THEY'LL JUST WANT REVENGE.
Jolt
ガバッ
NOW WHO'S THE MEAN OLD AUNTIE?!
I UNDER-STAND WANTING TO TAKE A CUTE LITTLE THING HOME WITH YOU.
ウガー
Gaaah!
DON'T LUMP ME IN WITH YOU!

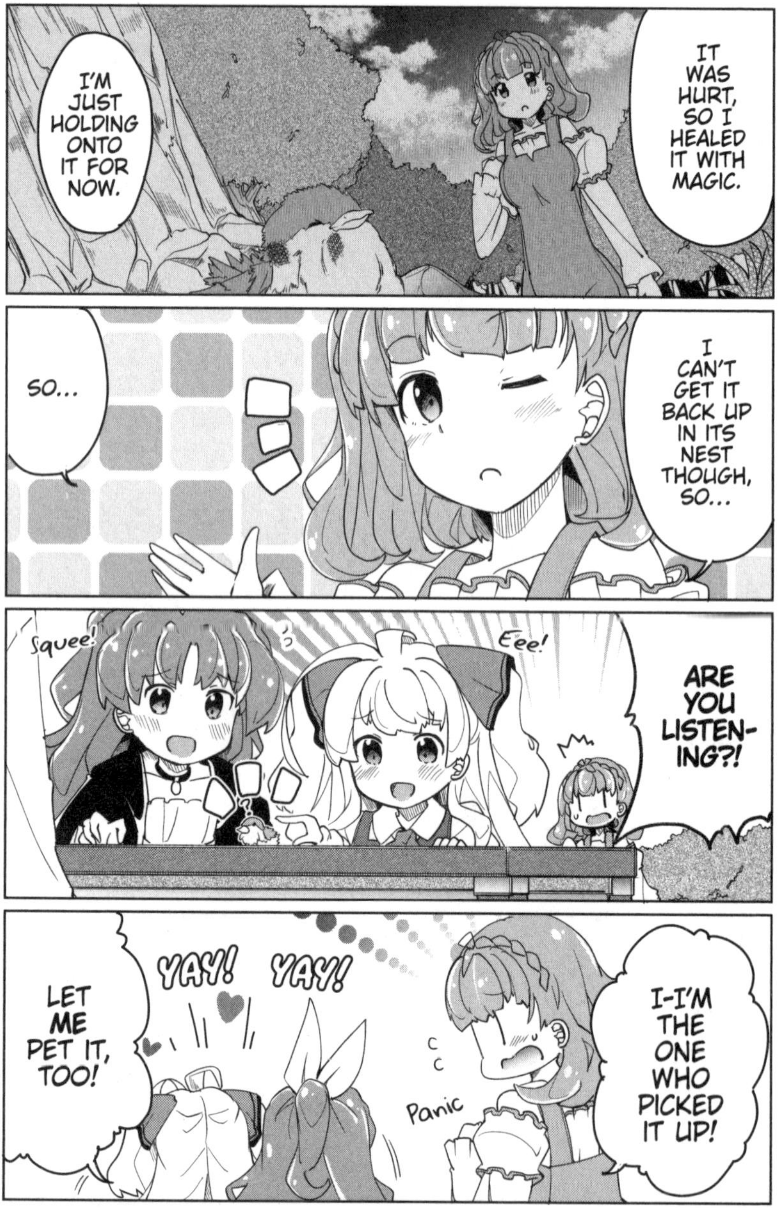

IT WAS HURT, SO I HEALED IT WITH MAGIC.
I'M JUST HOLDING ONTO IT FOR NOW.
I CAN'T GET IT BACK UP IN ITS NEST THOUGH, SO...
SO...
ARE YOU LISTENING?!
Eee!
Squee!
I-I'M THE ONE WHO PICKED IT UP!
Panic
YAY! YAY!
LET ME PET IT, TOO!

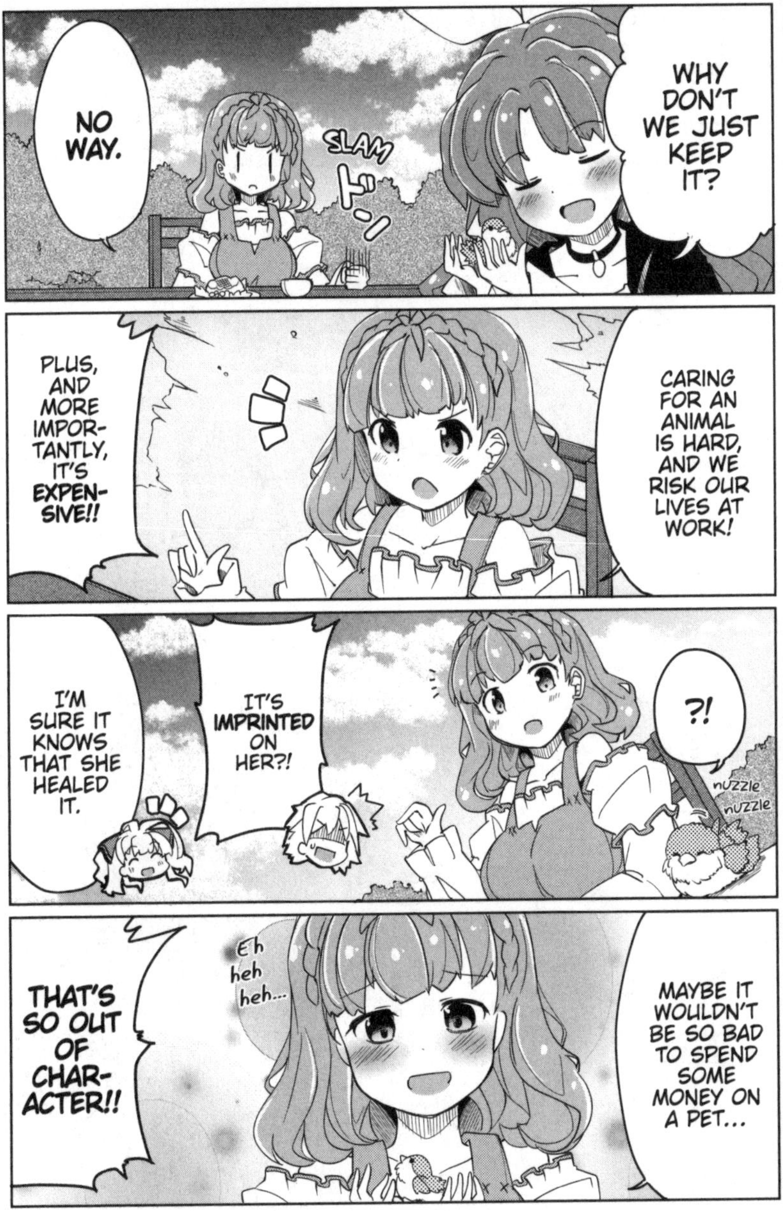
WHY DON'T WE JUST KEEP IT?
SLAM
ドーン
NO WAY.
CARING FOR AN ANIMAL IS HARD, AND WE RISK OUR LIVES AT WORK!
PLUS, AND MORE IMPOR-TANTLY, IT'S EXPEN-SIVE!!
?!
nuzzle nuzzle
IT'S IMPRINTED ON HER?!
I'M SURE IT KNOWS THAT SHE HEALED IT.
MAYBE IT WOULDN'T BE SO BAD TO SPEND SOME MONEY ON A PET...
Eh heh heh...
THAT'S SO OUT OF CHAR-ACTER!!

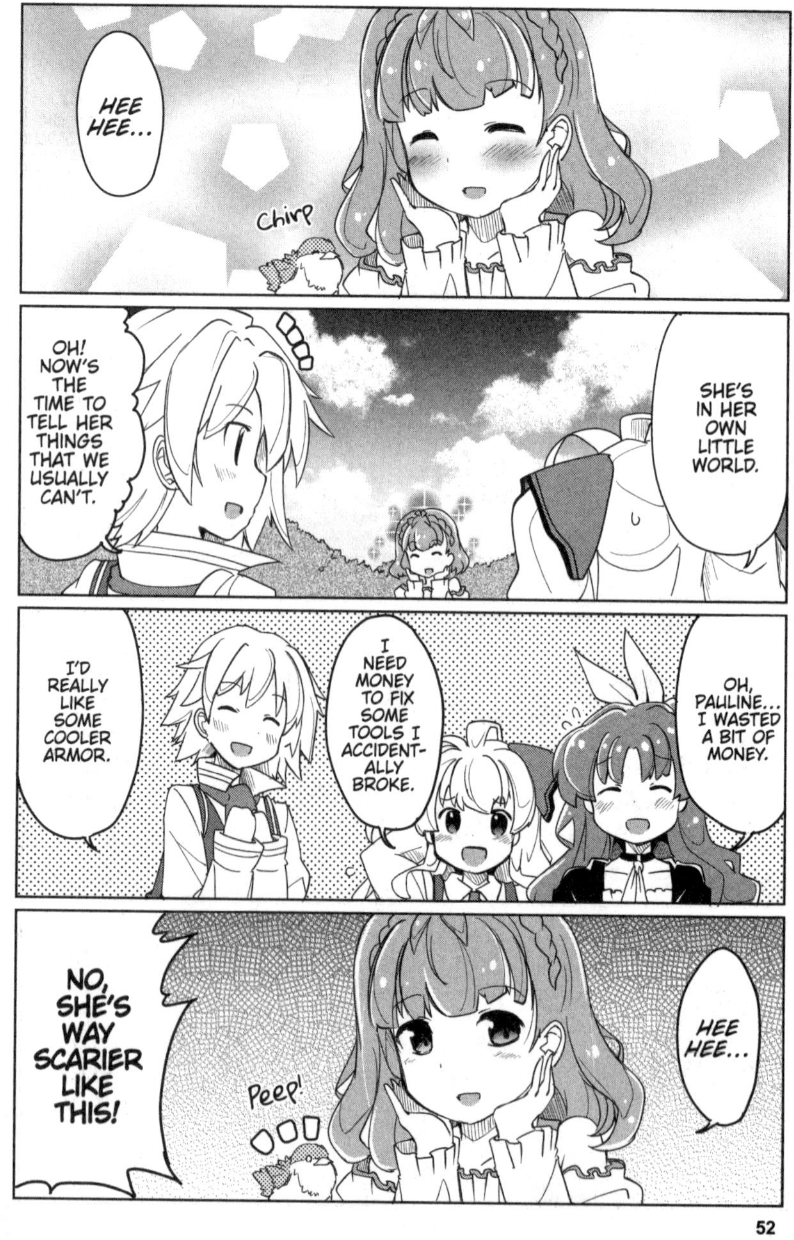
HEE HEE...
Chirp
SHE'S IN HER OWN LITTLE WORLD.
OH! NOW'S THE TIME TO TELL HER THINGS THAT WE USUALLY CAN'T.
OH, PAULINE... I WASTED A BIT OF MONEY.
I NEED MONEY TO FIX SOME TOOLS I ACCIDENT-ALLY BROKE.
I'D REALLY LIKE SOME COOLER ARMOR.
HEE HEE...
Peep!
NO, SHE'S WAY SCARIER LIKE THIS!

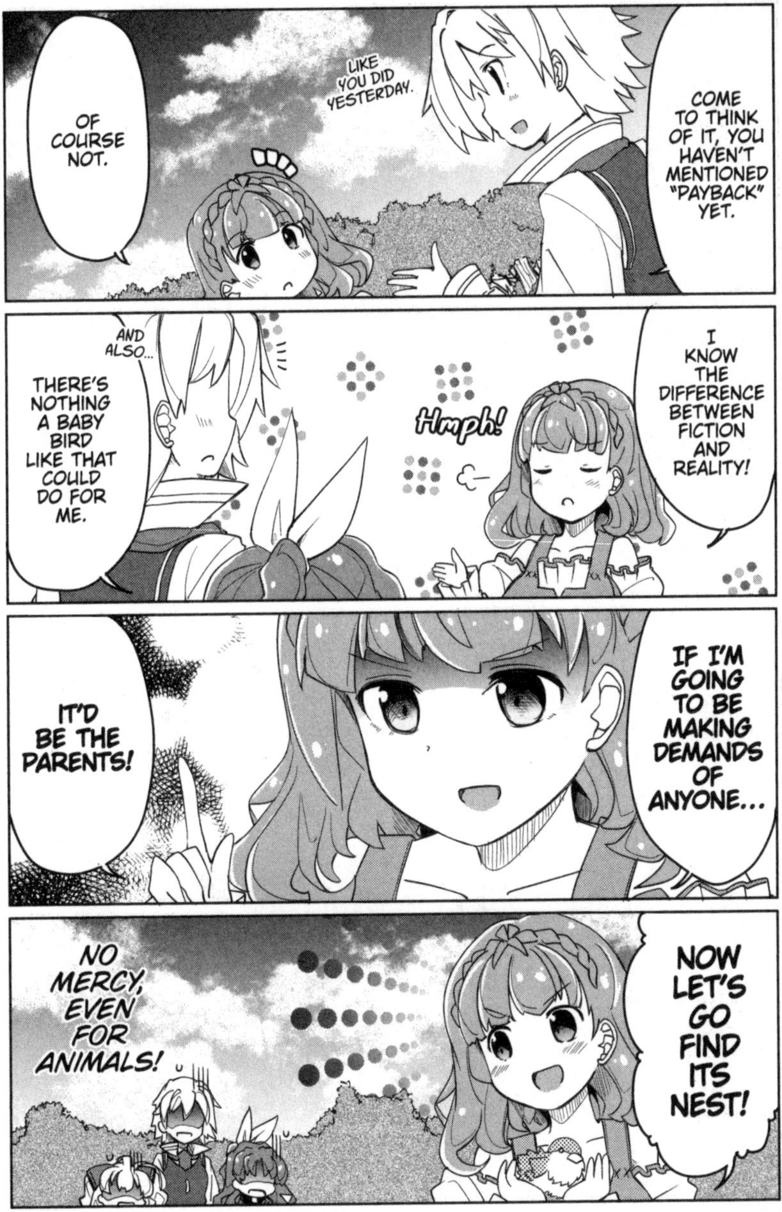
COME TO THINK OF IT, YOU HAVEN'T MENTIONED "PAYBACK" YET.
LIKE YOU DID YESTERDAY.
OF COURSE NOT.
I KNOW THE DIFFERENCE BETWEEN FICTION AND REALITY!
Hmph!
AND ALSO...
THERE'S NOTHING A BABY BIRD LIKE THAT COULD DO FOR ME.
IF I'M GOING TO BE MAKING DEMANDS OF ANYONE...
IT'D BE THE PARENTS!
NOW LET'S GO FIND ITS NEST!
NO MERCY, EVEN FOR ANIMALS!

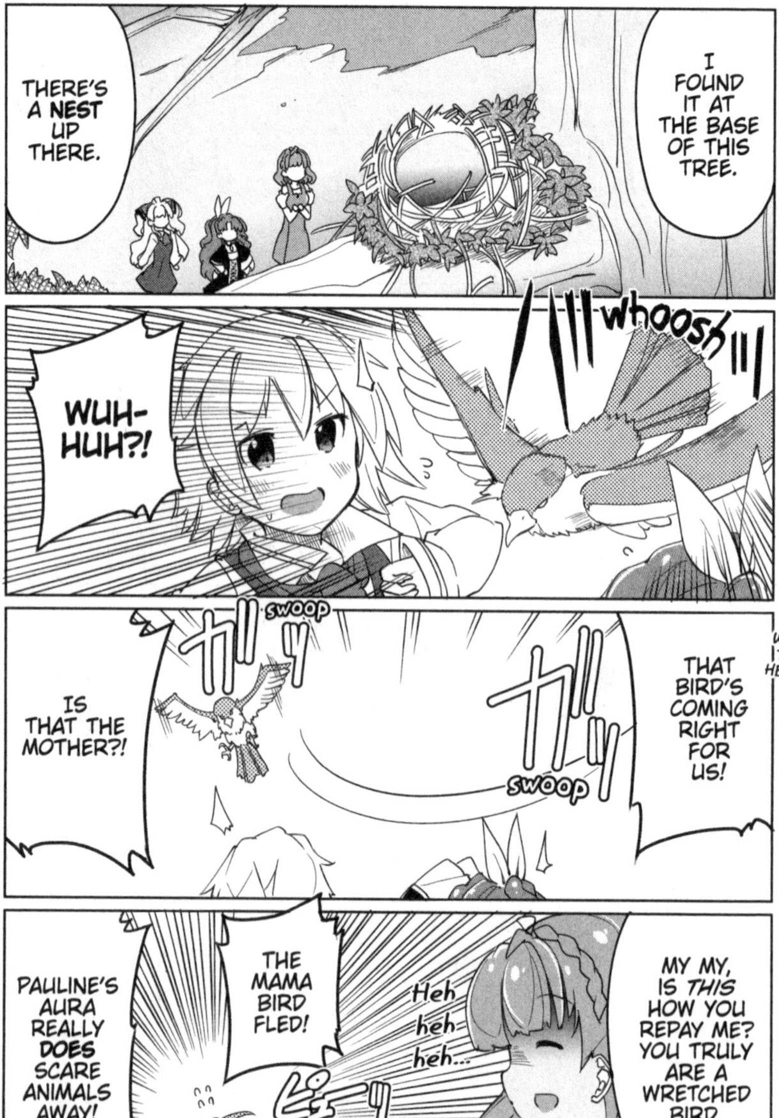
I FOUND IT AT THE BASE OF THIS TREE.
THERE'S A NEST UP THERE.
whoosh
WUH-HUH?!
WHAT THE HECK?
THAT BIRD'S COMING RIGHT FOR US!
swoop
swoop
IS THAT THE MOTHER?!
MY MY, IS THIS HOW YOU REPAY ME? YOU TRULY ARE A WRETCHED BIRD.
Heh heh heh...
ZOOM
THE MAMA BIRD FLED!
PAULINE'S AURA REALLY DOES SCARE ANIMALS AWAY!

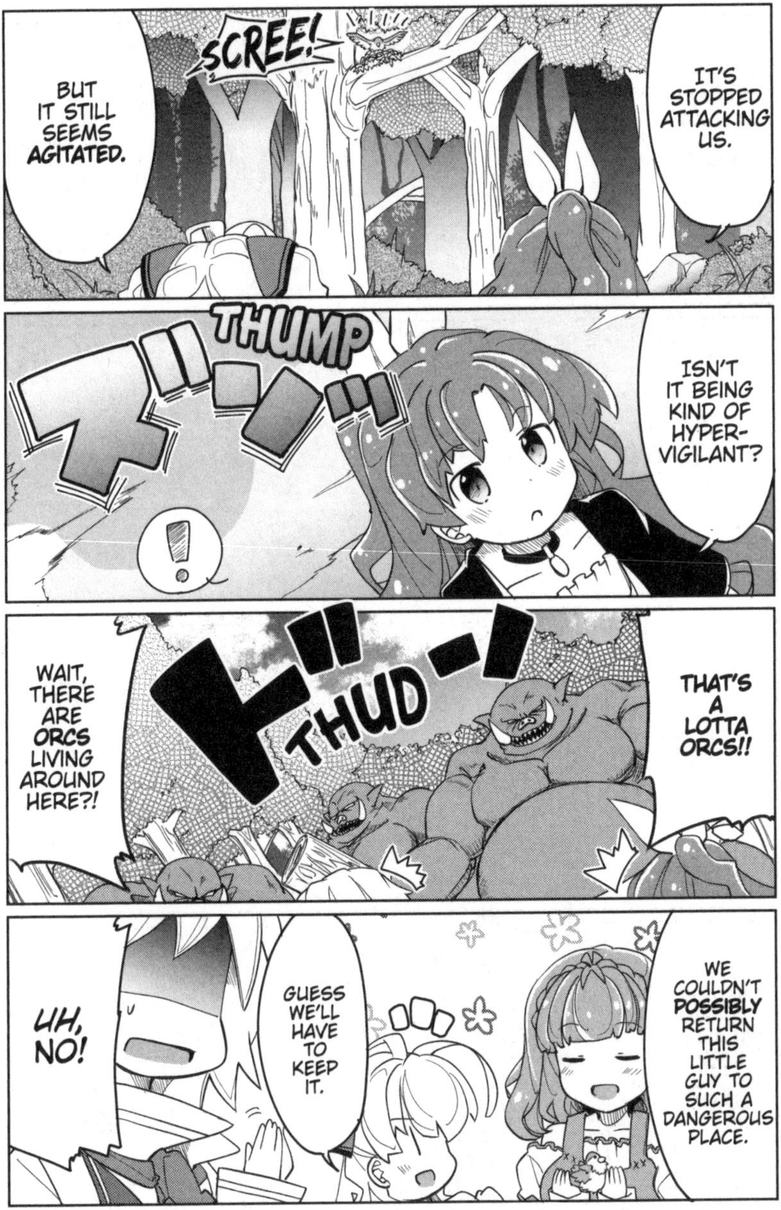
IT'S STOPPED ATTACKING US.
SCREE!
BUT IT STILL SEEMS AGITATED.
ISN'T IT BEING KIND OF HYPER-VIGILANT?
THUMP
!
THAT'S A LOTTA ORCS!!
THUD
WAIT, THERE ARE ORCS LIVING AROUND HERE?!
WE COULDN'T POSSIBLY RETURN THIS LITTLE GUY TO SUCH A DANGEROUS PLACE.
GUESS WE'LL HAVE TO KEEP IT.
UH, NO!

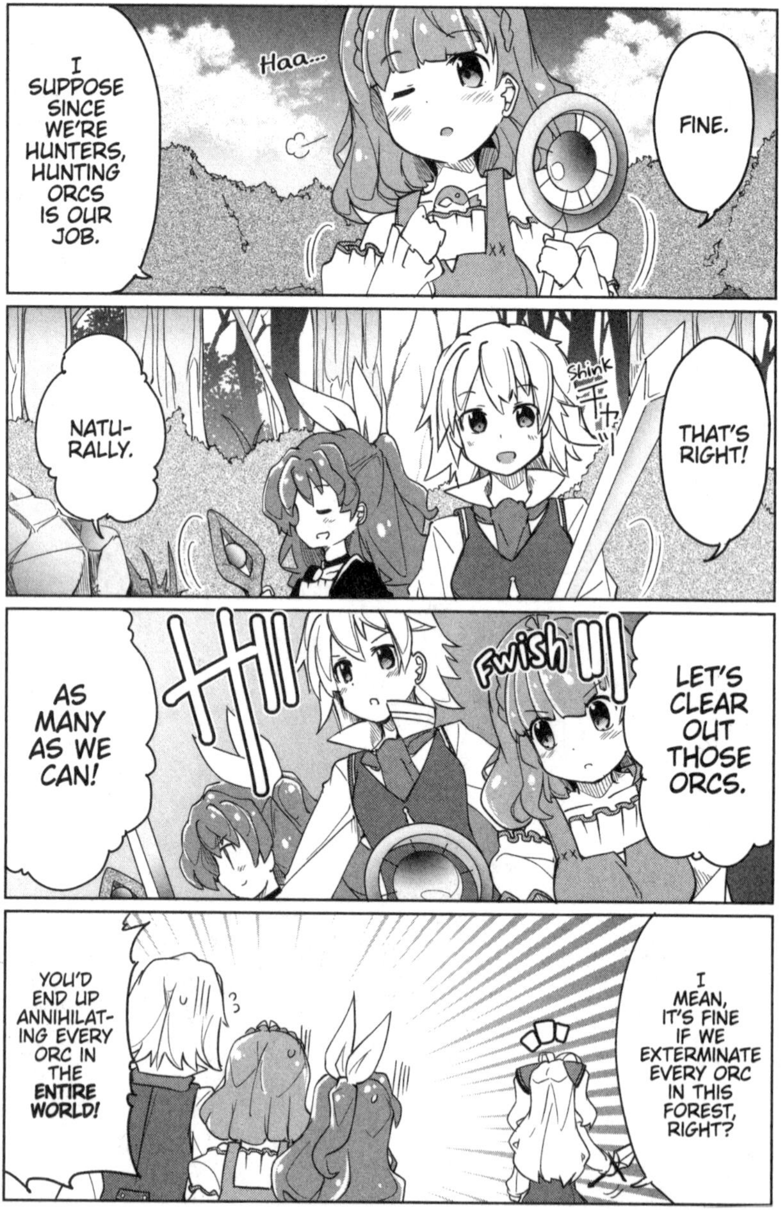
FINE.
Haa...
I SUPPOSE SINCE WE'RE HUNTERS, HUNTING ORCS IS OUR JOB.
THAT'S RIGHT!
Shink
NATU-RALLY.
LET'S CLEAR OUT THOSE ORCS.
Fwish
AS MANY AS WE CAN!
I MEAN, IT'S FINE IF WE EXTERMINATE EVERY ORC IN THIS FOREST, RIGHT?
YOU'D END UP ANNIHILAT-ING EVERY ORC IN THE **ENTIRE WORLD!**

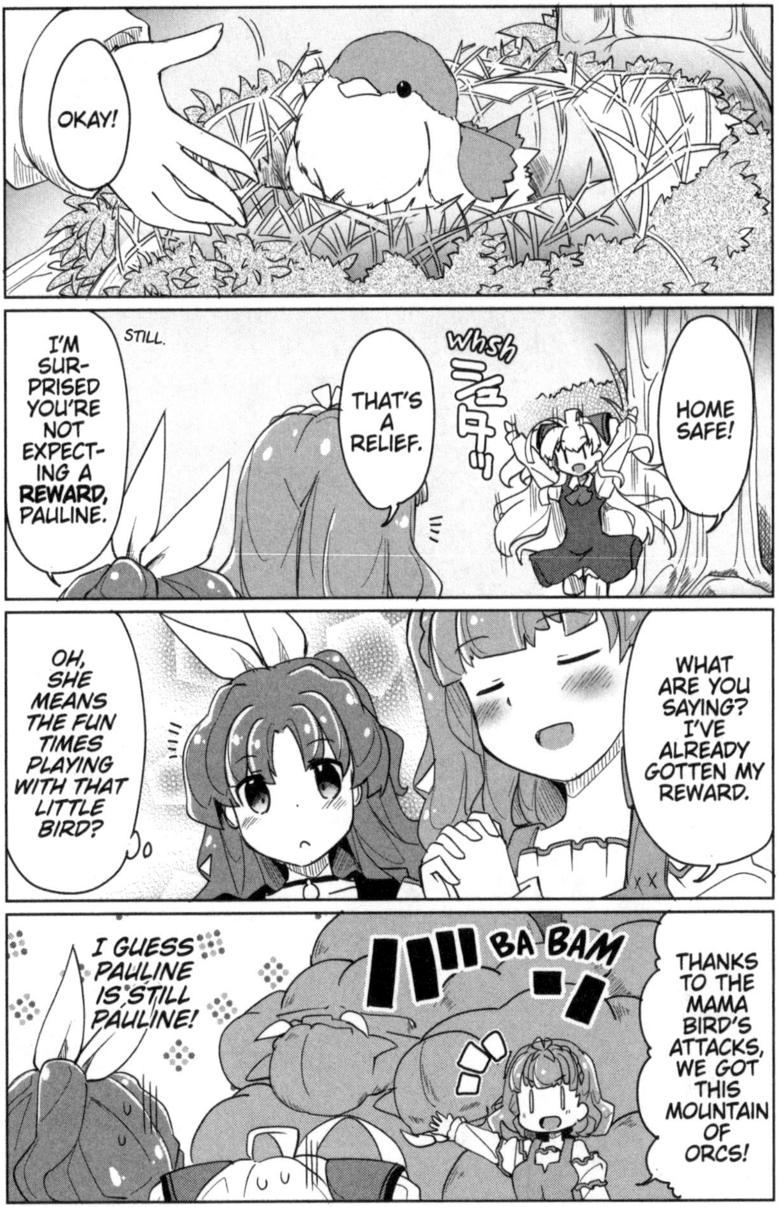
OKAY!
HOME SAFE!
Whsh
シュタッ
THAT'S A RELIEF.
STILL.
I'M SURPRISED YOU'RE NOT EXPECTING A **REWARD**, PAULINE.
WHAT ARE YOU SAYING? I'VE ALREADY GOTTEN MY REWARD.
OH, SHE MEANS THE FUN TIMES PLAYING WITH THAT LITTLE BIRD?
THANKS TO THE MAMA BIRD'S ATTACKS, WE GOT THIS MOUNTAIN OF ORCS!
BA BAM
I GUESS PAULINE IS STILL PAULINE!

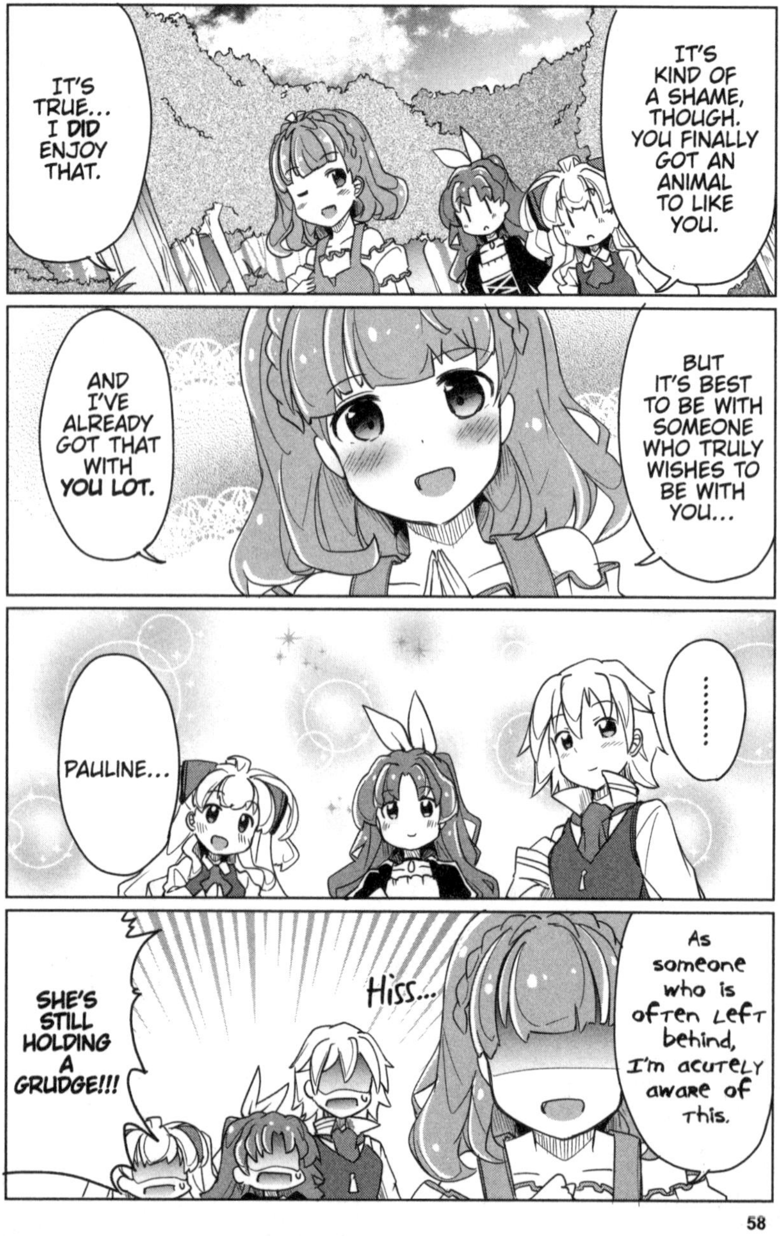

IT'S KIND OF A SHAME, THOUGH. YOU FINALLY GOT AN ANIMAL TO LIKE YOU.
IT'S TRUE... I DID ENJOY THAT.
BUT IT'S BEST TO BE WITH SOMEONE WHO TRULY WISHES TO BE WITH YOU...
AND I'VE ALREADY GOT THAT WITH YOU LOT.
....
PAULINE...
As someone who is often left behind, I'm acutely aware of this.
Hiss...
SHE'S STILL HOLDING A GRUDGE!!!

Didn't I Say to Make My Abilities Average in the Next Life?!

EVERYDAY MISADVENTURES!

Chirp

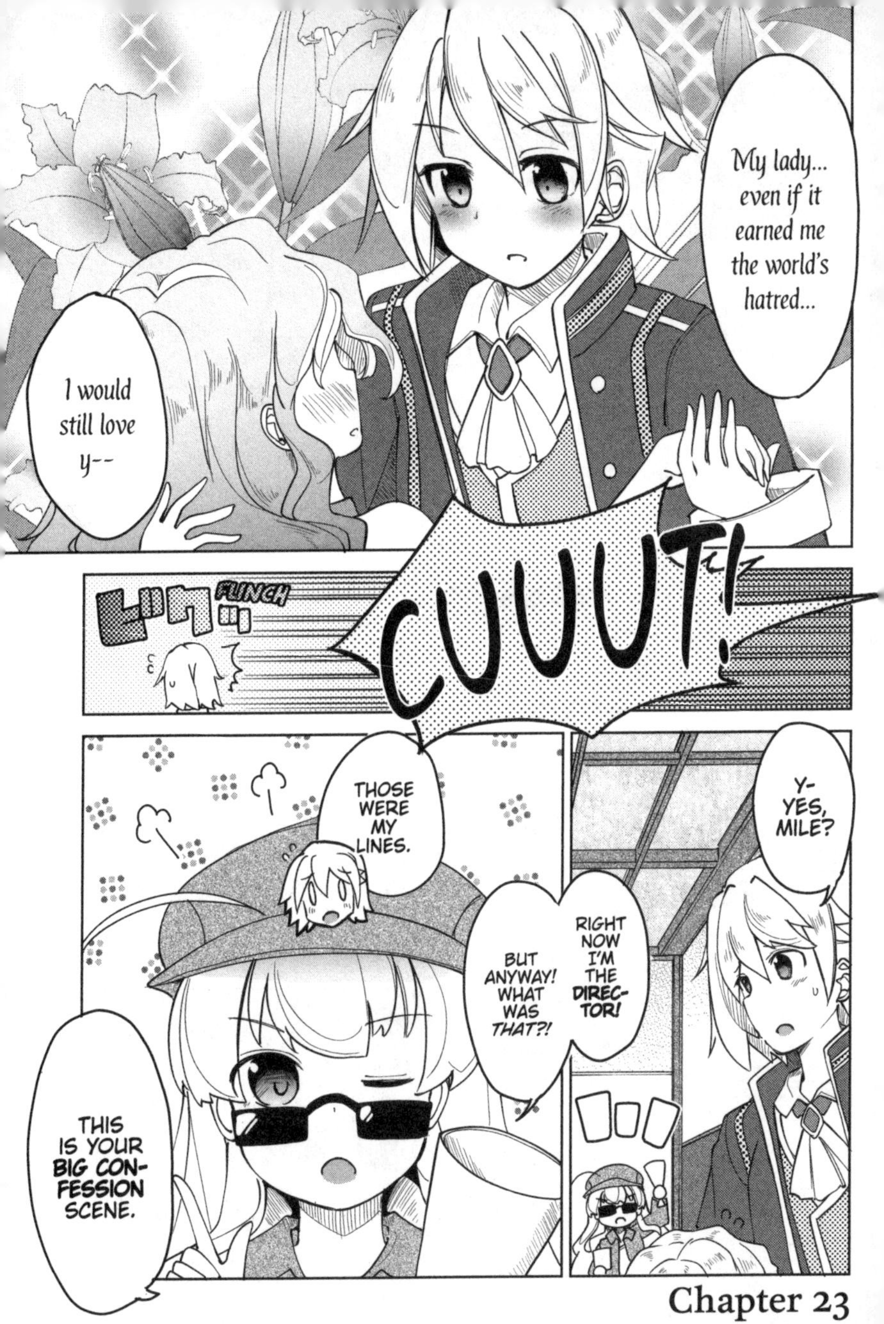
My lady... even if it earned me the world's hatred...
I would still love y--
FLINCH
CUUUT!
Y- YES, MILE?
RIGHT NOW I'M THE DIRECTOR!
BUT ANYWAY! WHAT WAS THAT?!
THOSE WERE MY LINES.
THIS IS YOUR BIG CONFESSION SCENE.

Chapter 23

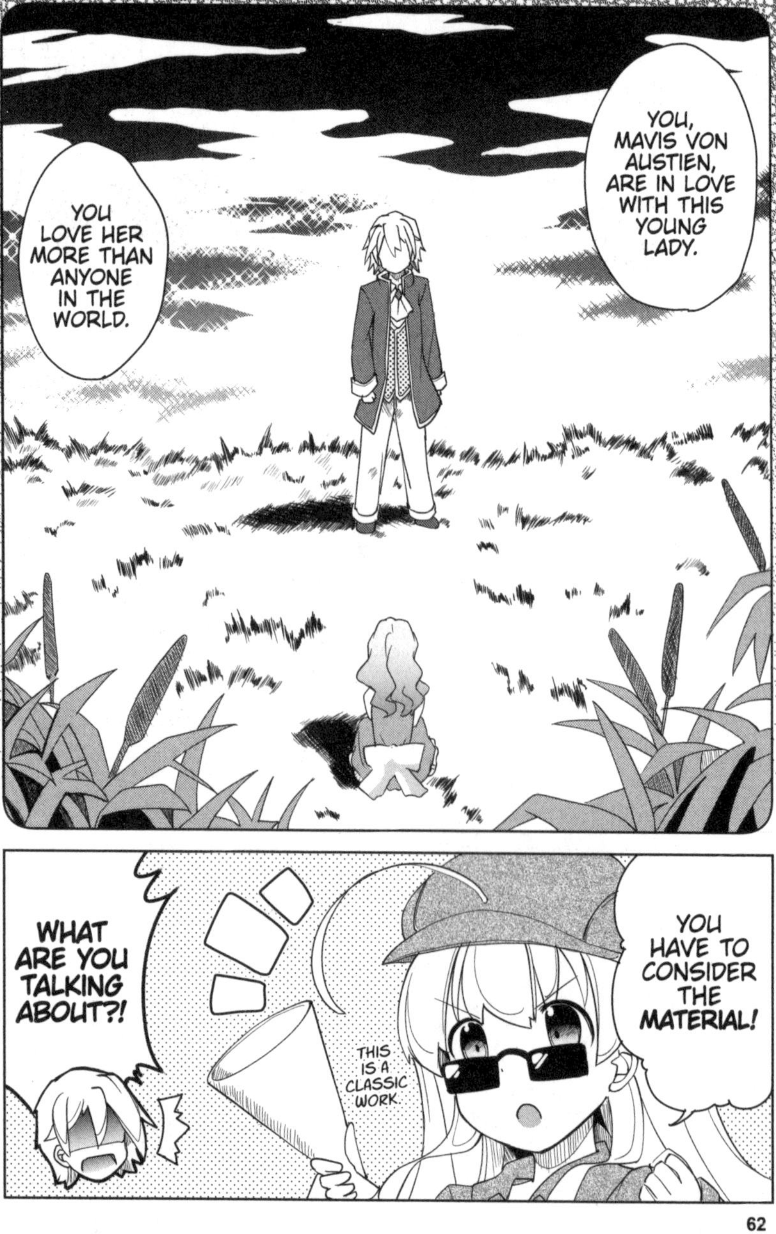
YOU, MAVIS VON AUSTIEN, ARE IN LOVE WITH THIS YOUNG LADY.
YOU LOVE HER MORE THAN ANYONE IN THE WORLD.
YOU HAVE TO CONSIDER THE MATERIAL!
THIS IS A CLASSIC WORK.
WHAT ARE YOU TALKING ABOUT?!

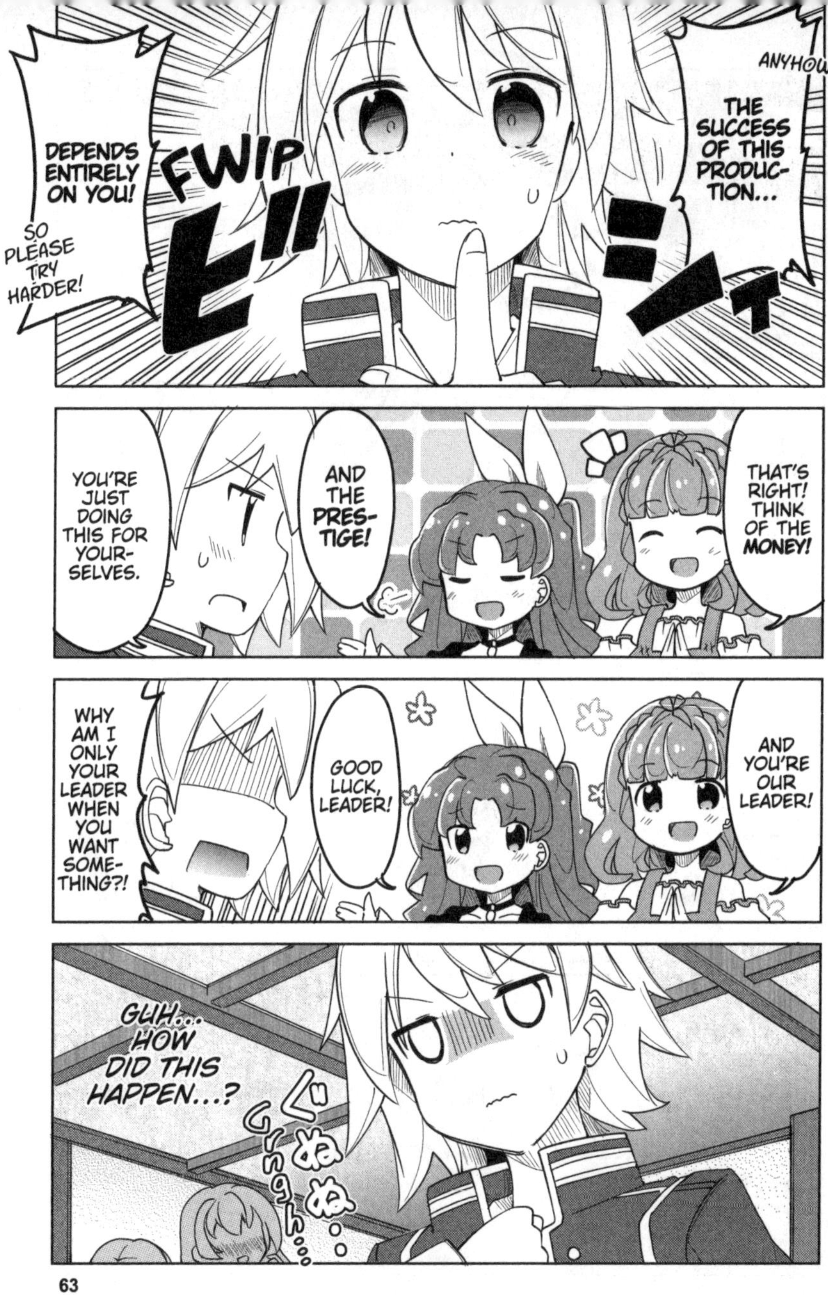
ANYHOW!
THE SUCCESS OF THIS PRODUCTION...
DEPENDS ENTIRELY ON YOU!
SO PLEASE TRY HARDER!
FWIP
ビシッ
THAT'S RIGHT! THINK OF THE MONEY!
AND THE PRESTIGE!
YOU'RE JUST DOING THIS FOR YOURSELVES.
AND YOU'RE OUR LEADER!
GOOD LUCK, LEADER!
WHY AM I ONLY YOUR LEADER WHEN YOU WANT SOMETHING?!
GUH... HOW DID THIS HAPPEN...?
ぐぬぬ。。
Grrngh...

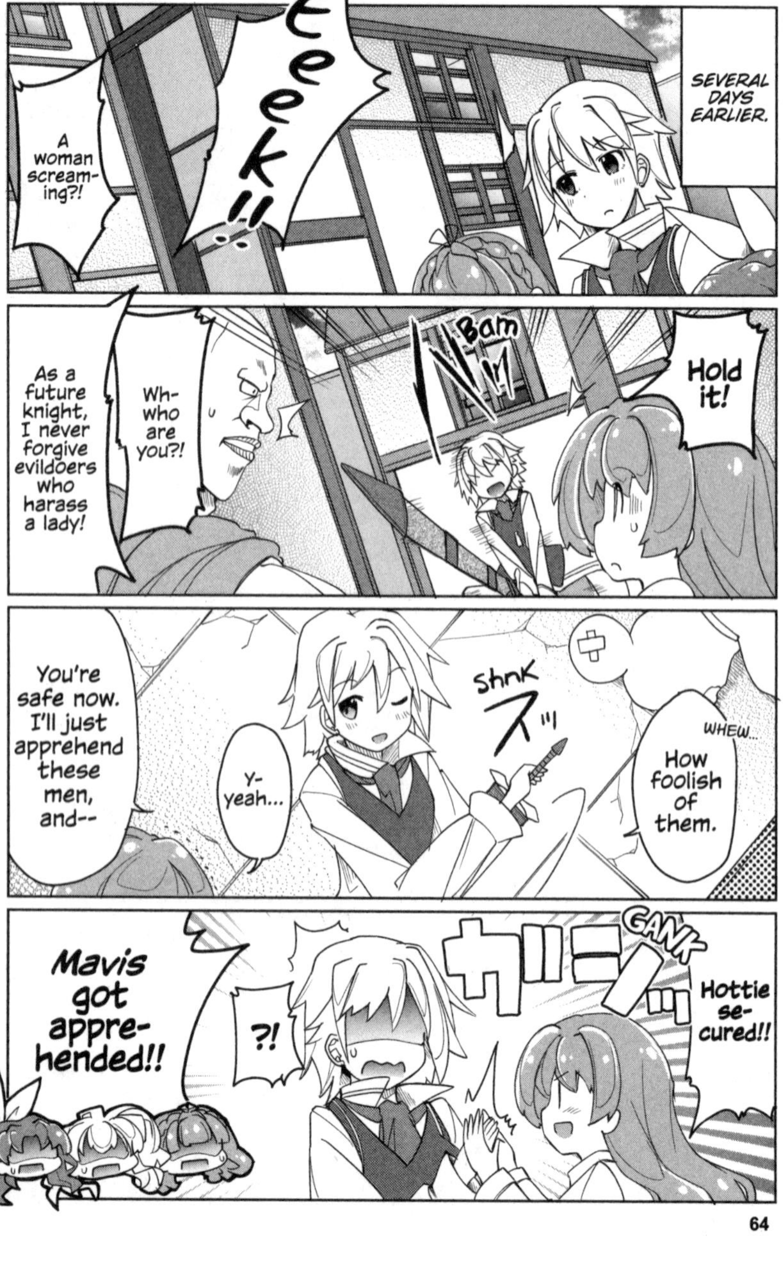
SEVERAL DAYS EARLIER.
Eeeek!!
A woman scream-ing?!
Hold it!
Bam
Wh-who are you?!
As a future knight, I never forgive evildoers who harass a lady!
WHEW... How foolish of them.
Shnk
Y-yeah...
You're safe now. I'll just apprehend these men, and--
Hottie se-cured!!
GANK
?!
Mavis got appre-hended!!

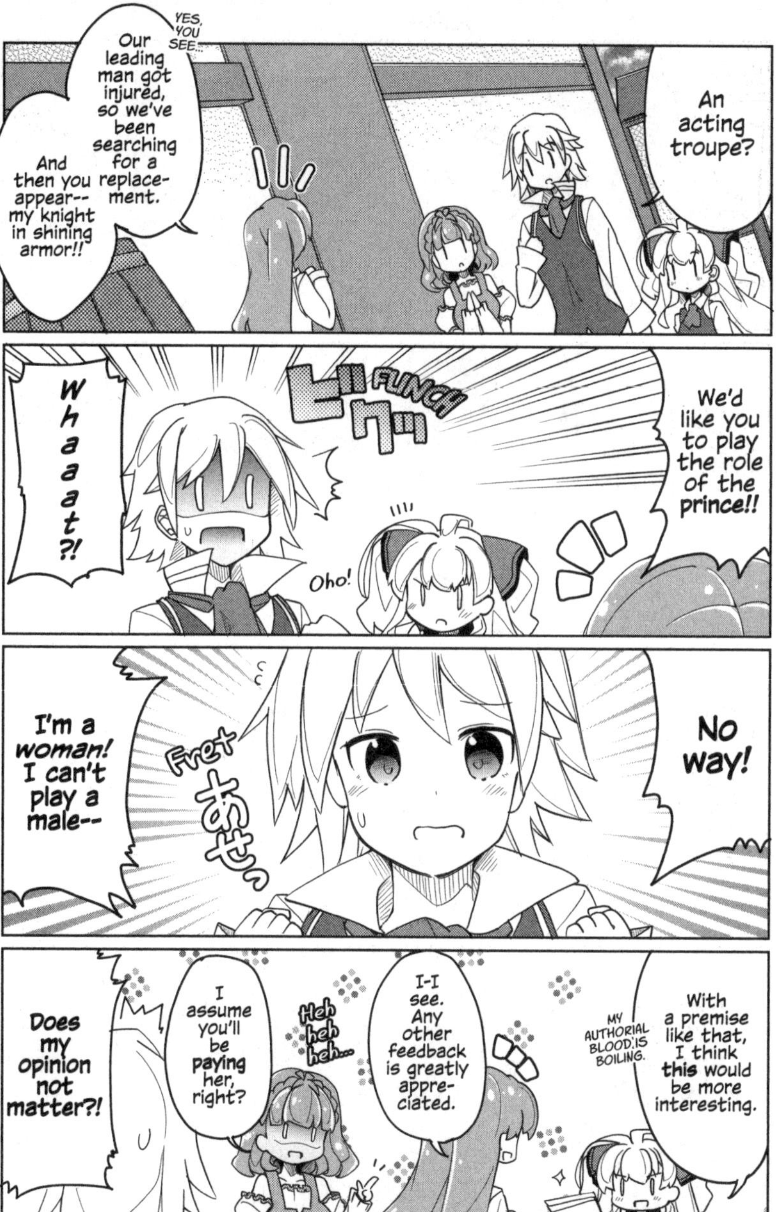
An acting troupe?
YES, YOU SEE...
Our leading man got injured, so we've been searching for a replacement.
And then you appear-- my knight in shining armor!!
We'd like you to play the role of the prince!!
ビクッ
FLINCH!
Oho!
Whaaaat?!
No way!
Fret
あせっ
I'm a woman! I can't play a male--
With a premise like that, I think this would be more interesting.
MY AUTHORIAL BLOOD IS BOILING.
I-I see. Any other feedback is greatly appreciated.
Heh heh heh...
I assume you'll be paying her, right?
Does my opinion not matter?!

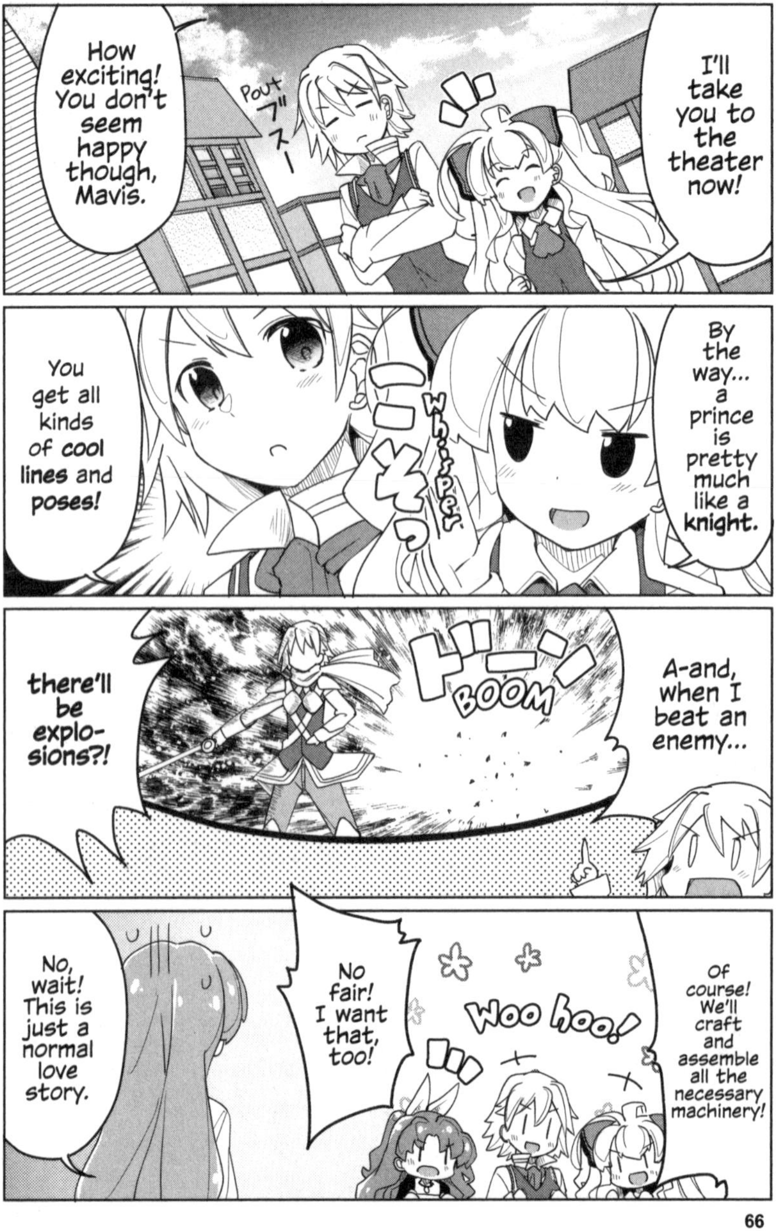
I'll take you to the theater now!
How exciting! You don't seem happy though, Mavis.
Pout
By the way... a prince is pretty much like a knight.
Whisper
You get all kinds of cool lines and poses!
A-and, when I beat an enemy...
BOOM
there'll be explosions?!
Of course! We'll craft and assemble all the necessary machinery!
Woo hoo!
No fair! I want that, too!
No, wait! This is just a normal love story.

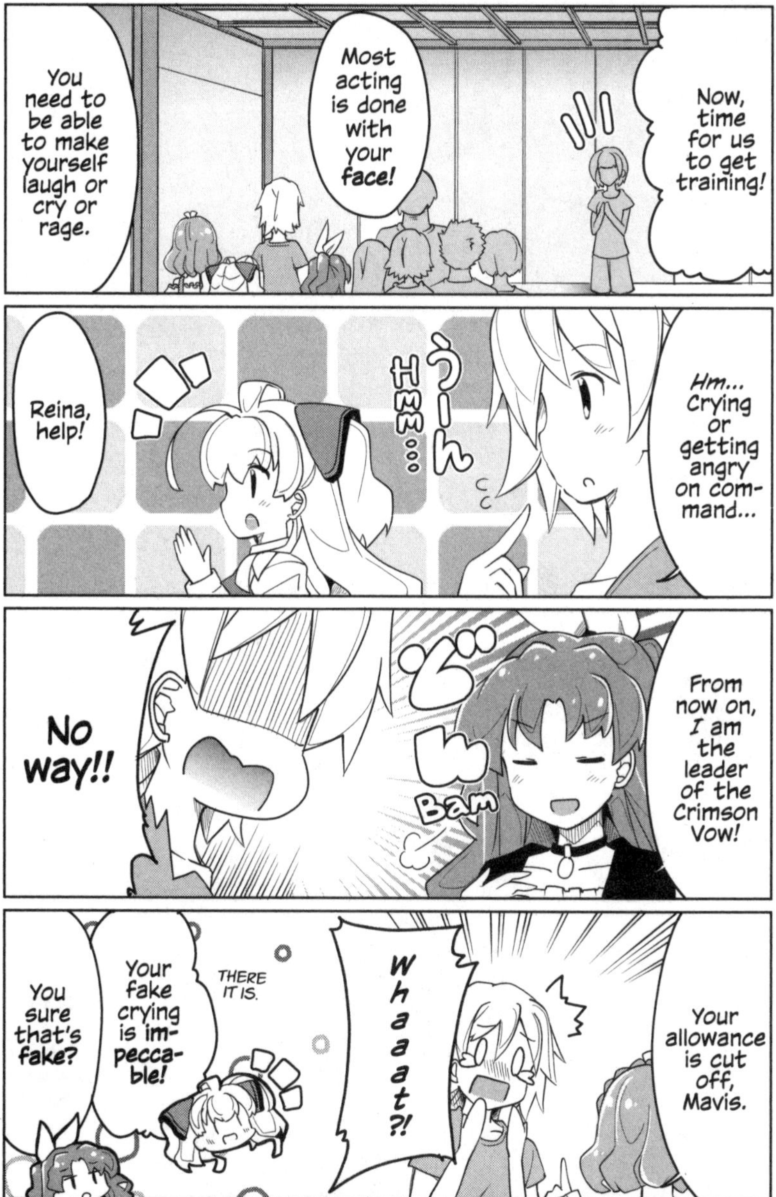
Now, time for us to get training!
Most acting is done with your face!
You need to be able to make yourself laugh or cry or rage.
Hm... Crying or getting angry on command...
うーん
Hmm...
Reina, help!
From now on, I am the leader of the Crimson Vow!
どん
Bam
No way!!
Your allowance is cut off, Mavis.
Whaaaat?!
THERE IT IS.
Your fake crying is impeccable!
You sure that's fake?

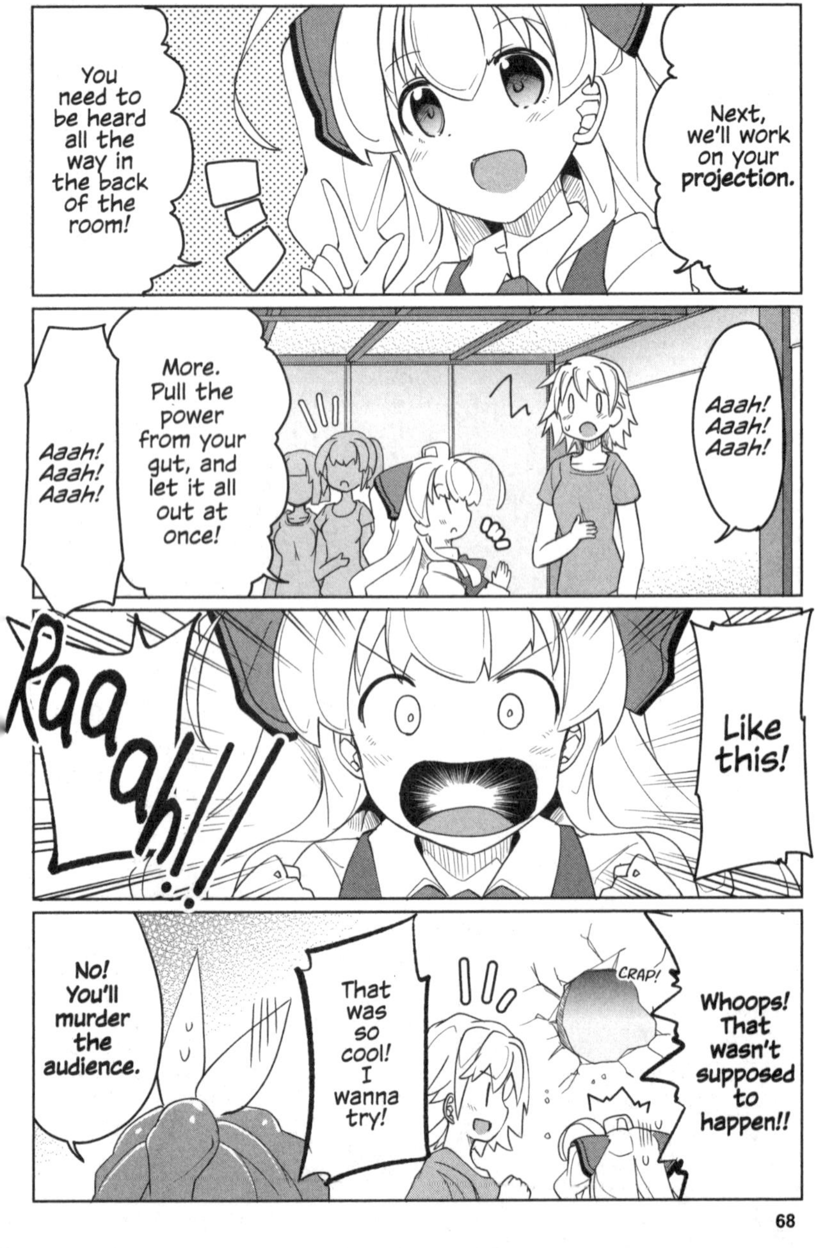

Next, we'll work on your projection.
You need to be heard all the way in the back of the room!
Aaah! Aaah! Aaah!
More. Pull the power from your gut, and let it all out at once!
Aaah! Aaah! Aaah!
Like this!
Raaah!!
Whoops! That wasn't supposed to happen!!
CRAP!
That was so cool! I wanna try!
No! You'll murder the audience.

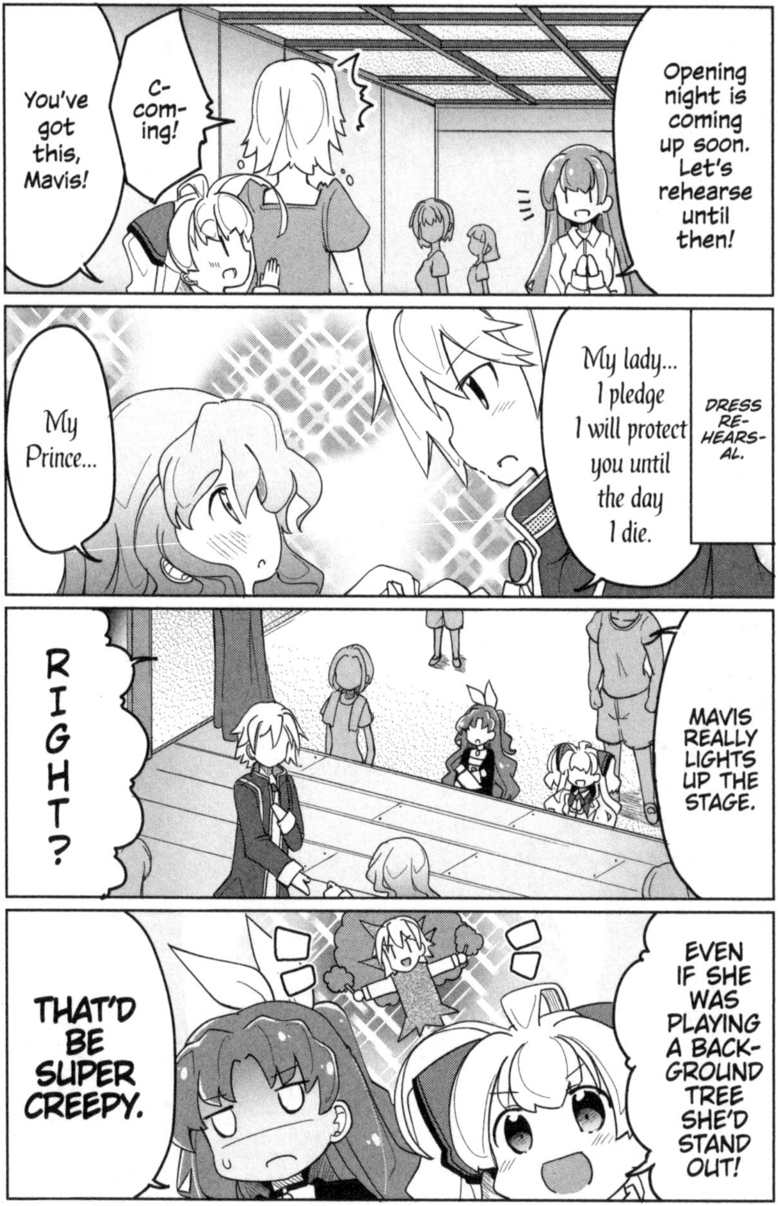
Opening night is coming up soon. Let's rehearse until then!
C-coming!
You've got this, Mavis!
DRESS REHEARSAL.
My lady... I pledge I will protect you until the day I die.
My Prince...
MAVIS REALLY LIGHTS UP THE STAGE.
RIGHT?
EVEN IF SHE WAS PLAYING A BACKGROUND TREE SHE'D STAND OUT!
THAT'D BE SUPER CREEPY.

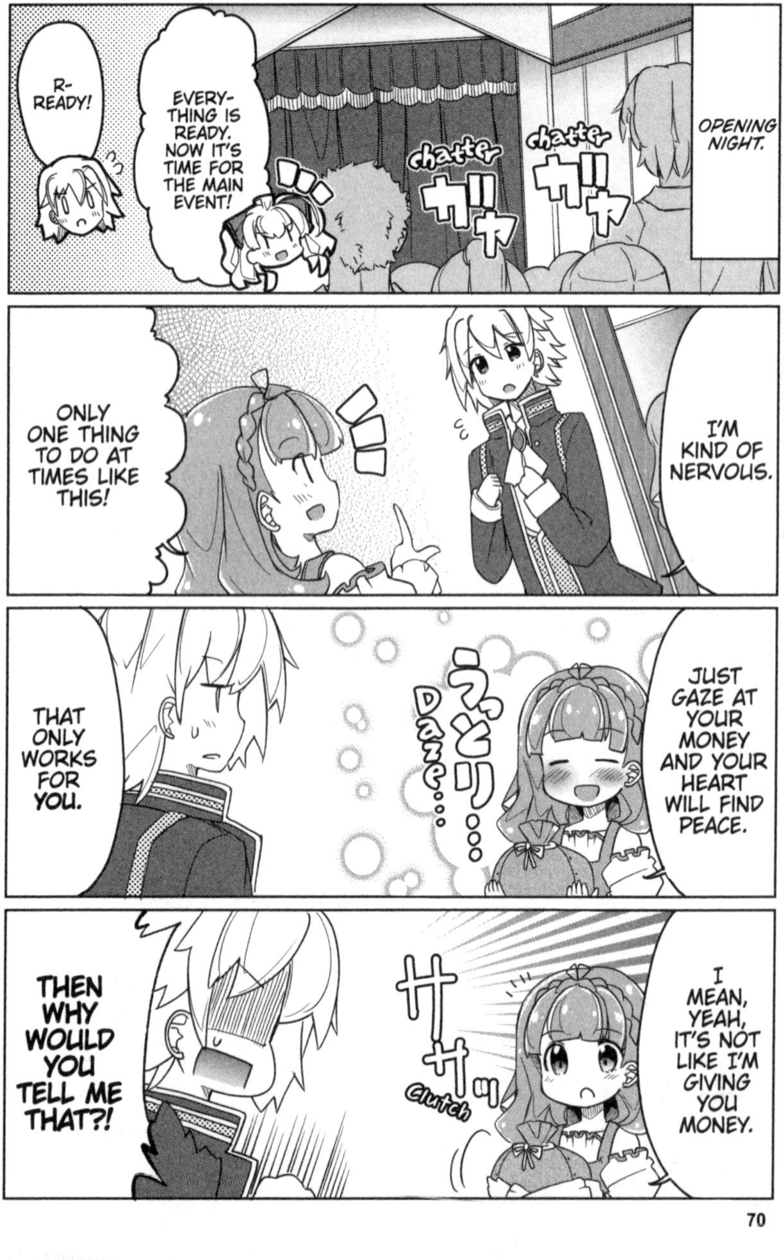
OPENING NIGHT.
chatter ガヤ
chatter ガヤ
EVERY-THING IS READY. NOW IT'S TIME FOR THE MAIN EVENT!
R-READY!
I'M KIND OF NERVOUS.
ONLY ONE THING TO DO AT TIMES LIKE THIS!
JUST GAZE AT YOUR MONEY AND YOUR HEART WILL FIND PEACE.
うっとり… Daze…
THAT ONLY WORKS FOR YOU.
I MEAN, YEAH, IT'S NOT LIKE I'M GIVING YOU MONEY.
ササッ Clutch
THEN WHY WOULD YOU TELL ME THAT?!

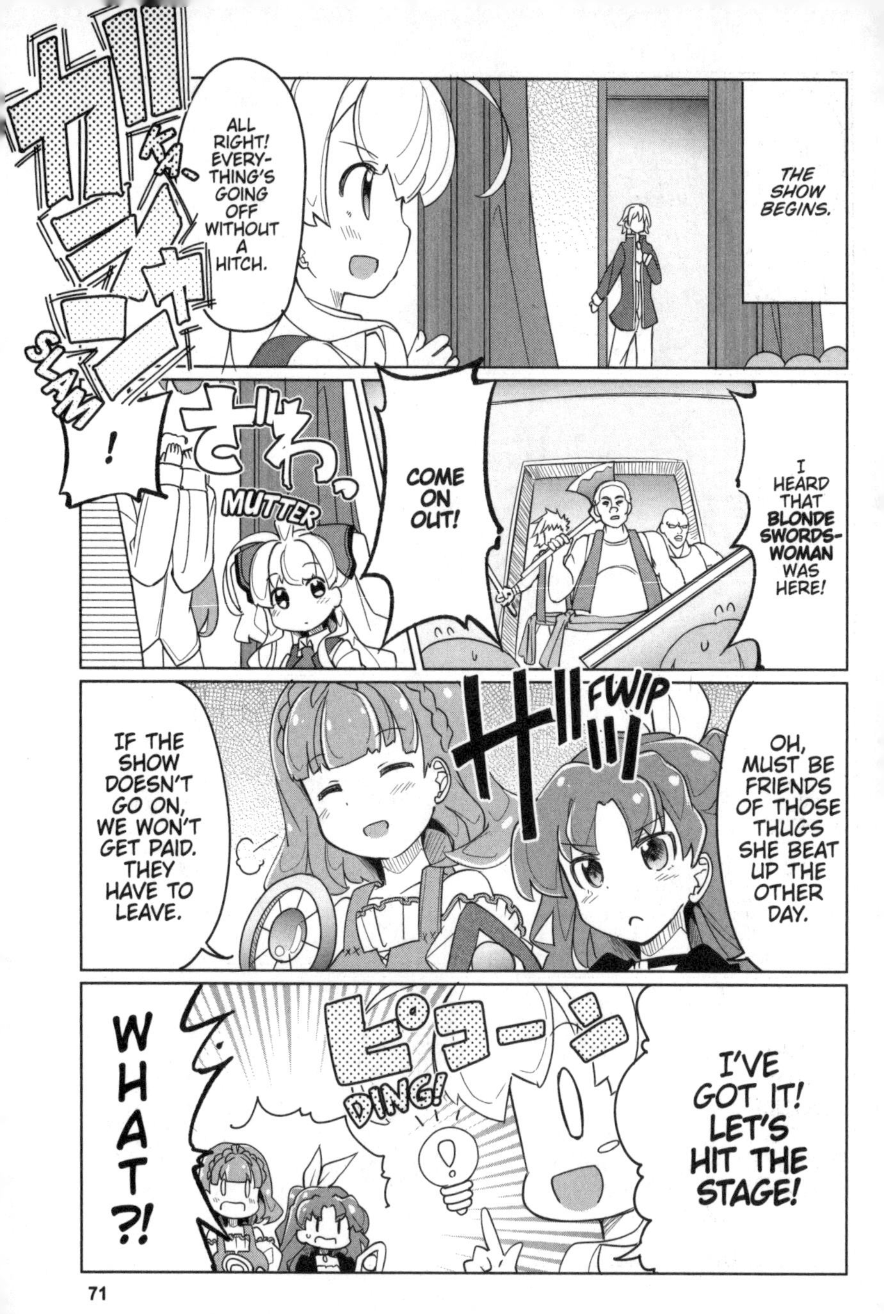
THE SHOW BEGINS.
ALL RIGHT! EVERYTHING'S GOING OFF WITHOUT A HITCH.
SLAM
!
I HEARD THAT BLONDE SWORDSWOMAN WAS HERE!
COME ON OUT!
MUTTER
OH, MUST BE FRIENDS OF THOSE THUGS SHE BEAT UP THE OTHER DAY.
FWIP
IF THE SHOW DOESN'T GO ON, WE WON'T GET PAID. THEY HAVE TO LEAVE.
I'VE GOT IT! LET'S HIT THE STAGE!
DING!
WHAT?!

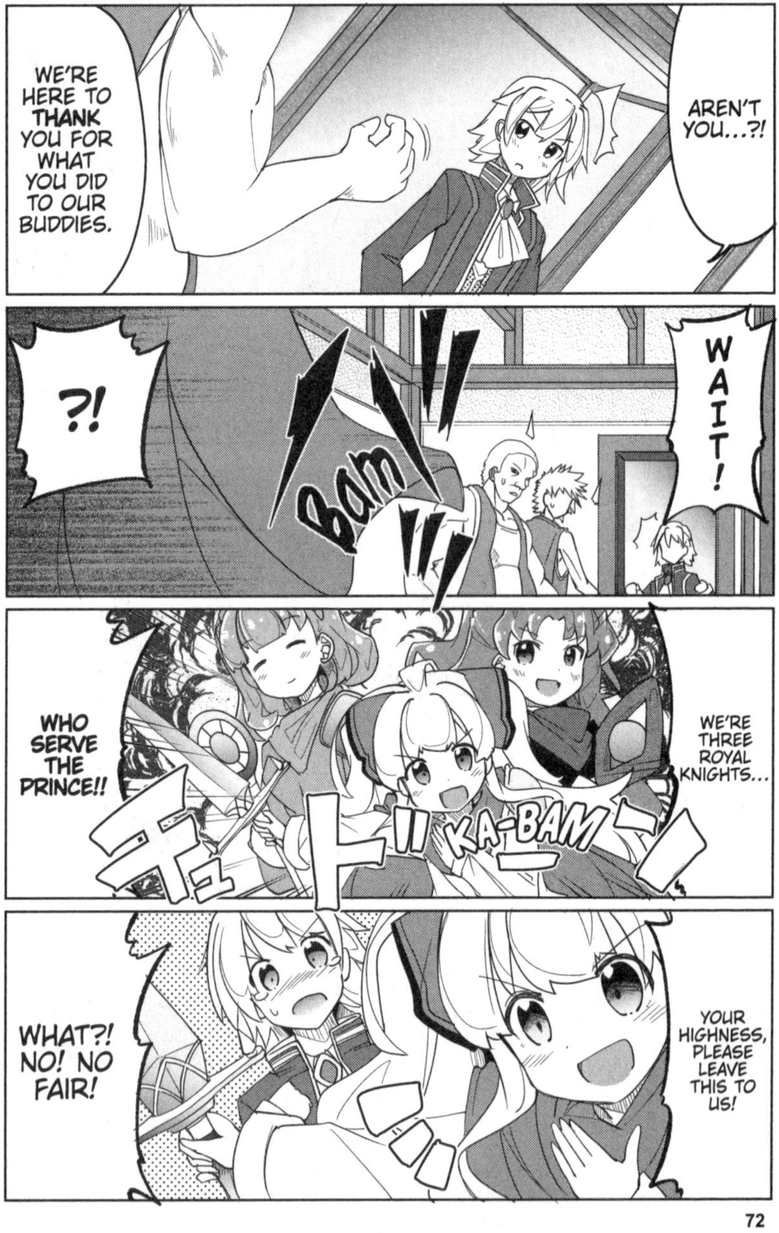
WE'RE HERE TO THANK YOU FOR WHAT YOU DID TO OUR BUDDIES.
AREN'T YOU...?!
WAIT!
?!
BAM
WE'RE THREE ROYAL KNIGHTS...
WHO SERVE THE PRINCE!!
KA-BAM
YOUR HIGHNESS, PLEASE LEAVE THIS TO US!
WHAT?! NO! NO FAIR!

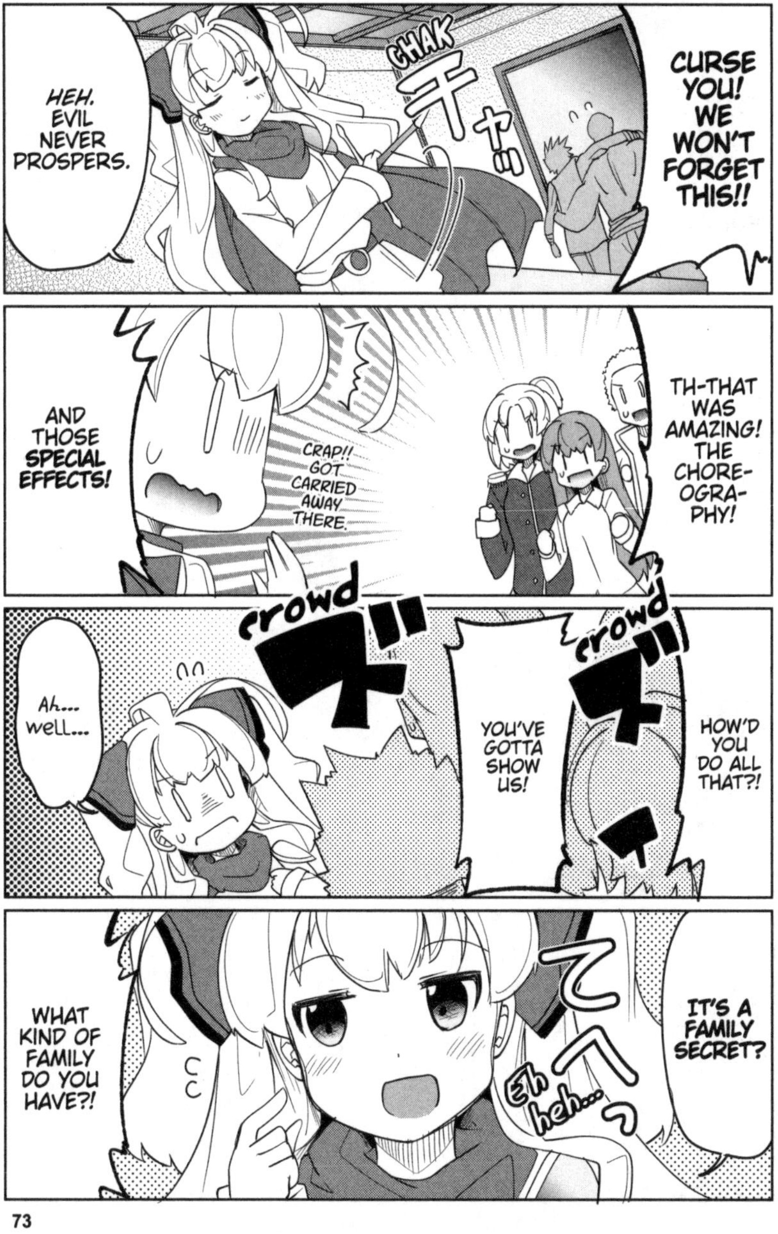
CURSE YOU! WE WON'T FORGET THIS!!
CHAK
HEH. EVIL NEVER PROSPERS.
TH-THAT WAS AMAZING! THE CHORE-OGRA-PHY!
CRAP!! GOT CARRIED AWAY THERE.
AND THOSE SPECIAL EFFECTS!
HOW'D YOU DO ALL THAT?!
crowd
YOU'VE GOTTA SHOW US!
crowd
Ah... well...
IT'S A FAMILY SECRET?
Eh heh...
WHAT KIND OF FAMILY DO YOU HAVE?!

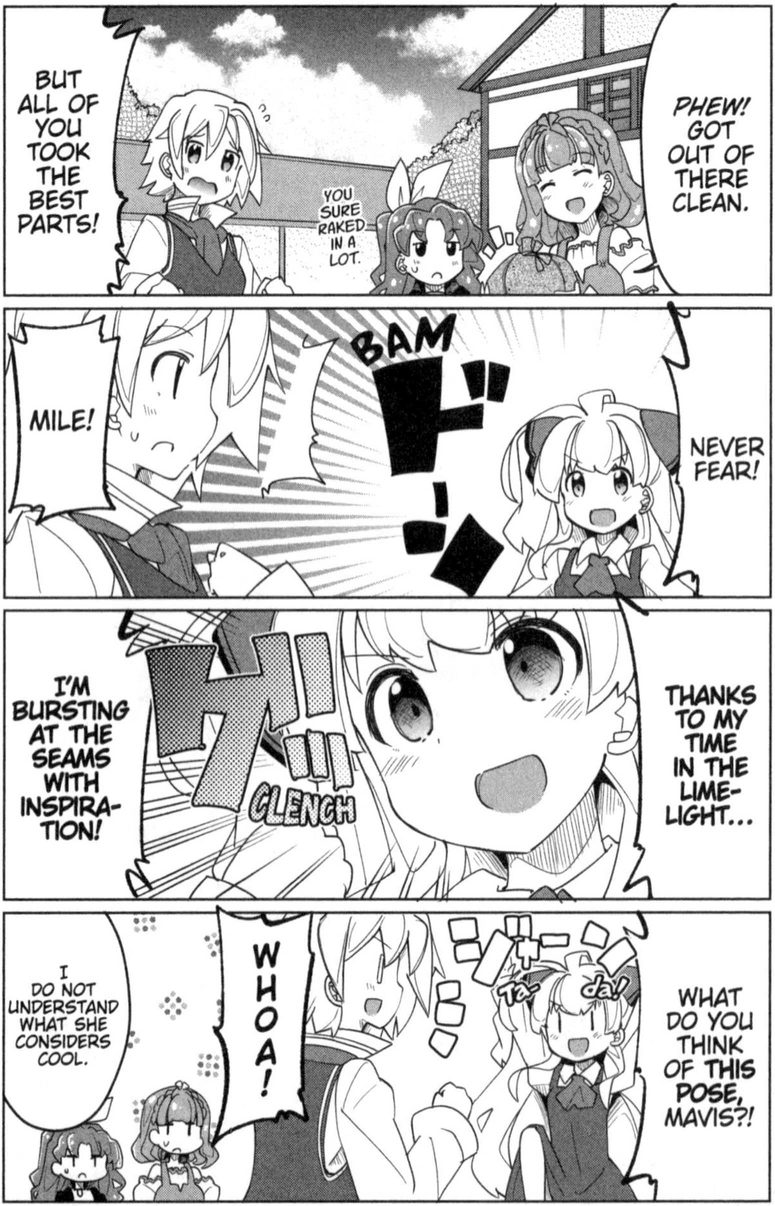
PHEW! GOT OUT OF THERE CLEAN.
YOU SURE RAKED IN A LOT.
BUT ALL OF YOU TOOK THE BEST PARTS!
NEVER FEAR!
BAM
MILE!
THANKS TO MY TIME IN THE LIME-LIGHT...
CLENCH
I'M BURSTING AT THE SEAMS WITH INSPIRA-TION!
WHAT DO YOU THINK OF THIS POSE, MAVIS?!
Ta-da!
WHOA!
I DO NOT UNDERSTAND WHAT SHE CONSIDERS COOL.

Didn't I Say to Make My Abilities Average in the Next Life?!

EVERYDAY MISADVENTURES!

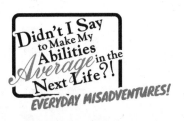

Oho!

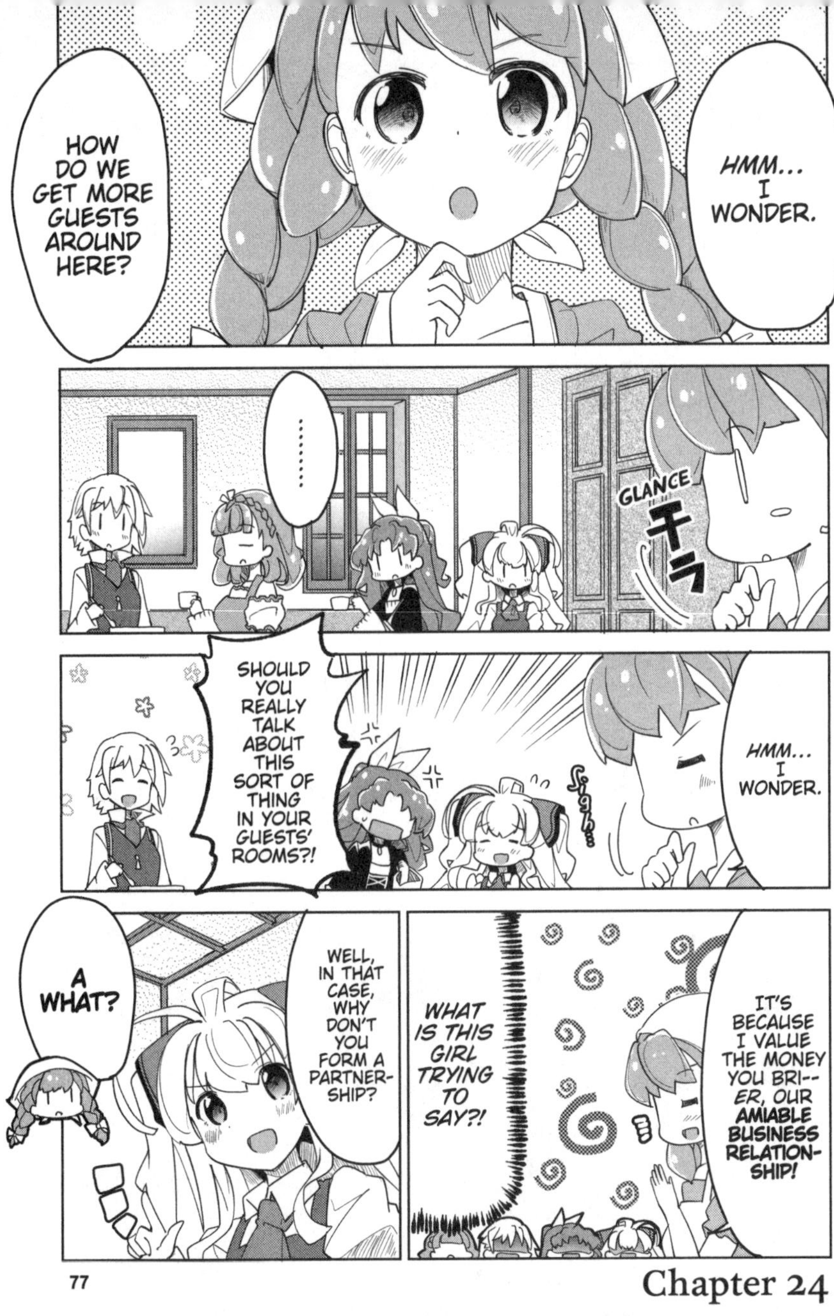
HMM… I WONDER.
HOW DO WE GET MORE GUESTS AROUND HERE?
GLANCE
チラ
……
HMM… I WONDER.
SIGH…
SHOULD YOU REALLY TALK ABOUT THIS SORT OF THING IN YOUR GUESTS' ROOMS?!
IT'S BECAUSE I VALUE THE MONEY YOU BRI-- ER, OUR AMIABLE BUSINESS RELATIONSHIP!
WHAT IS THIS GIRL TRYING TO SAY?!
WELL, IN THAT CASE, WHY DON'T YOU FORM A PARTNERSHIP?
A WHAT?

Chapter 24

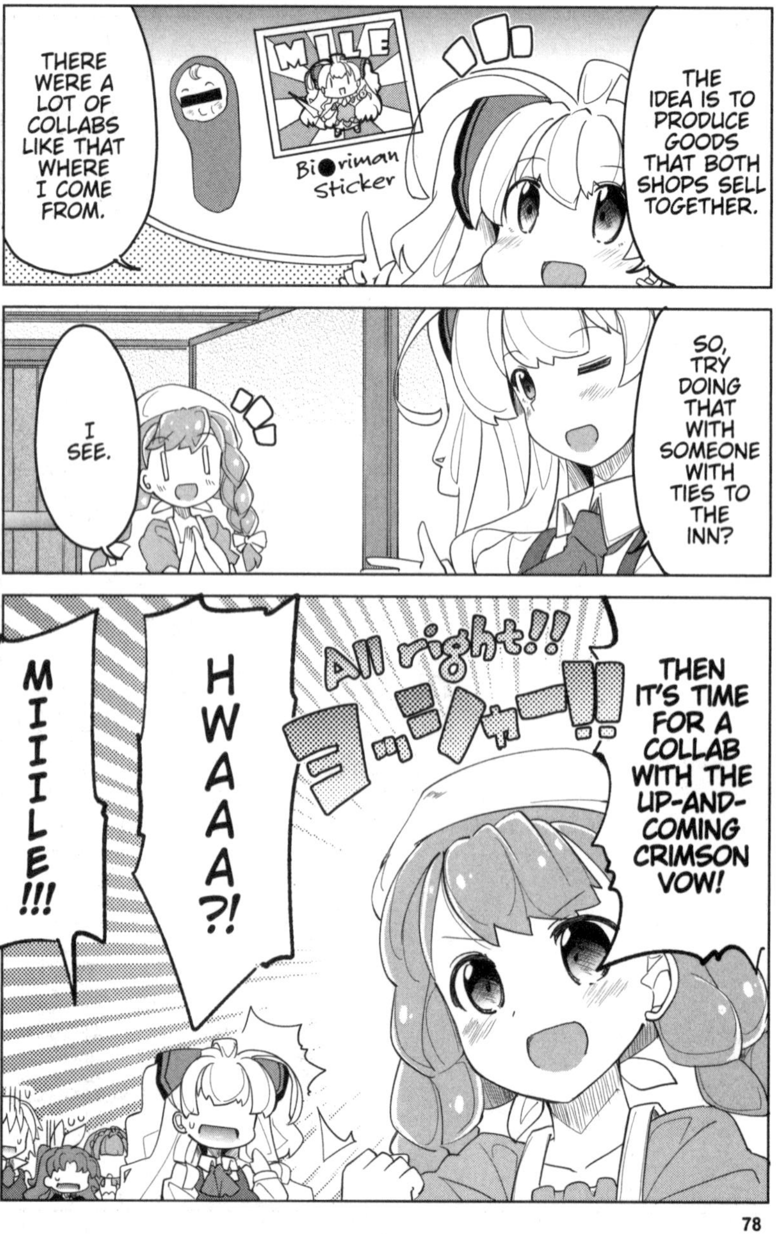
THE IDEA IS TO PRODUCE GOODS THAT BOTH SHOPS SELL TOGETHER.
MILE
Bi●riman Sticker
THERE WERE A LOT OF COLLABS LIKE THAT WHERE I COME FROM.
SO, TRY DOING THAT WITH SOMEONE WITH TIES TO THE INN?
I SEE.
All right!!
ヨッシャー!!
THEN IT'S TIME FOR A COLLAB WITH THE UP-AND-COMING CRIMSON VOW!
HWAAAA?!
MIIIILE!!!

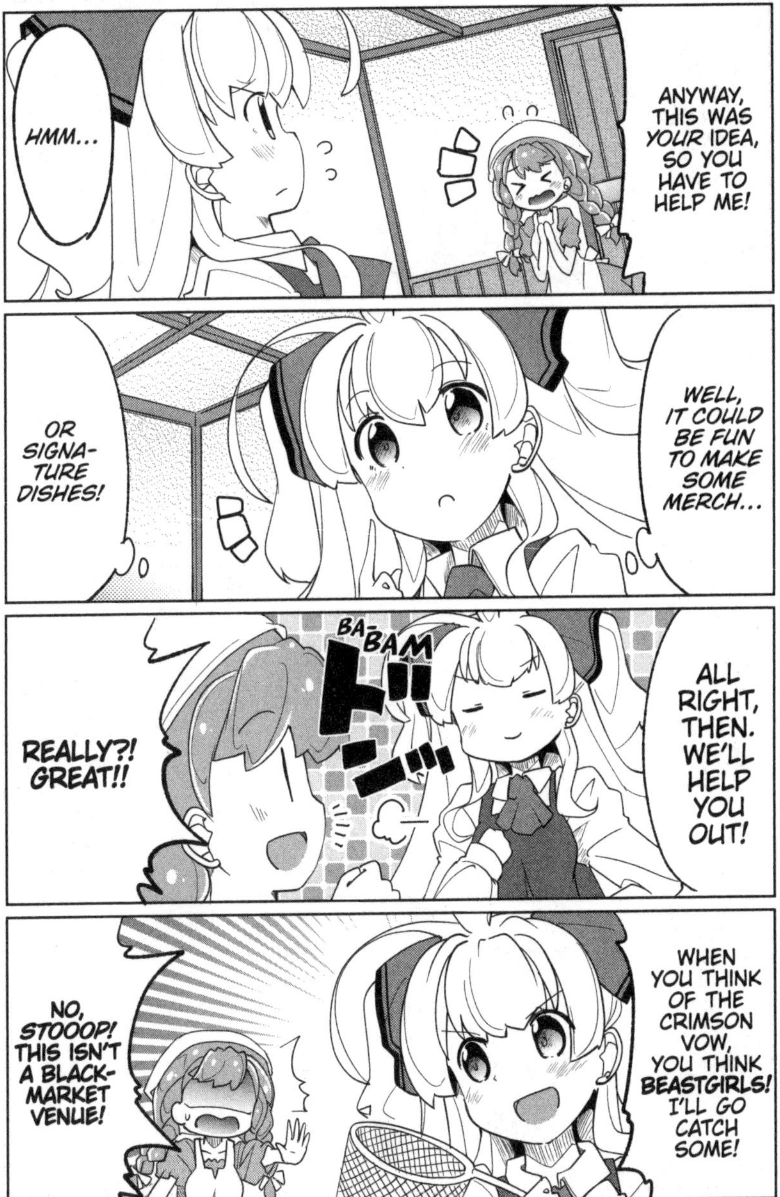
ANYWAY, THIS WAS *YOUR* IDEA, SO YOU HAVE TO HELP ME!
HMM...
WELL, IT COULD BE FUN TO MAKE SOME MERCH...
OR SIGNATURE DISHES!
ALL RIGHT, THEN. WE'LL HELP YOU OUT!
BA-BAM
トッ
REALLY?! GREAT!!
WHEN YOU THINK OF THE CRIMSON VOW, YOU THINK **BEASTGIRLS!** *I'LL GO CATCH* SOME!
NO, *STOOOP!* THIS ISN'T A BLACK-MARKET VENUE!

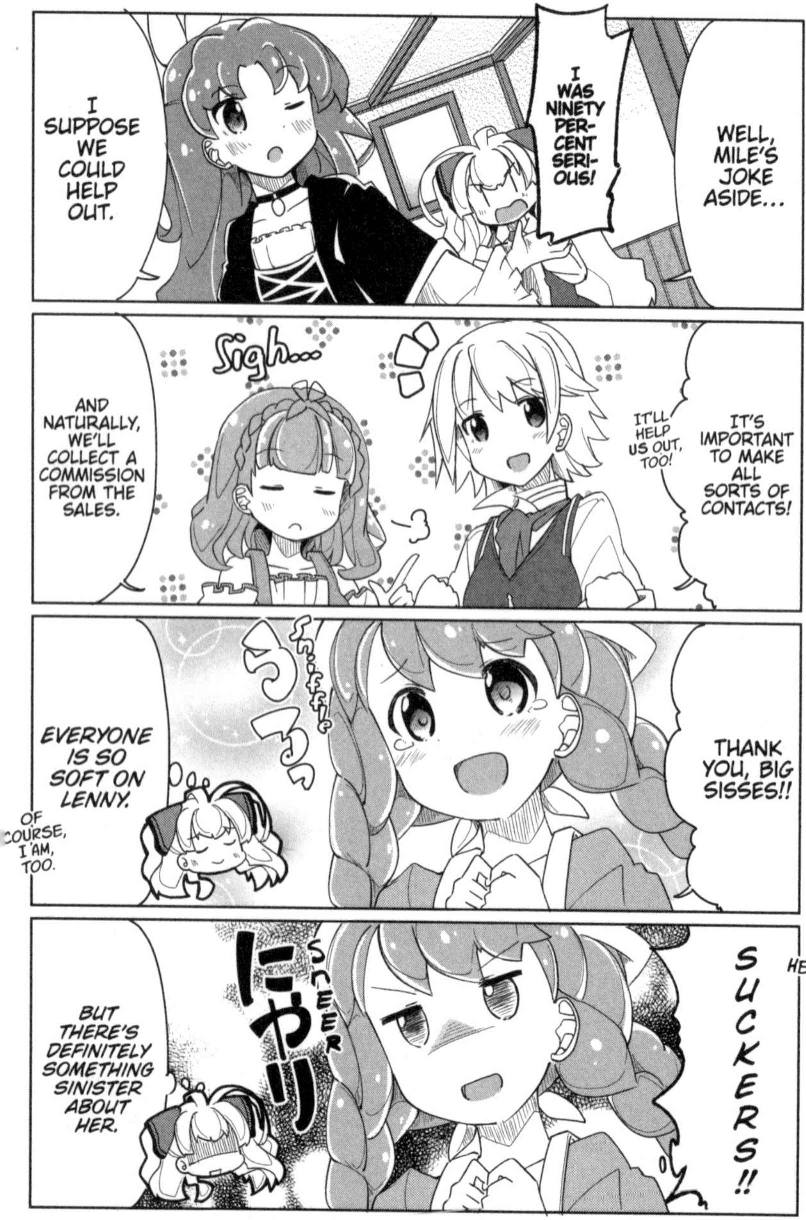

WELL, MILE'S JOKE ASIDE...
I WAS NINETY PERCENT SERIOUS!
I SUPPOSE WE COULD HELP OUT.
IT'S IMPORTANT TO MAKE ALL SORTS OF CONTACTS!
IT'LL HELP US OUT, TOO!
Sigh...
AND NATURALLY, WE'LL COLLECT A COMMISSION FROM THE SALES.
THANK YOU, BIG SISSES!!
うるっ
sniffle
EVERYONE IS SO SOFT ON LENNY.
OF COURSE, I AM, TOO.
HEH.
SUCKERS!!
にやり
SNEER
BUT THERE'S DEFINITELY SOMETHING SINISTER ABOUT HER.

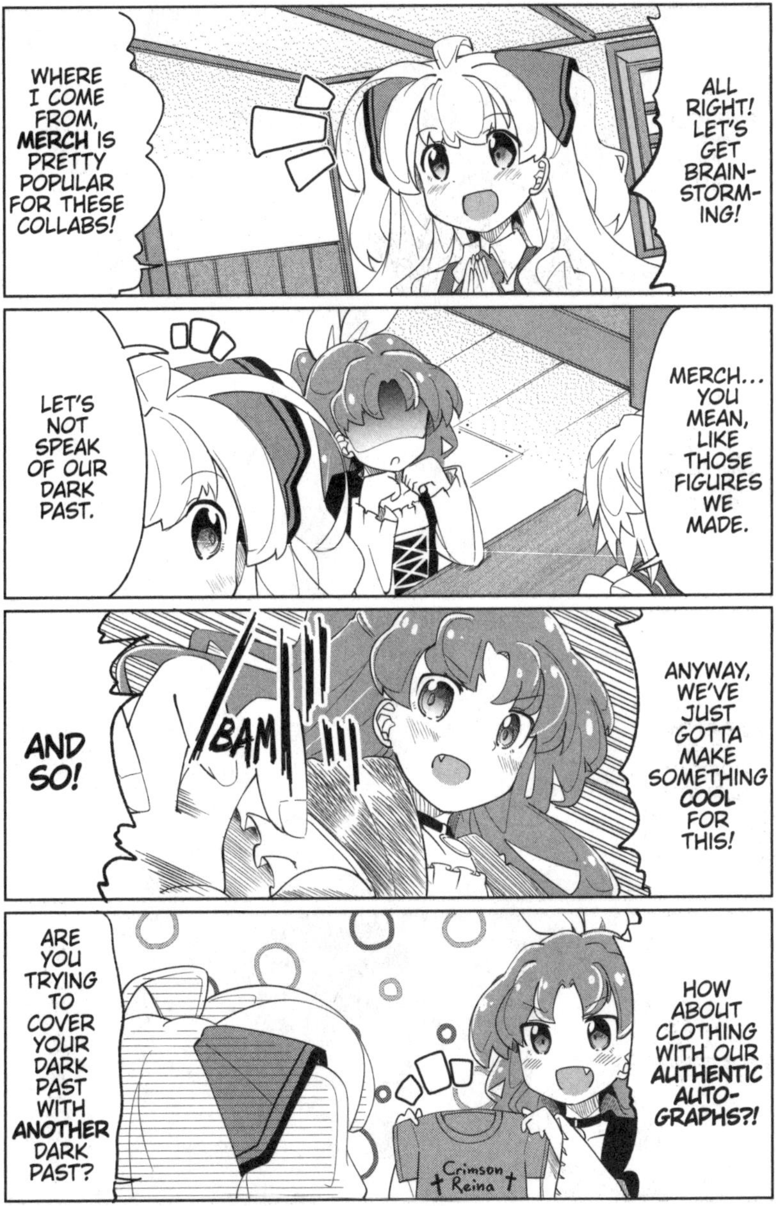
ALL RIGHT! LET'S GET BRAIN-STORMING!
WHERE I COME FROM, **MERCH** IS PRETTY POPULAR FOR THESE COLLABS!
MERCH... YOU MEAN, LIKE THOSE FIGURES WE MADE.
LET'S NOT SPEAK OF OUR DARK PAST.
AND SO!
BAM
ANYWAY, WE'VE JUST GOTTA MAKE SOMETHING **COOL** FOR THIS!
HOW ABOUT CLOTHING WITH OUR **AUTHENTIC AUTO-GRAPHS?!**
Crimson Reina
ARE YOU TRYING TO COVER YOUR DARK PAST WITH **ANOTHER** DARK PAST?

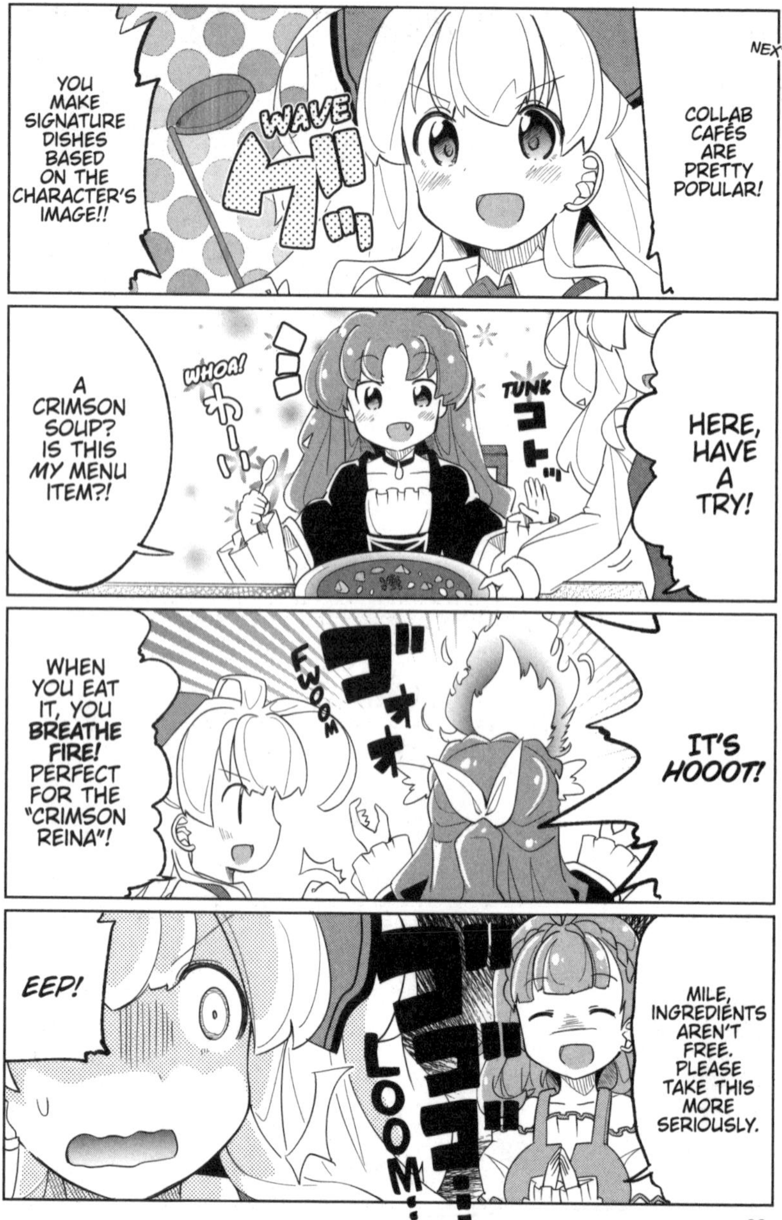
NEXT!
COLLAB CAFÉS ARE PRETTY POPULAR!
WAVE
YOU MAKE SIGNATURE DISHES BASED ON THE CHARACTER'S IMAGE!!
HERE, HAVE A TRY!
TUNK
WHOA!
A CRIMSON SOUP? IS THIS *MY* MENU ITEM?!
IT'S HOOOT!
FWOOM
WHEN YOU EAT IT, YOU **BREATHE FIRE!** PERFECT FOR THE "CRIMSON REINA"!
MILE, INGREDIENTS AREN'T FREE. PLEASE TAKE THIS MORE SERIOUSLY.
LOOM!!
EEP!

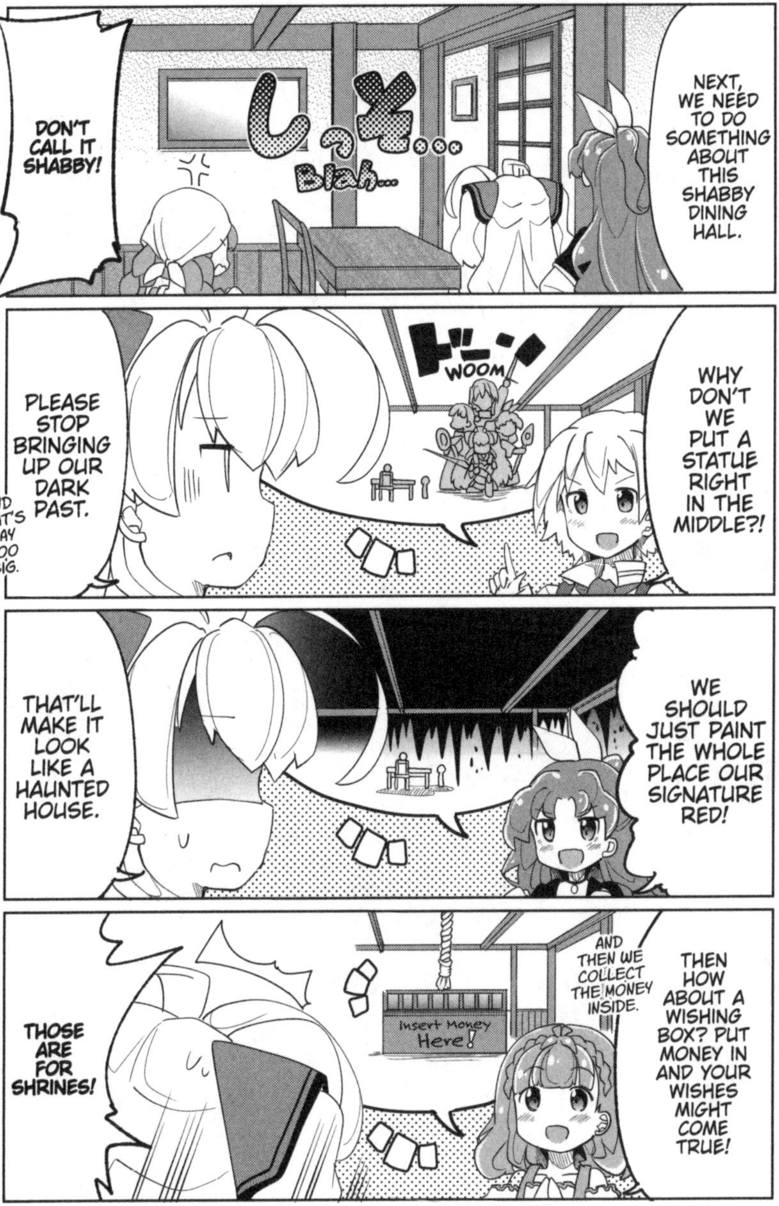
NEXT, WE NEED TO DO SOMETHING ABOUT THIS SHABBY DINING HALL.
Blah...
DON'T CALL IT SHABBY!
WHY DON'T WE PUT A STATUE RIGHT IN THE MIDDLE?!
WOOM
PLEASE STOP BRINGING UP OUR DARK PAST.
AND THAT'S WAY TOO BIG.
WE SHOULD JUST PAINT THE WHOLE PLACE OUR SIGNATURE RED!
THAT'LL MAKE IT LOOK LIKE A HAUNTED HOUSE.
THEN HOW ABOUT A WISHING BOX? PUT MONEY IN AND YOUR WISHES MIGHT COME TRUE!
AND THEN WE COLLECT THE MONEY INSIDE.
Insert Money Here!
THOSE ARE FOR SHRINES!

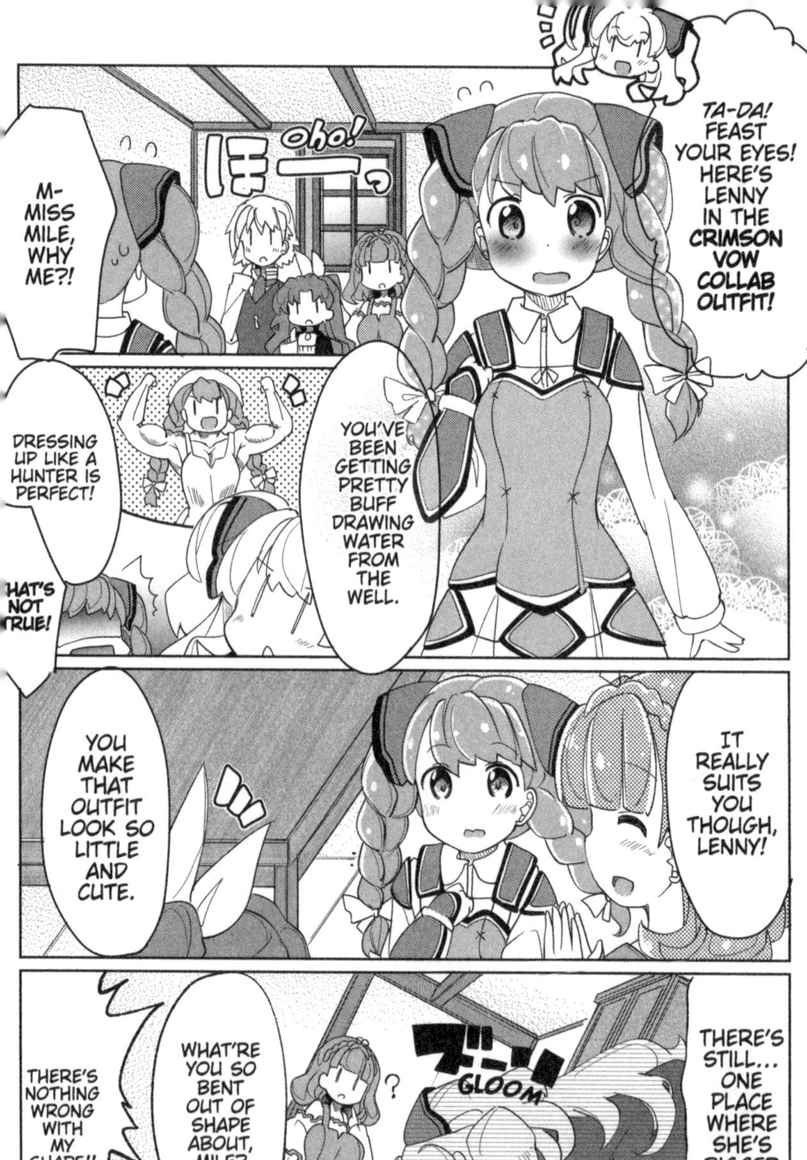
TA-DA! FEAST YOUR EYES! HERE'S LENNY IN THE CRIMSON VOW COLLAB OUTFIT!
oho!
M-MISS MILE, WHY ME?!
YOU'VE BEEN GETTING PRETTY BUFF DRAWING WATER FROM THE WELL.
DRESSING UP LIKE A HUNTER IS PERFECT!
HAT'S NOT TRUE!
IT REALLY SUITS YOU THOUGH, LENNY!
YOU MAKE THAT OUTFIT LOOK SO LITTLE AND CUTE.
THERE'S STILL... ONE PLACE WHERE SHE'S BIGGER THAN ME...
GLOOM
WHAT'RE YOU SO BENT OUT OF SHAPE ABOUT, MILE?
THERE'S NOTHING WRONG WITH MY SHAPE!!

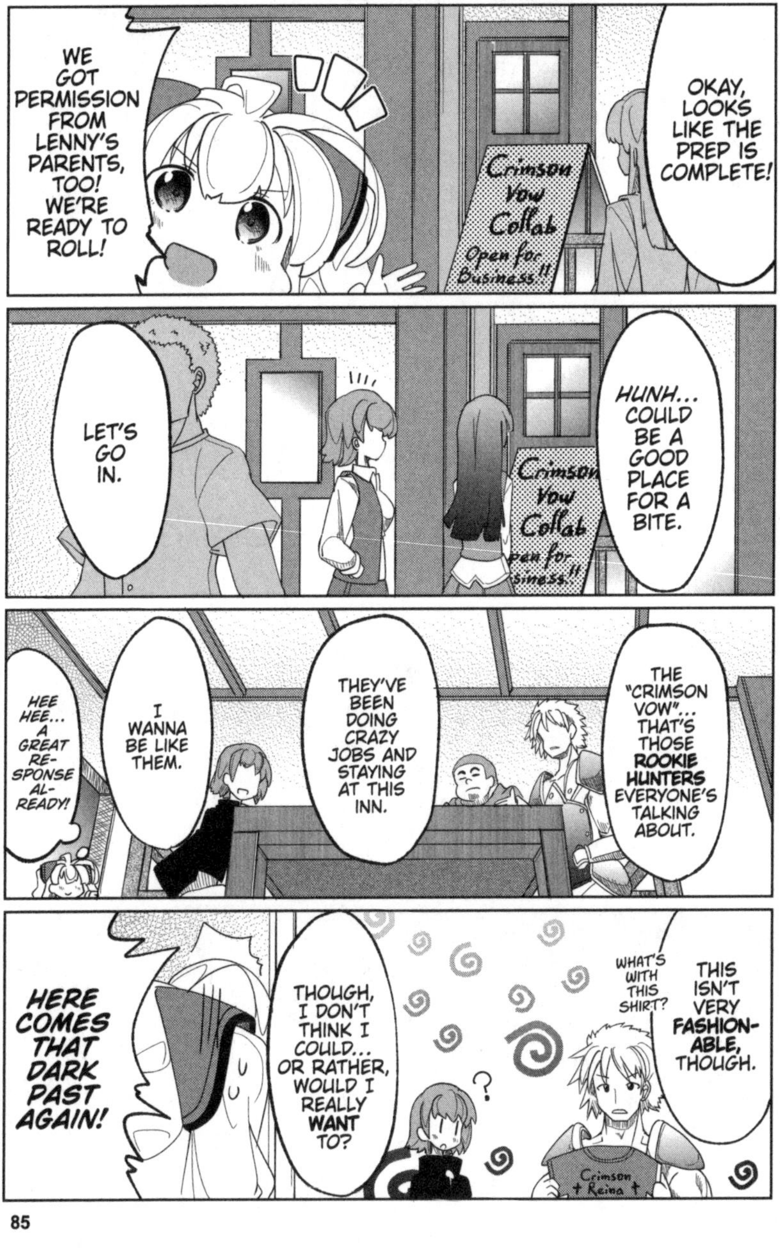
OKAY, LOOKS LIKE THE PREP IS COMPLETE!
Crimson Vow Collab Open for Business!!
WE GOT PERMISSION FROM LENNY'S PARENTS, TOO! WE'RE READY TO ROLL!
HUNH... COULD BE A GOOD PLACE FOR A BITE.
LET'S GO IN.
THE "CRIMSON VOW"... THAT'S THOSE ROOKIE HUNTERS EVERYONE'S TALKING ABOUT.
THEY'VE BEEN DOING CRAZY JOBS AND STAYING AT THIS INN.
I WANNA BE LIKE THEM.
HEE HEE... A GREAT RE-SPONSE AL-READY!
THIS ISN'T VERY FASHION-ABLE, THOUGH.
WHAT'S WITH THIS SHIRT?
Crimson Reina
THOUGH, I DON'T THINK I COULD... OR RATHER, WOULD I REALLY WANT TO?
HERE COMES THAT DARK PAST AGAIN!

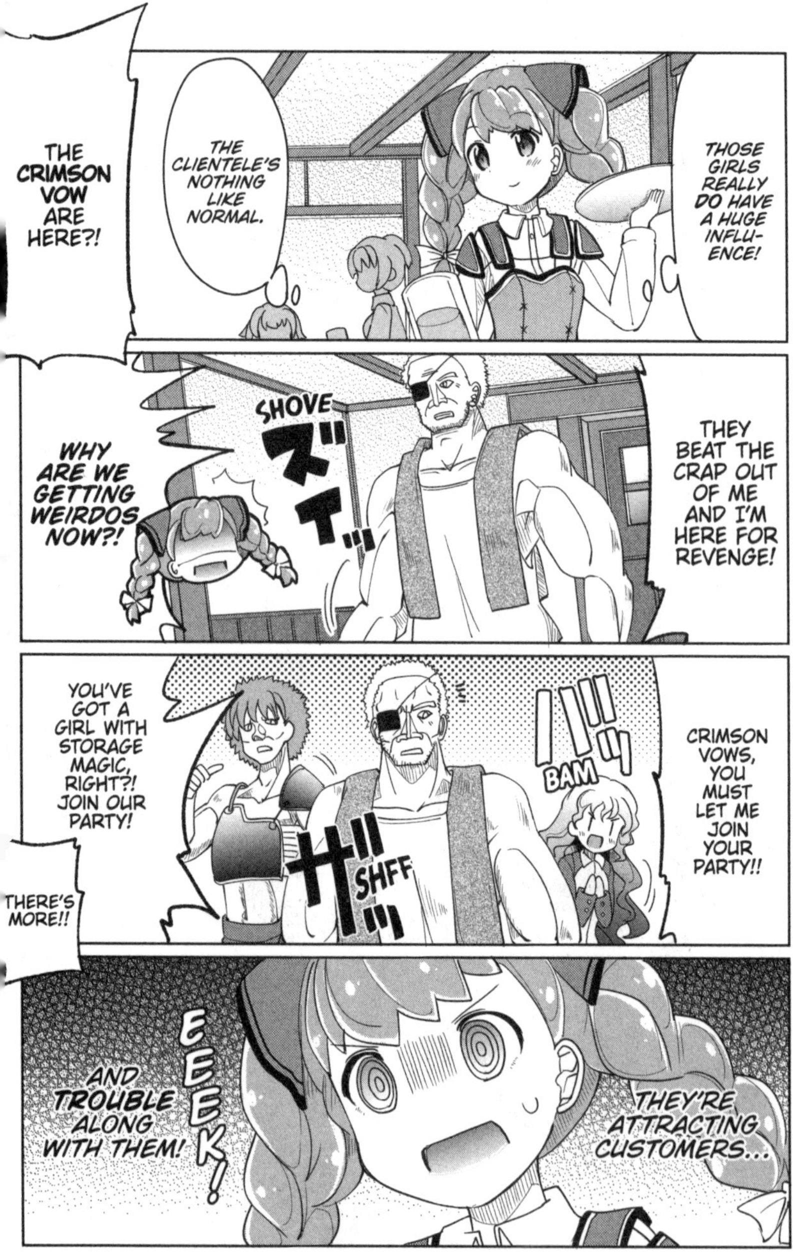
THOSE GIRLS REALLY DO HAVE A HUGE INFLU-ENCE!
THE CLIENTELE'S NOTHING LIKE NORMAL.
THE CRIMSON VOW ARE HERE?!
THEY BEAT THE CRAP OUT OF ME AND I'M HERE FOR REVENGE!
SHOVE
WHY ARE WE GETTING WEIRDOS NOW?!
CRIMSON VOWS, YOU MUST LET ME JOIN YOUR PARTY!!
BAM
SHFF
YOU'VE GOT A GIRL WITH STORAGE MAGIC, RIGHT?! JOIN OUR PARTY!
THERE'S MORE!!
THEY'RE ATTRACTING CUSTOMERS...
EEEEK!
AND TROUBLE ALONG WITH THEM!

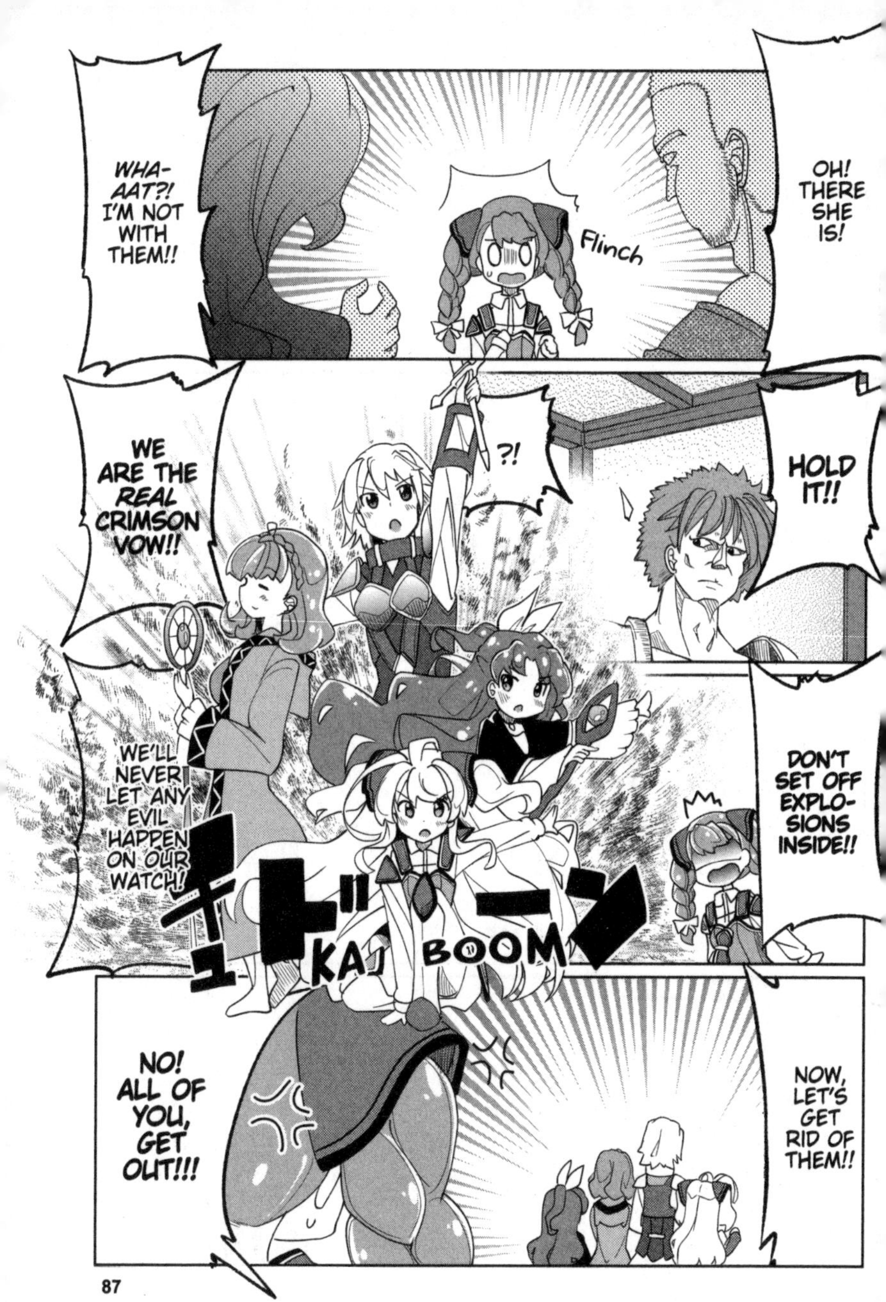
OH! THERE SHE IS!
Flinch
WHA-AAT?! I'M NOT WITH THEM!!
HOLD IT!!
?!
WE ARE THE REAL CRIMSON VOW!!
DON'T SET OFF EXPLOSIONS INSIDE!!
WE'LL NEVER LET ANY EVIL HAPPEN ON OUR WATCH!
KA BOOM
NOW, LET'S GET RID OF THEM!!
NO! ALL OF YOU, GET OUT!!!

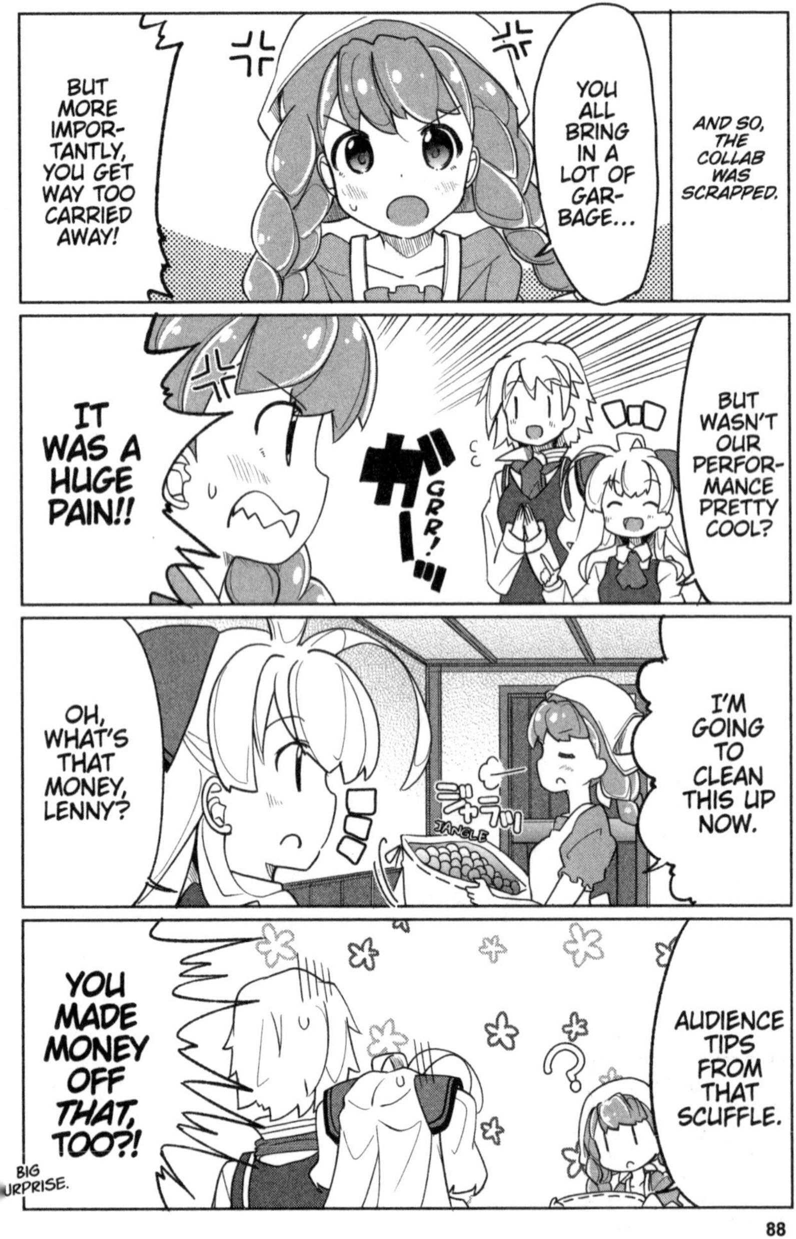

AND SO, THE COLLAB WAS SCRAPPED.
YOU ALL BRING IN A LOT OF GAR-BAGE...
BUT MORE IMPOR-TANTLY, YOU GET WAY TOO CARRIED AWAY!
BUT WASN'T OUR PERFOR-MANCE PRETTY COOL?
GRR!!
IT WAS A HUGE PAIN!!
I'M GOING TO CLEAN THIS UP NOW.
JANGLE
OH, WHAT'S THAT MONEY, LENNY?
AUDIENCE TIPS FROM THAT SCUFFLE.
YOU MADE MONEY OFF *THAT*, TOO?!
BIG URPRISE.

Didn't I Say to Make My Abilities Average in the Next Life?!
EVERYDAY MISADVENTURES!

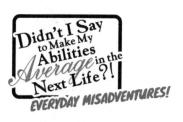

Flinch

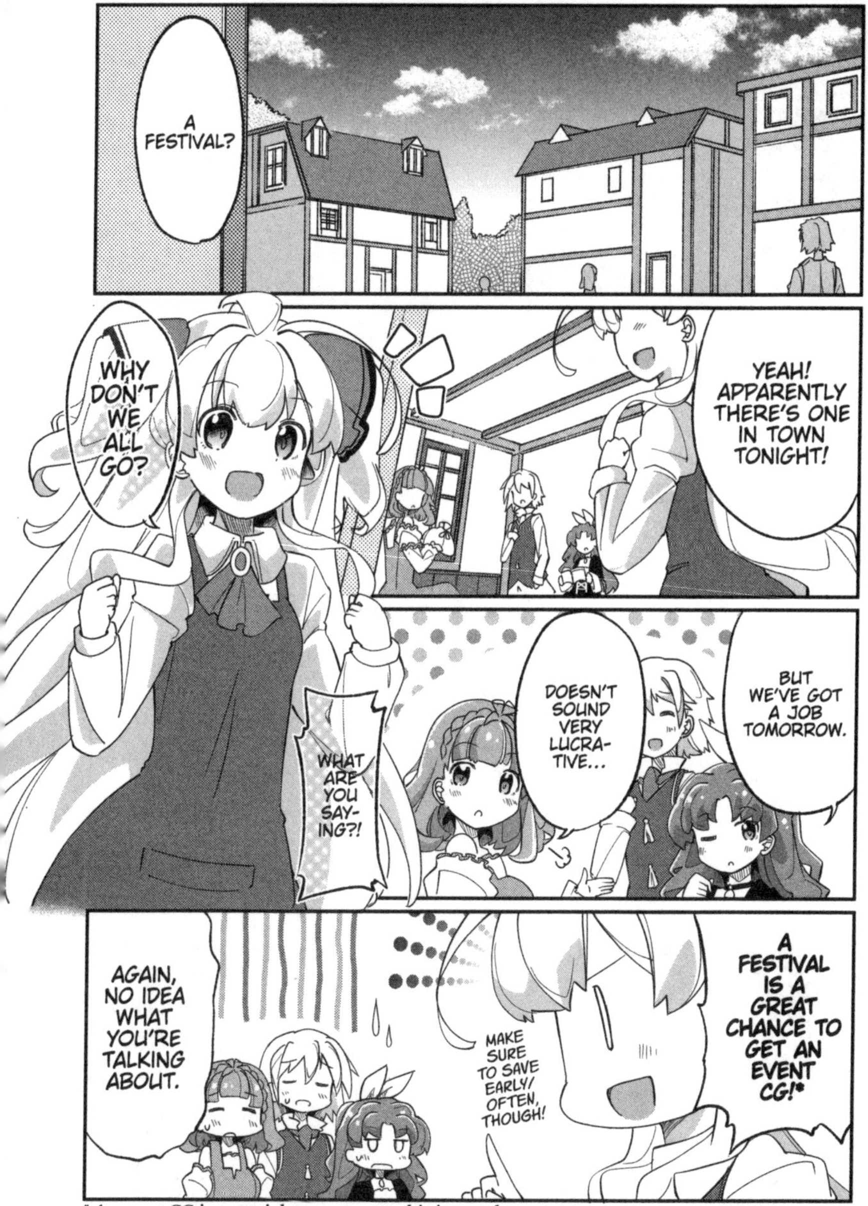
A FESTIVAL?
YEAH! APPARENTLY THERE'S ONE IN TOWN TONIGHT!
WHY DON'T WE ALL GO?
BUT WE'VE GOT A JOB TOMORROW.
DOESN'T SOUND VERY LUCRA-TIVE...
WHAT ARE YOU SAY-ING?!
A FESTIVAL IS A GREAT CHANCE TO GET AN EVENT CG!*
MAKE SURE TO SAVE EARLY/OFTEN, THOUGH!
AGAIN, NO IDEA WHAT YOU'RE TALKING ABOUT.

* An event CG is a special computer graphic image that includes both a detailed background and character designs. Usually distributed to promote special events in games.

Chapter 25

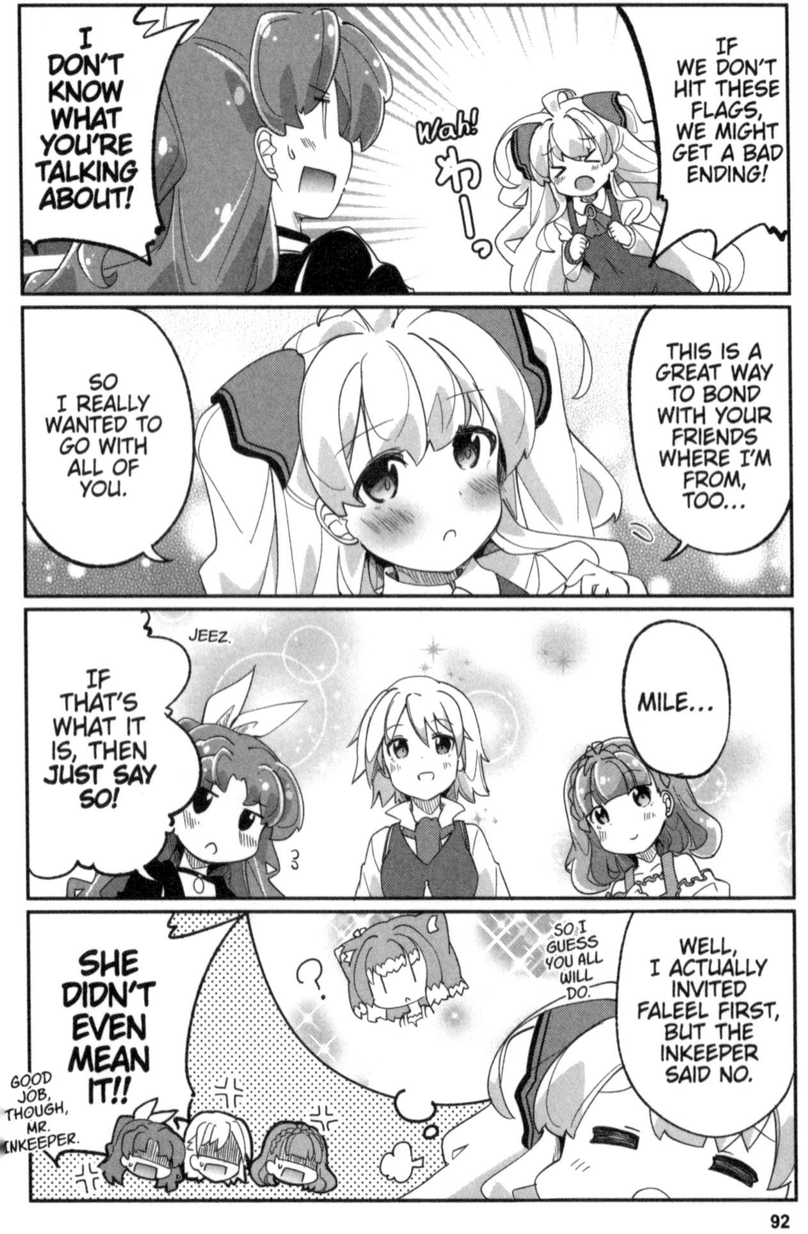
IF WE DON'T HIT THESE FLAGS, WE MIGHT GET A BAD ENDING!
Wah!
わー
I DON'T KNOW WHAT YOU'RE TALKING ABOUT!
THIS IS A GREAT WAY TO BOND WITH YOUR FRIENDS WHERE I'M FROM, TOO...
SO I REALLY WANTED TO GO WITH ALL OF YOU.
MILE...
JEEZ.
IF THAT'S WHAT IT IS, THEN JUST SAY SO!
WELL, I ACTUALLY INVITED FALEEL FIRST, BUT THE INKEEPER SAID NO.
SO I GUESS YOU ALL WILL DO.
SHE DIDN'T EVEN MEAN IT!!
GOOD JOB, THOUGH, MR. INKEEPER.

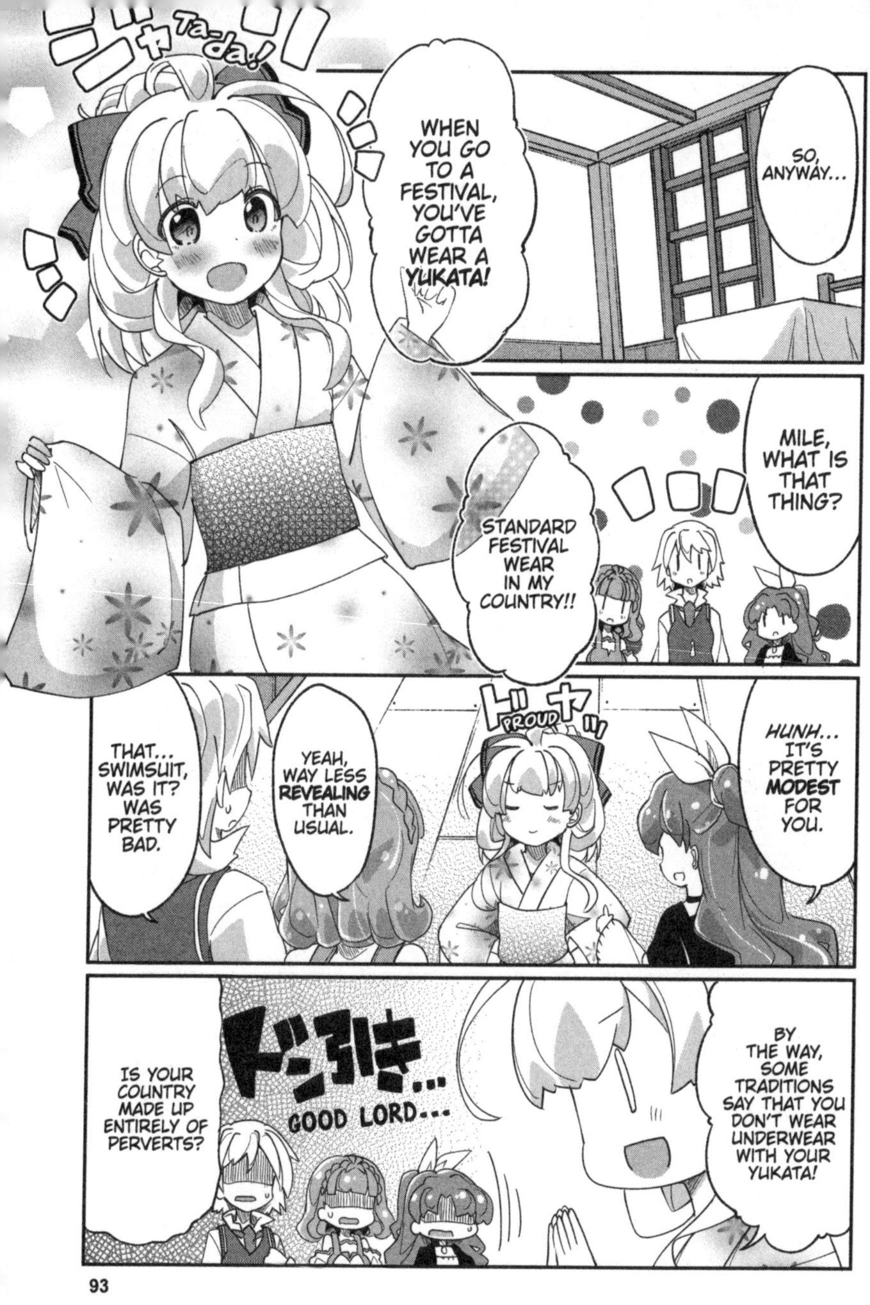
SO, ANYWAY...
Ta-da!
WHEN YOU GO TO A FESTIVAL, YOU'VE GOTTA WEAR A **YUKATA!**
MILE, WHAT IS THAT THING?
STANDARD FESTIVAL WEAR IN MY COUNTRY!!
HUNH... IT'S PRETTY **MODEST** FOR YOU.
ドヤッ
PROUD
YEAH, WAY LESS **REVEALING** THAN USUAL.
THAT... SWIMSUIT, WAS IT? WAS PRETTY BAD.
BY THE WAY, SOME TRADITIONS SAY THAT YOU DON'T WEAR UNDERWEAR WITH YOUR YUKATA!
ドン引き…
GOOD LORD...
IS YOUR COUNTRY MADE UP ENTIRELY OF PERVERTS?

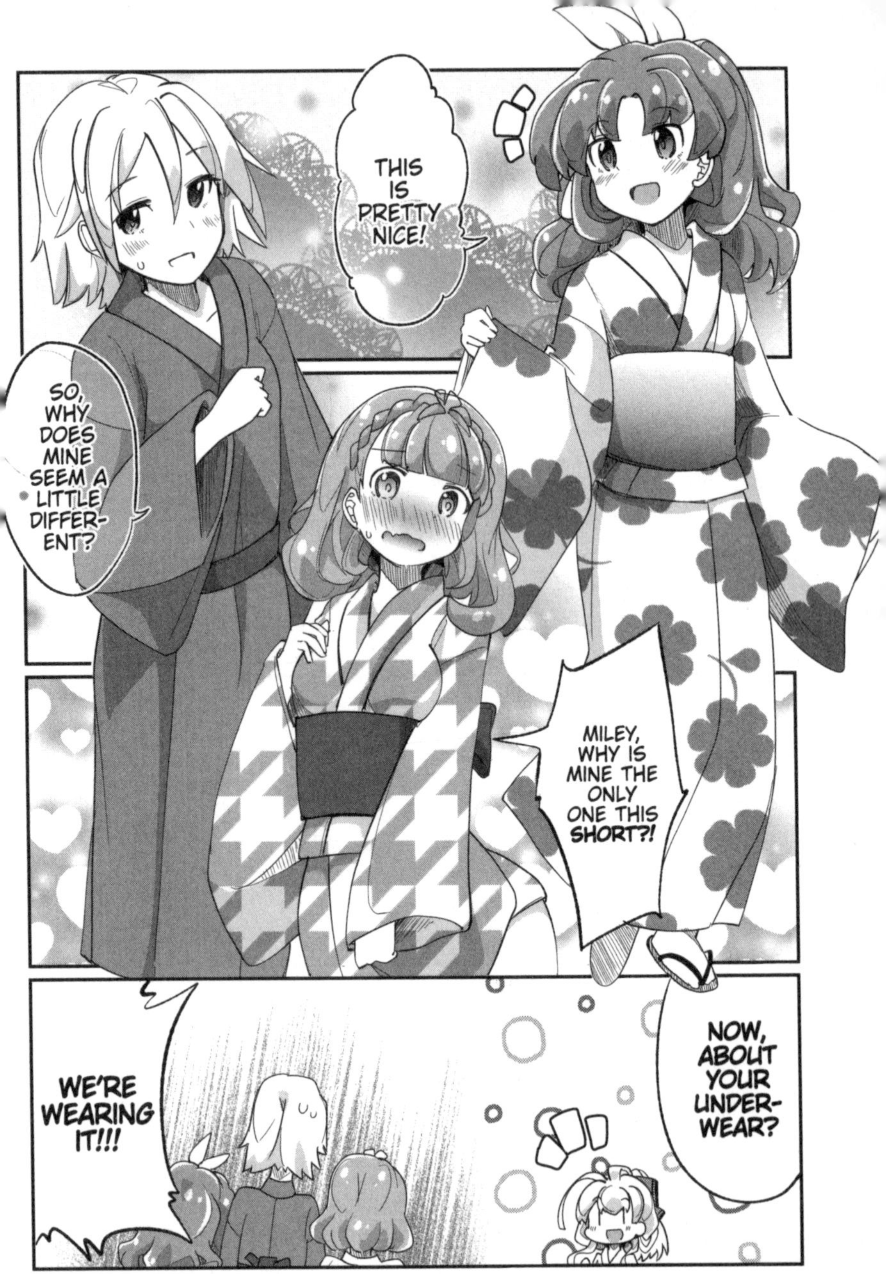
THIS IS PRETTY NICE!
SO, WHY DOES MINE SEEM A LITTLE DIFFERENT?
MILEY, WHY IS MINE THE ONLY ONE THIS **SHORT?!**
NOW, ABOUT YOUR UNDERWEAR?
WE'RE WEARING IT!!!

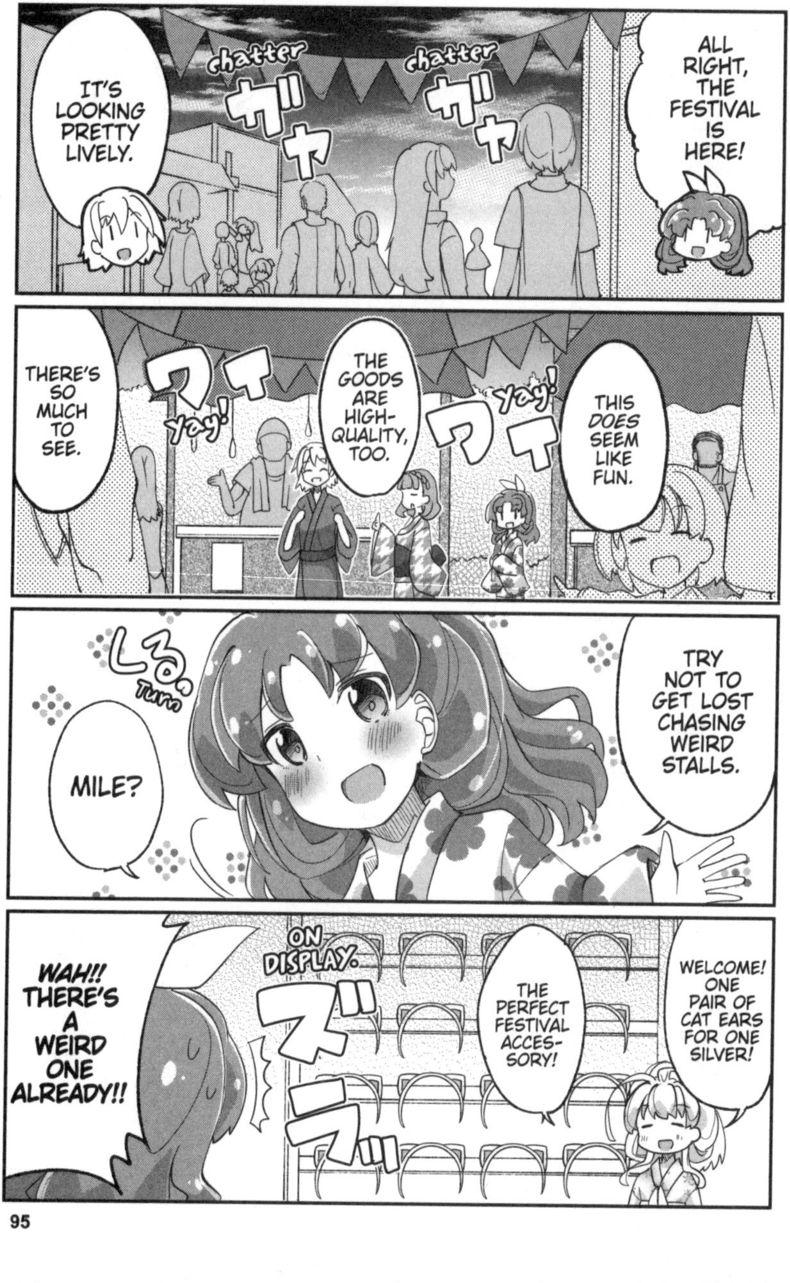
ALL RIGHT, THE FESTIVAL IS HERE!
chatter chatter
IT'S LOOKING PRETTY LIVELY.
THIS *DOES* SEEM LIKE FUN.
yay! yay!
THE GOODS ARE HIGH-QUALITY, TOO.
THERE'S SO MUCH TO SEE.
TRY NOT TO GET LOST CHASING WEIRD STALLS.
Turn
MILE?
WELCOME! ONE PAIR OF CAT EARS FOR ONE SILVER!
THE PERFECT FESTIVAL ACCES-SORY!
ON DISPLAY.
WAH!! THERE'S A WEIRD ONE ALREADY!!

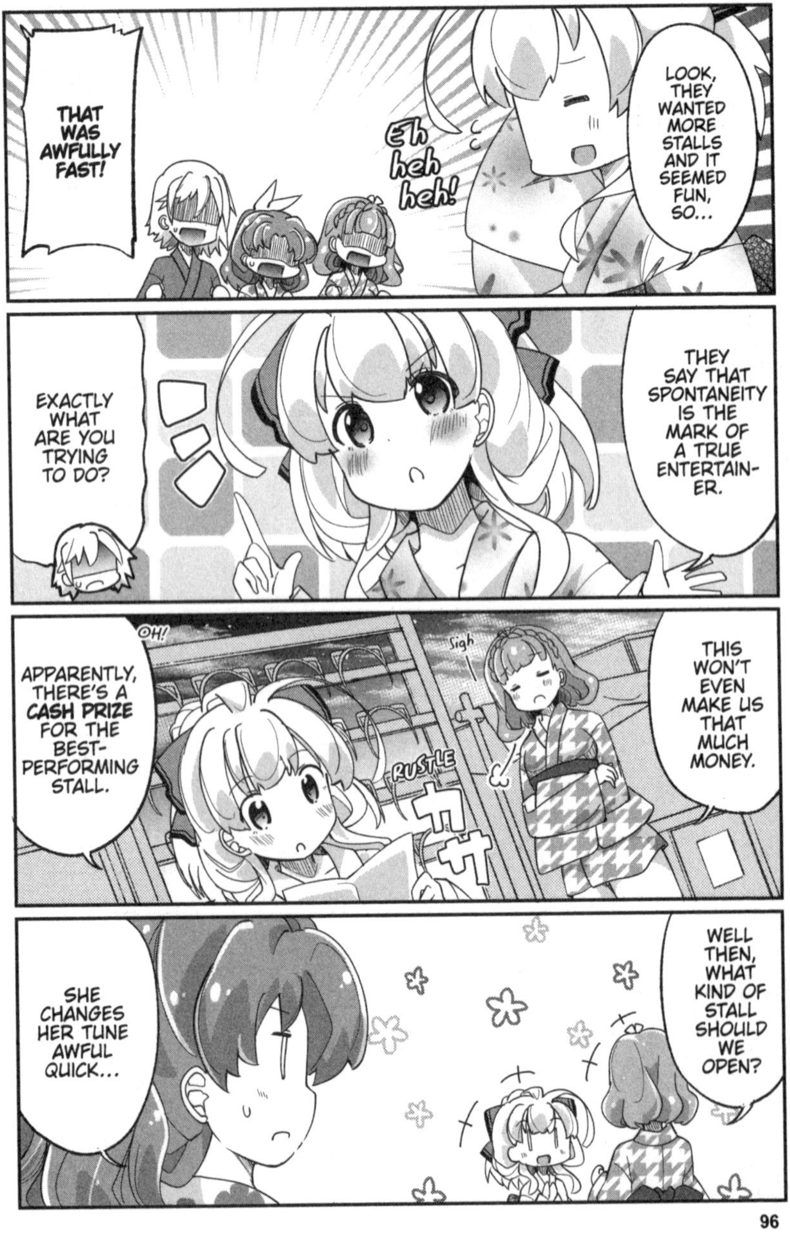
LOOK, THEY WANTED MORE STALLS AND IT SEEMED FUN, SO...
Eh heh heh!
THAT WAS AWFULLY FAST!
THEY SAY THAT SPONTANEITY IS THE MARK OF A TRUE ENTERTAINER.
EXACTLY WHAT ARE YOU TRYING TO DO?
THIS WON'T EVEN MAKE US THAT MUCH MONEY.
Sigh
RUSTLE
OH!
APPARENTLY, THERE'S A CASH PRIZE FOR THE BEST-PERFORMING STALL.
WELL THEN, WHAT KIND OF STALL SHOULD WE OPEN?
SHE CHANGES HER TUNE AWFUL QUICK...

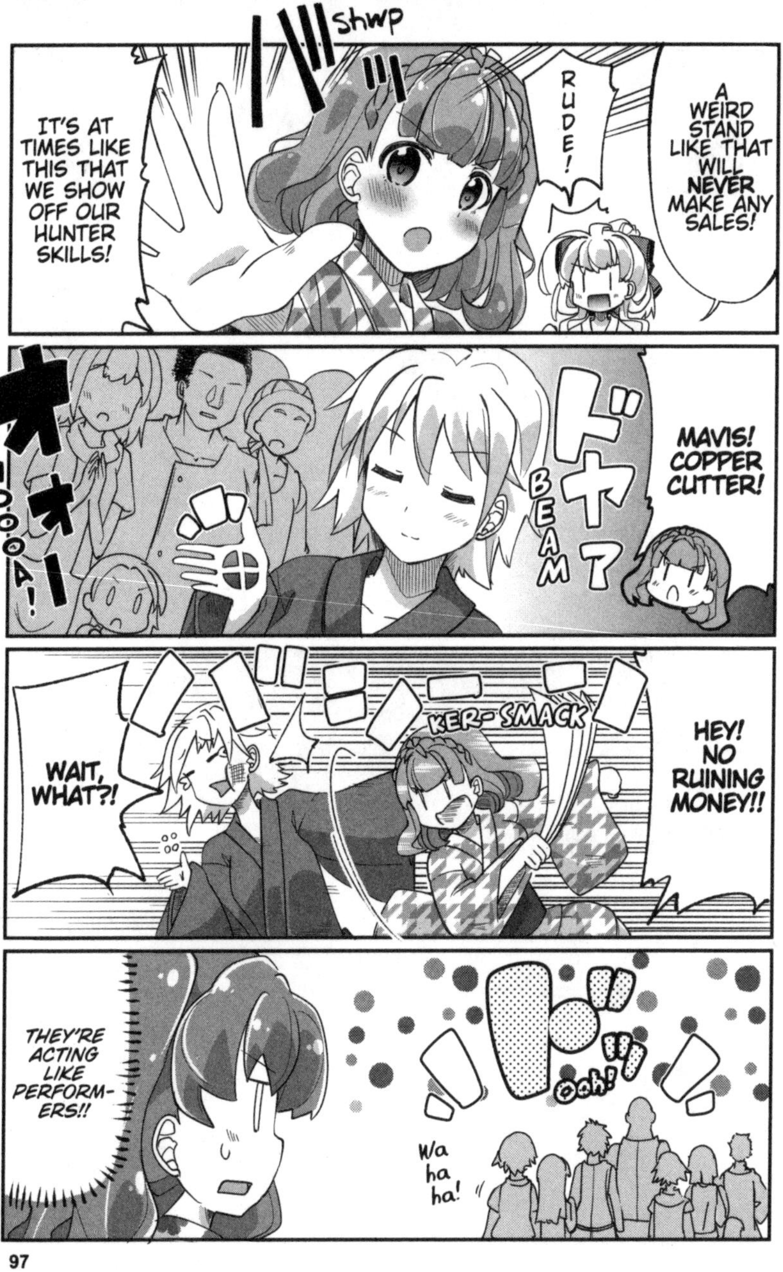

SHWP
A WEIRD STAND LIKE THAT WILL NEVER MAKE ANY SALES!
RUDE!
IT'S AT TIMES LIKE THIS THAT WE SHOW OFF OUR HUNTER SKILLS!
MAVIS! COPPER CUTTER!
ドヤァ
BEAM
WHOOOOA!
HEY! NO RUINING MONEY!!
KER-SMACK
WAIT, WHAT?!
ooh!
Wa ha ha!
THEY'RE ACTING LIKE PERFORMERS!!

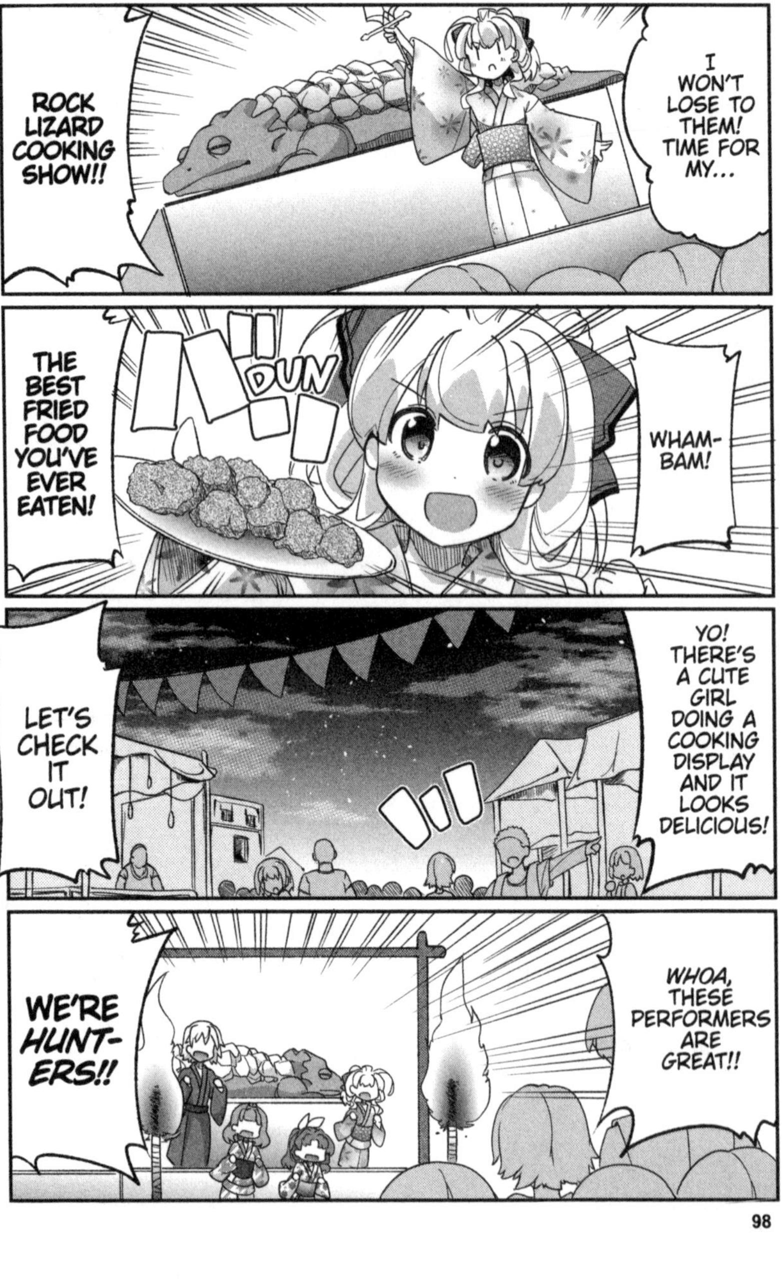
I WON'T LOSE TO THEM! TIME FOR MY...
ROCK LIZARD COOKING SHOW!!
WHAM-BAM!
DUN
THE BEST FRIED FOOD YOU'VE EVER EATEN!
YO! THERE'S A CUTE GIRL DOING A COOKING DISPLAY AND IT LOOKS DELICIOUS!
LET'S CHECK IT OUT!
WHOA, THESE PERFORMERS ARE GREAT!!
WE'RE HUNTERS!!

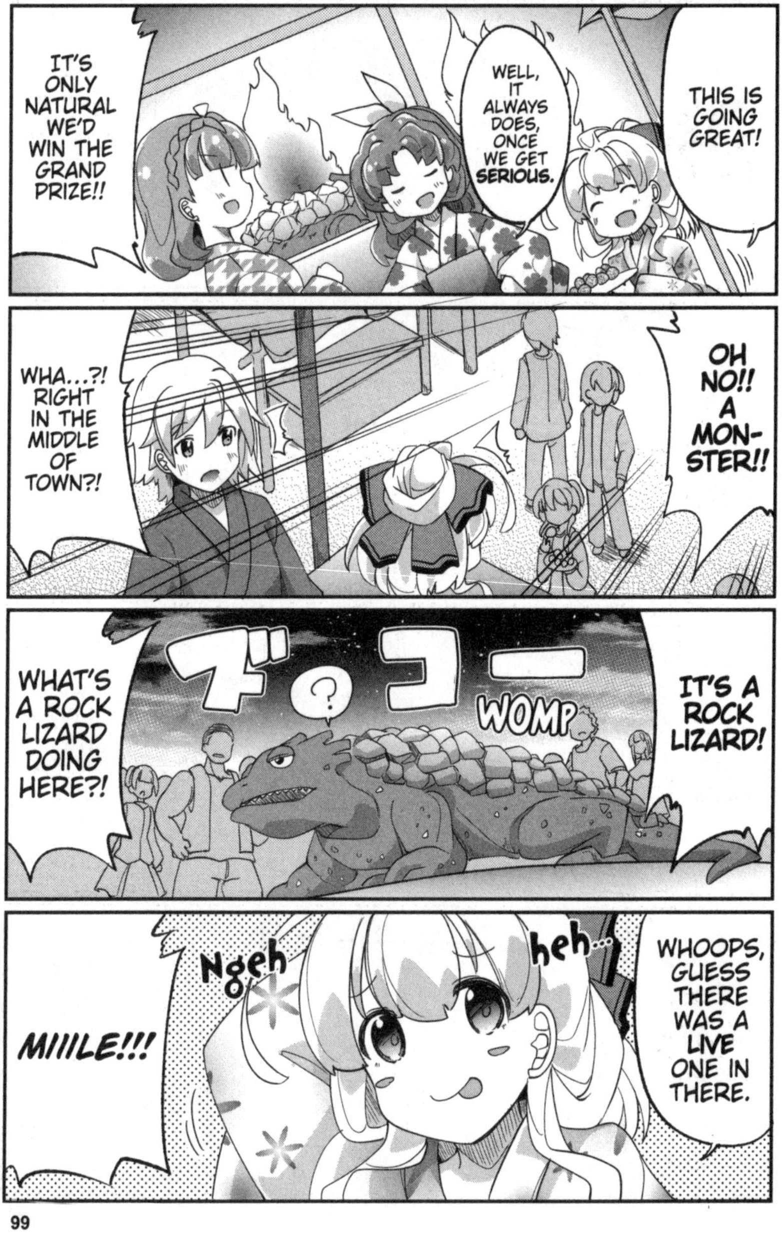
THIS IS GOING GREAT!
WELL, IT ALWAYS DOES, ONCE WE GET **SERIOUS**.
IT'S ONLY NATURAL WE'D WIN THE GRAND PRIZE!!
OH NO!! A MON-STER!!
WHA...?! RIGHT IN THE MIDDLE OF TOWN?!
WOMP
IT'S A ROCK LIZARD!
?
WHAT'S A ROCK LIZARD DOING HERE?!
WHOOPS, GUESS THERE WAS A **LIVE** ONE IN THERE.
heh...
Ngeh
MIIILE!!!

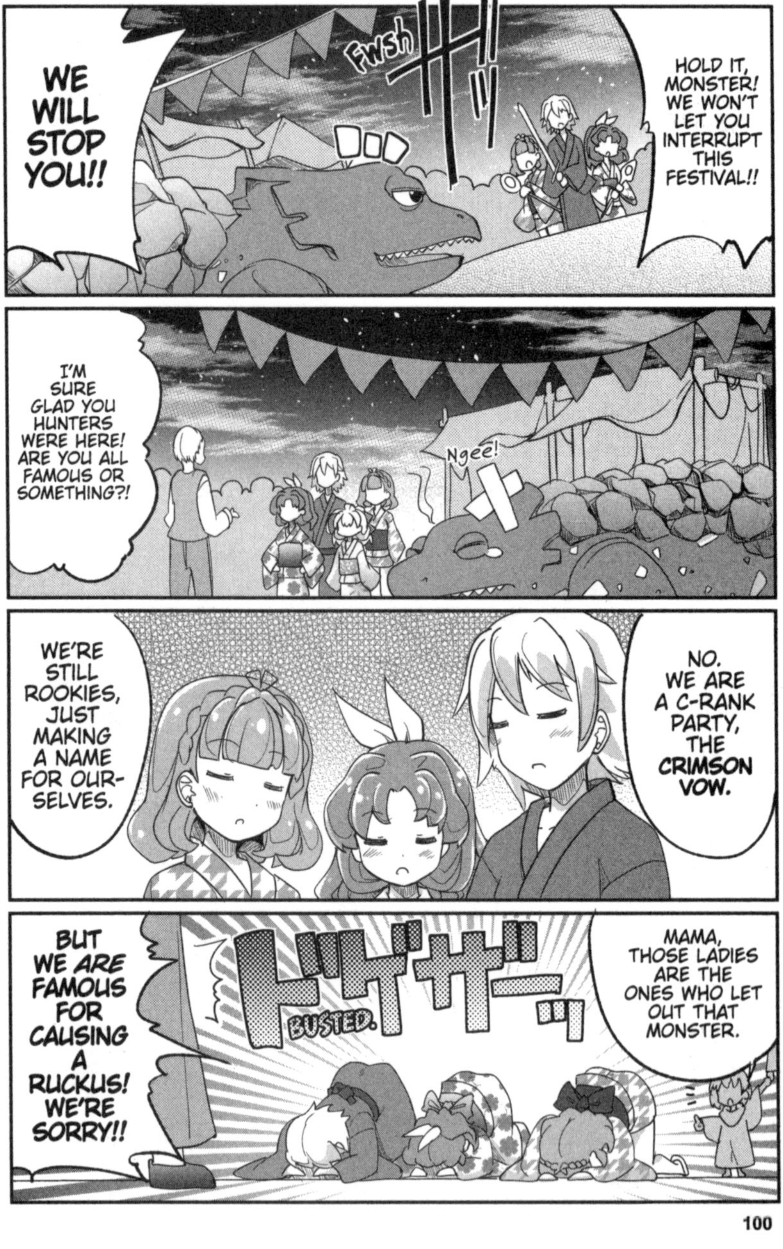

HOLD IT, MONSTER! WE WON'T LET YOU INTERRUPT THIS FESTIVAL!!
Fwsh
WE WILL STOP YOU!!
Ngee!
I'M SURE GLAD YOU HUNTERS WERE HERE! ARE YOU ALL FAMOUS OR SOMETHING?!
NO. WE ARE A C-RANK PARTY, THE CRIMSON VOW.
WE'RE STILL ROOKIES, JUST MAKING A NAME FOR OUR-SELVES.
MAMA, THOSE LADIES ARE THE ONES WHO LET OUT THAT MONSTER.
ドゲザーッ
BUSTED.
BUT WE ARE FAMOUS FOR CAUSING A RUCKUS! WE'RE SORRY!!

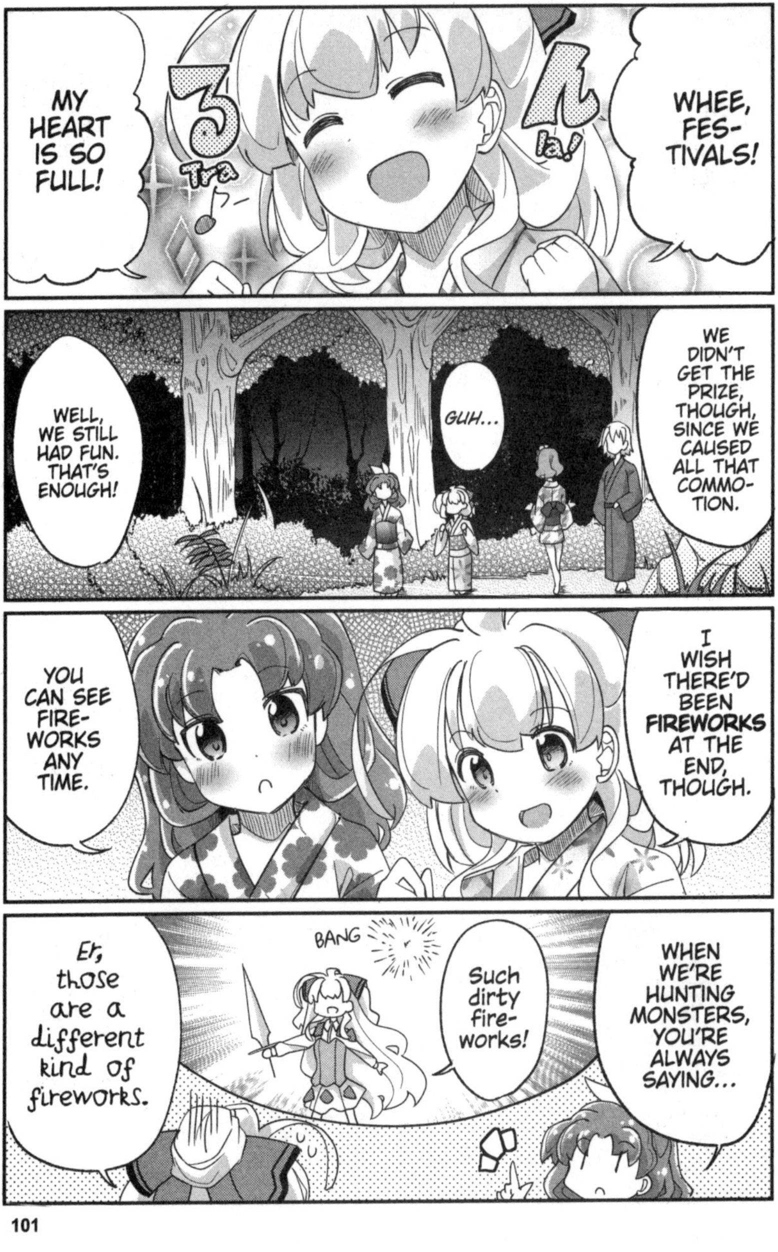
WHEE, FES-TIVALS!
la!
Tra
MY HEART IS SO FULL!
WE DIDN'T GET THE PRIZE, THOUGH, SINCE WE CAUSED ALL THAT COMMO-TION.
GUH...
WELL, WE STILL HAD FUN. THAT'S ENOUGH!
I WISH THERE'D BEEN **FIREWORKS** AT THE END, THOUGH.
YOU CAN SEE FIRE-WORKS ANY TIME.
WHEN WE'RE HUNTING MONSTERS, YOU'RE ALWAYS SAYING...
BANG
Such dirty fire-works!
Er, those are a different kind of fireworks.

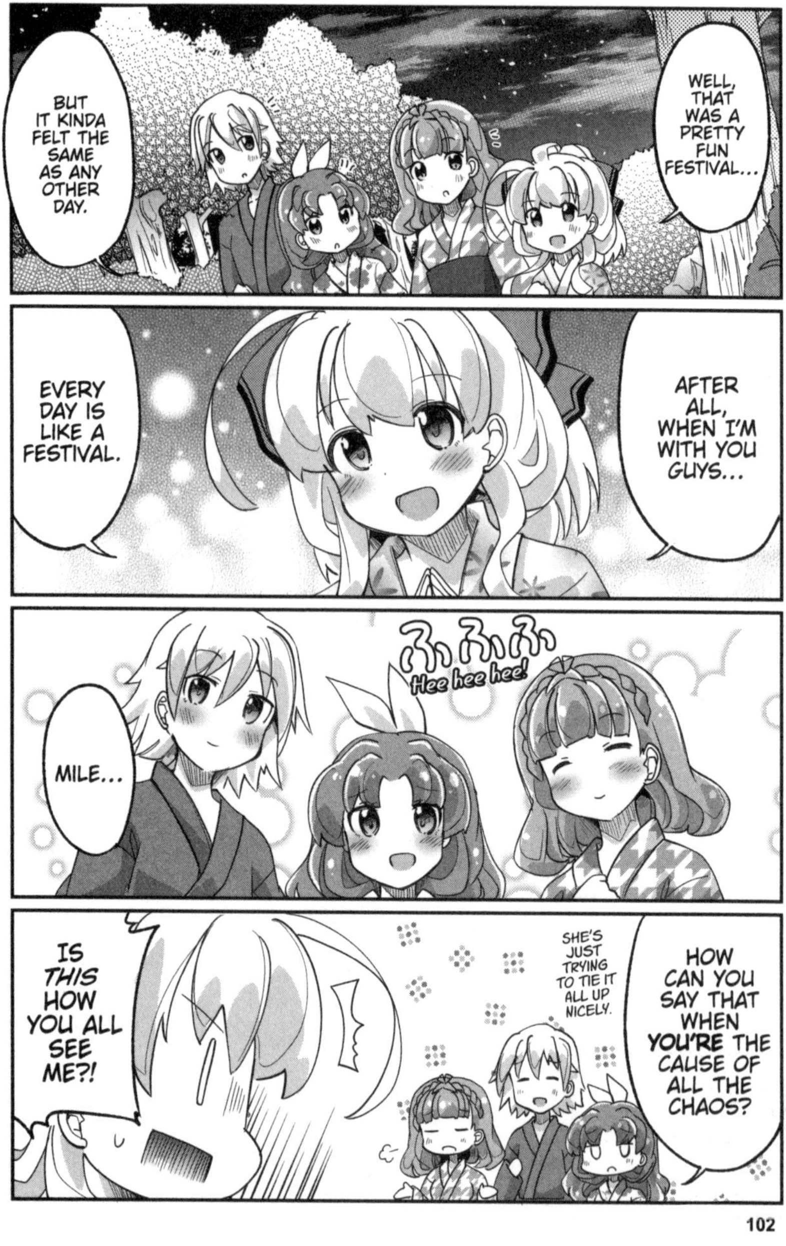
WELL, THAT WAS A PRETTY FUN FESTIVAL...
BUT IT KINDA FELT THE SAME AS ANY OTHER DAY.
AFTER ALL, WHEN I'M WITH YOU GUYS...
EVERY DAY IS LIKE A FESTIVAL.
ふふふ
Hee hee hee!
MILE...
HOW CAN YOU SAY THAT WHEN **YOU'RE** THE CAUSE OF ALL THE CHAOS?
SHE'S JUST TRYING TO TIE IT ALL UP NICELY.
IS *THIS* HOW YOU ALL SEE ME?!

Didn't I Say to Make My Abilities Average in the Next Life?!
EVERYDAY MISADVENTURES!

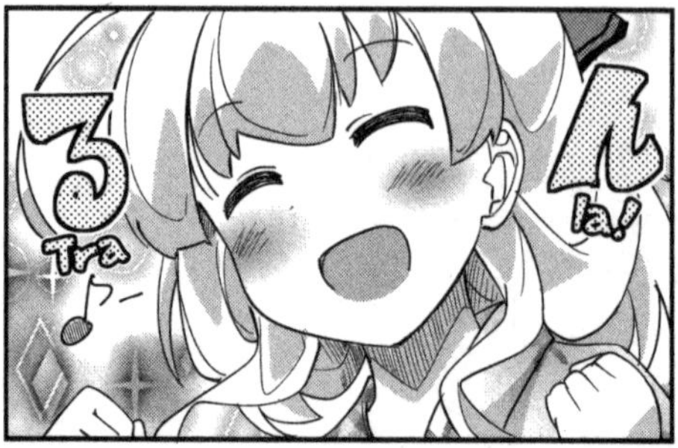

ら Tra
ん la!

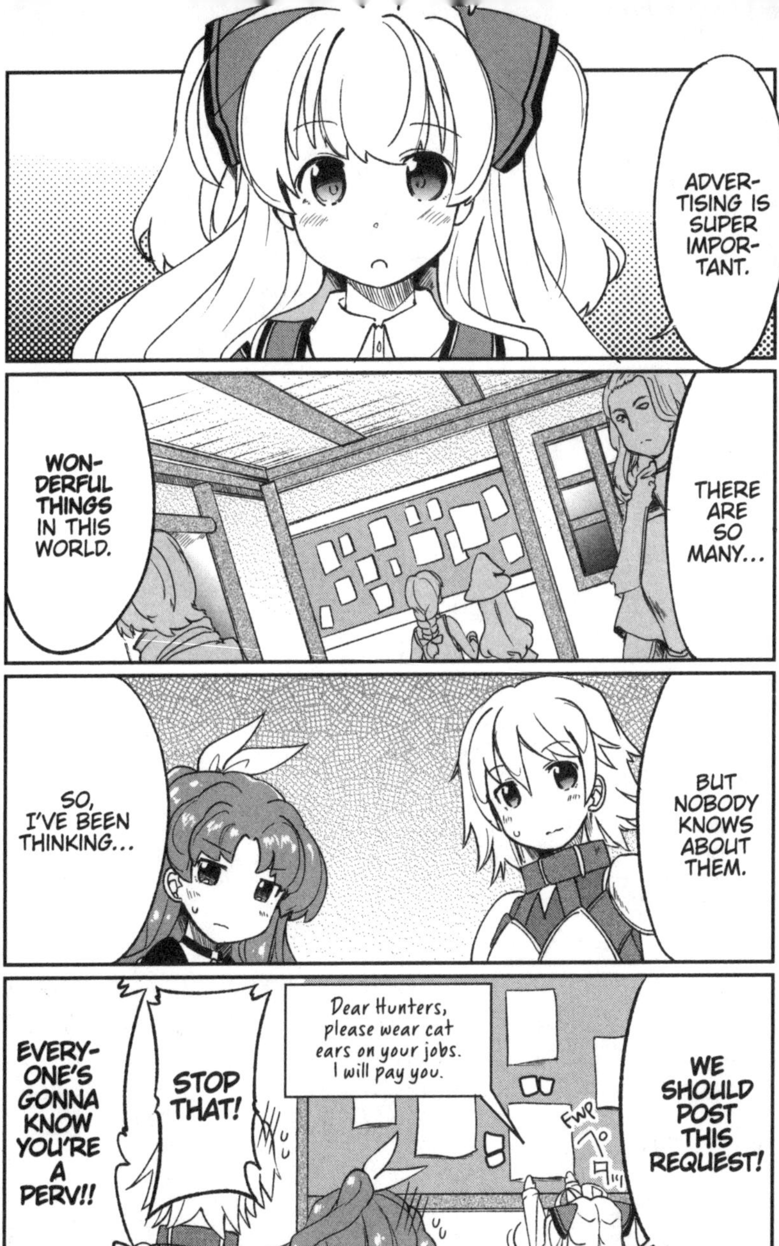
ADVERTISING IS SUPER IMPORTANT.
THERE ARE SO MANY...
WONDERFUL THINGS IN THIS WORLD.
BUT NOBODY KNOWS ABOUT THEM.
SO, I'VE BEEN THINKING...
WE SHOULD POST THIS REQUEST!
FWP
Dear Hunters, please wear cat ears on your jobs. I will pay you.
STOP THAT!
EVERYONE'S GONNA KNOW YOU'RE A PERV!!

Chapter 26

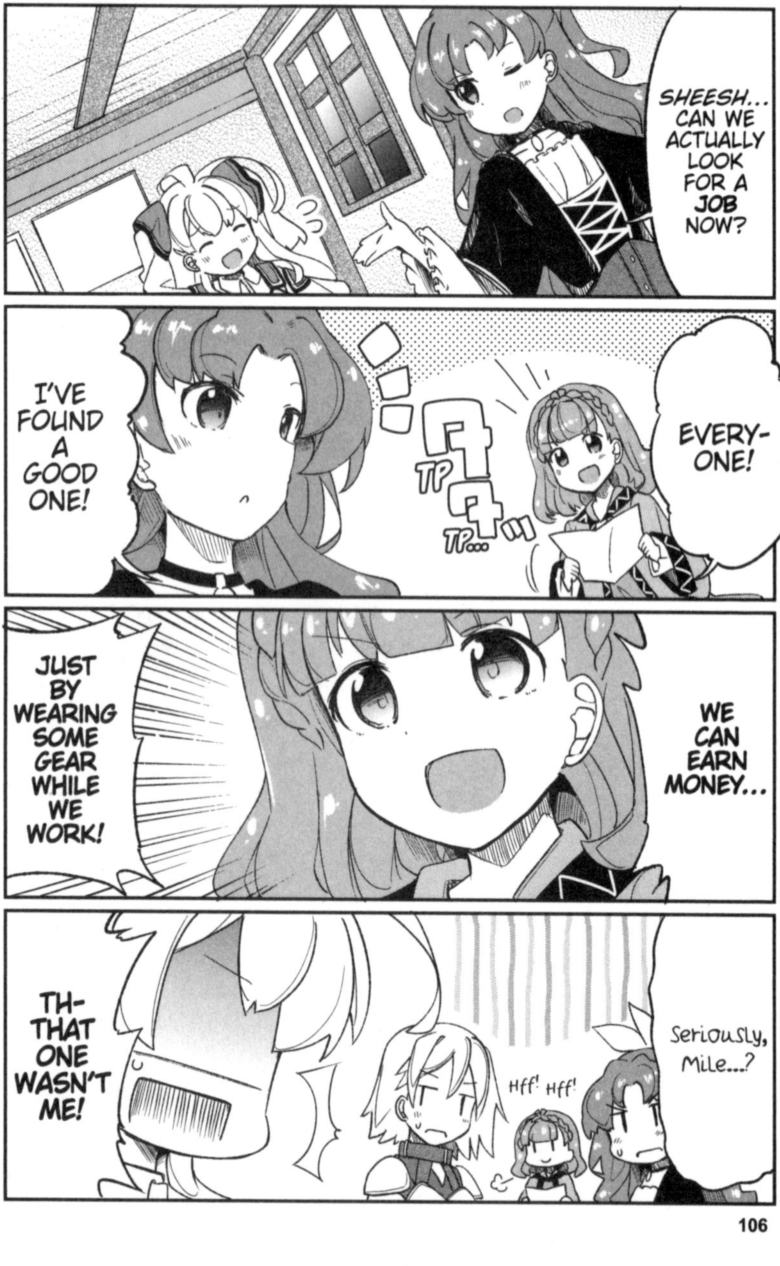
SHEESH... CAN WE ACTUALLY LOOK FOR A JOB NOW?
EVERY-ONE!
TP TP...
I'VE FOUND A GOOD ONE!
WE CAN EARN MONEY...
JUST BY WEARING SOME GEAR WHILE WE WORK!
Seriously, Mile...?
Hff! Hff!
TH-THAT ONE WASN'T ME!

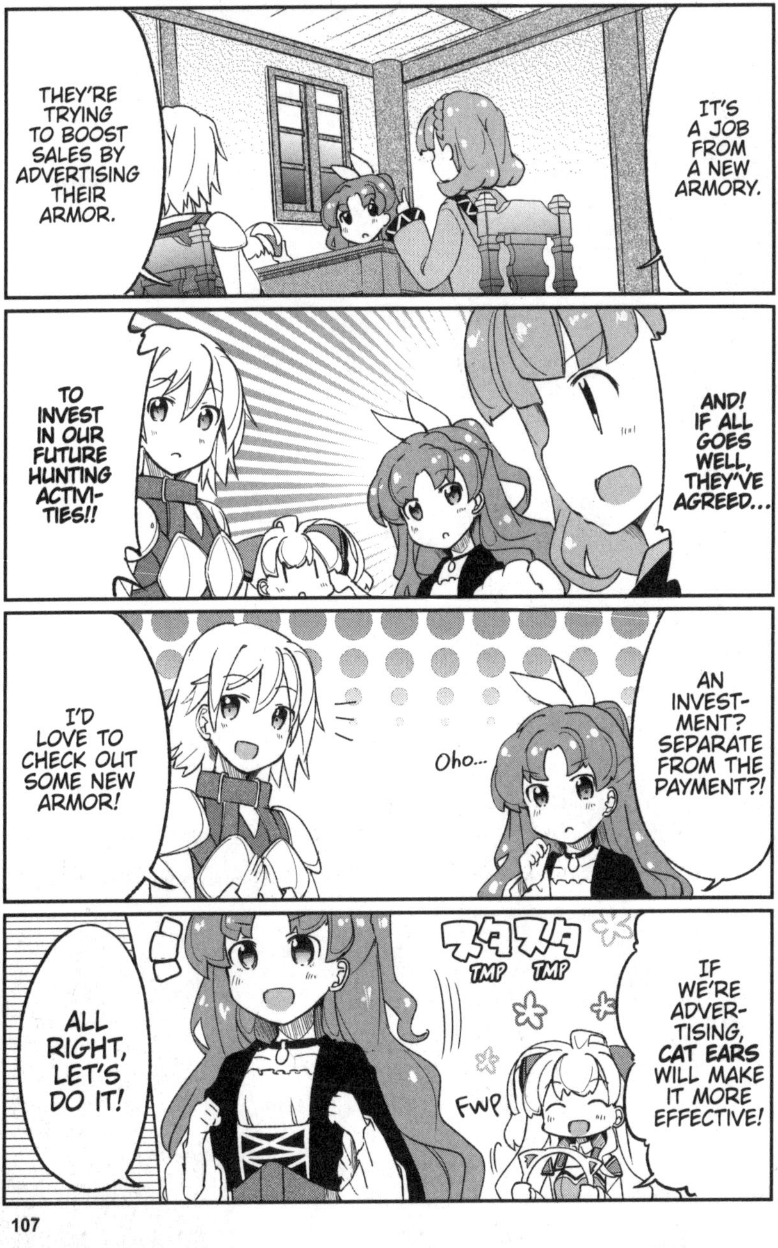
IT'S A JOB FROM A NEW ARMORY.
THEY'RE TRYING TO BOOST SALES BY ADVERTISING THEIR ARMOR.
AND! IF ALL GOES WELL, THEY'VE AGREED...
TO INVEST IN OUR FUTURE HUNTING ACTIVI-TIES!!
AN INVEST-MENT? SEPARATE FROM THE PAYMENT?!
Oho...
I'D LOVE TO CHECK OUT SOME NEW ARMOR!
IF WE'RE ADVER-TISING, **CAT EARS** WILL MAKE IT MORE EFFECTIVE!
スタスタ
TMP TMP
Fwp
ALL RIGHT, LET'S DO IT!

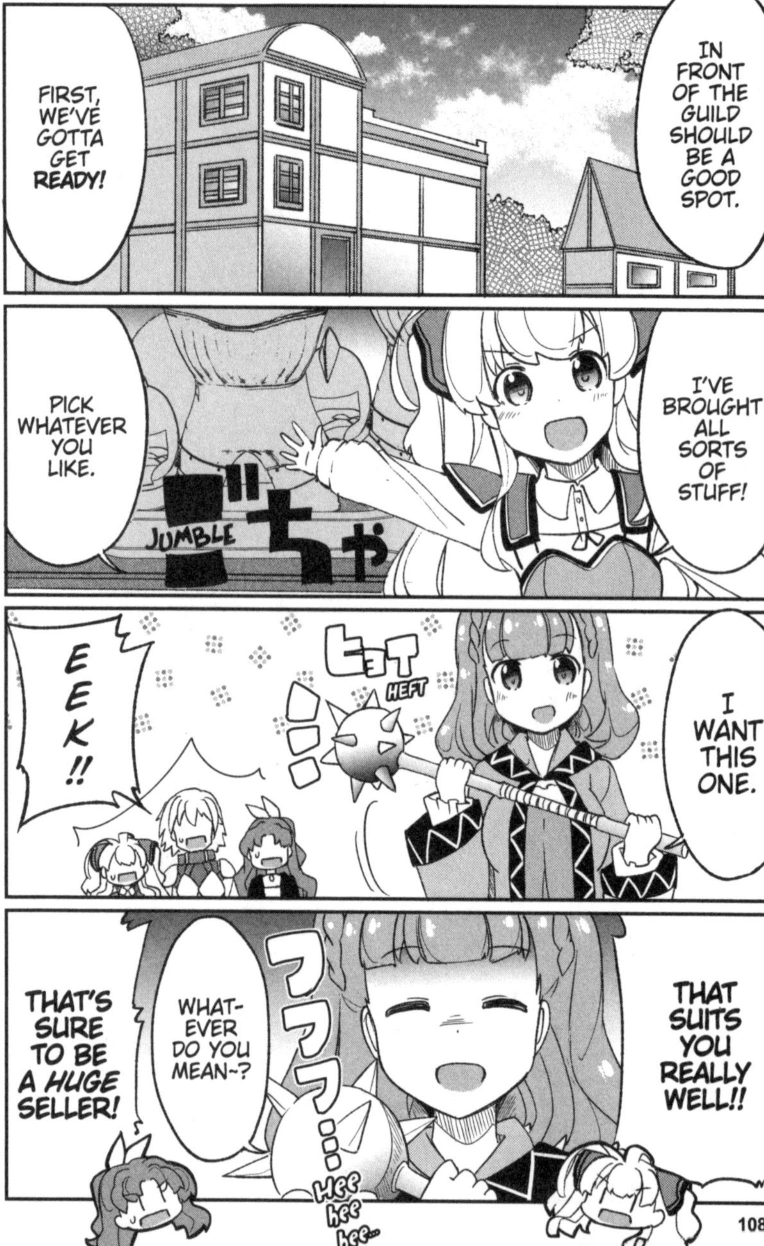
IN FRONT OF THE GUILD SHOULD BE A GOOD SPOT.
FIRST, WE'VE GOTTA GET READY!
I'VE BROUGHT ALL SORTS OF STUFF!
PICK WHATEVER YOU LIKE.
JUMBLE
I WANT THIS ONE.
HEFT
EEK!!
THAT SUITS YOU REALLY WELL!!
WHAT-EVER DO YOU MEAN~?
THAT'S SURE TO BE A *HUGE* SELLER!
Hee hee hee...

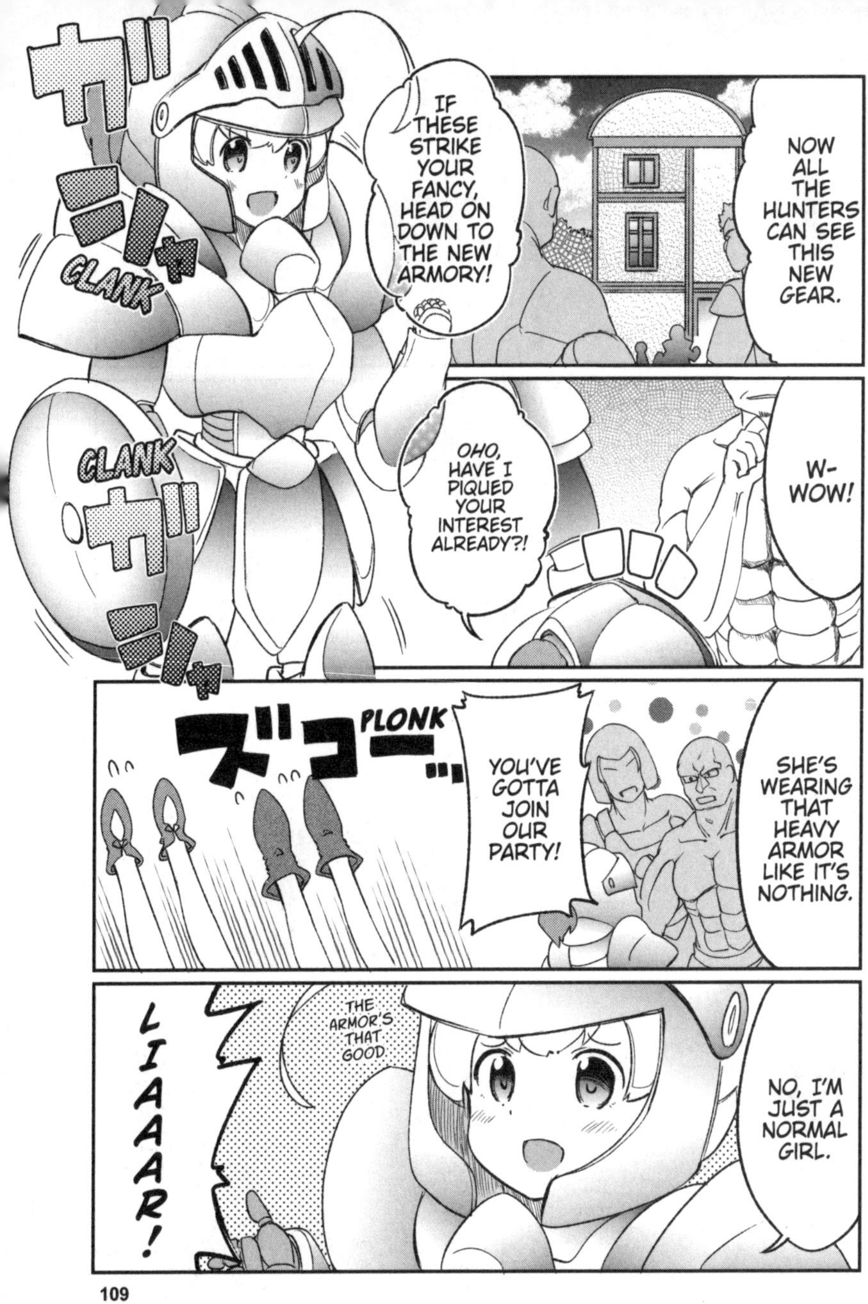
NOW ALL THE HUNTERS CAN SEE THIS NEW GEAR.
IF THESE STRIKE YOUR FANCY, HEAD ON DOWN TO THE NEW ARMORY!
CLANK
W-WOW!
OHO, HAVE I PIQUED YOUR INTEREST ALREADY?!
CLANK
SHE'S WEARING THAT HEAVY ARMOR LIKE IT'S NOTHING.
YOU'VE GOTTA JOIN OUR PARTY!
PLONK
NO, I'M JUST A NORMAL GIRL.
THE ARMOR'S THAT GOOD.
LIAAAAR!

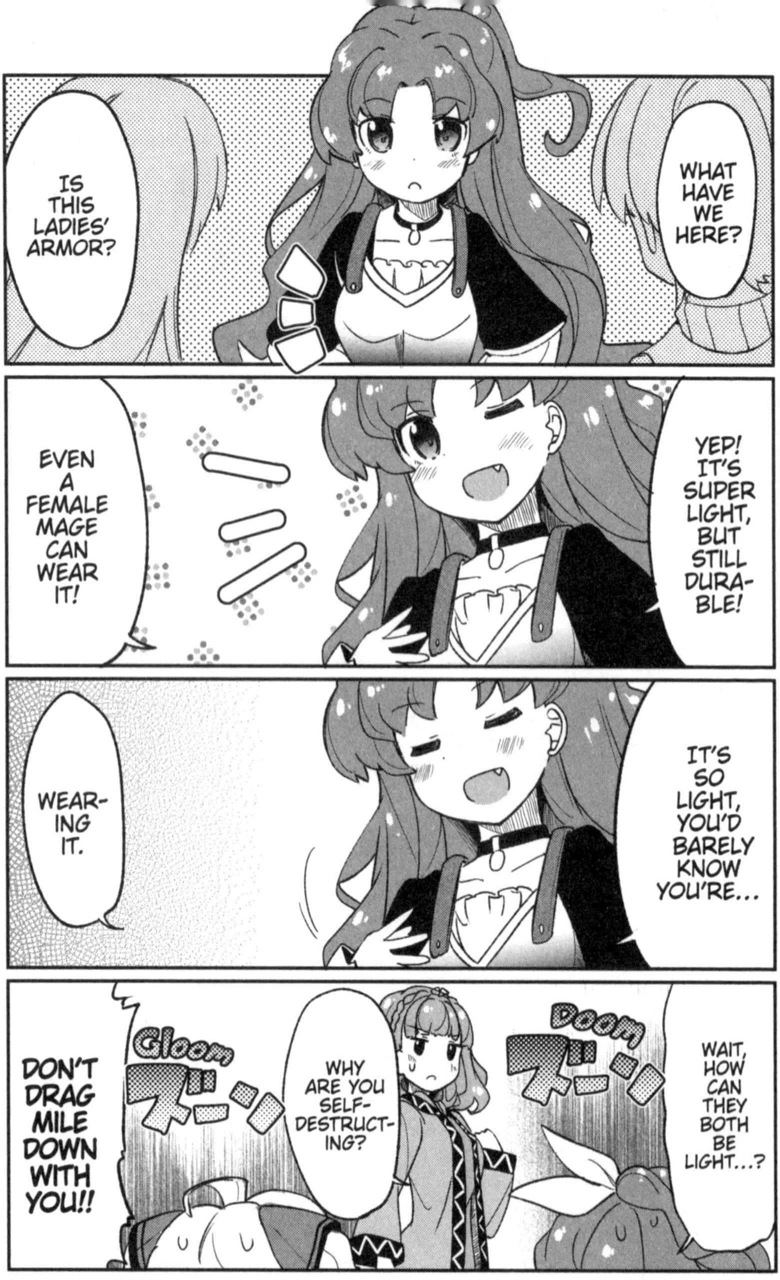
WHAT HAVE WE HERE?
IS THIS LADIES' ARMOR?
YEP! IT'S SUPER LIGHT, BUT STILL DURA-BLE!
EVEN A FEMALE MAGE CAN WEAR IT!
IT'S SO LIGHT, YOU'D BARELY KNOW YOU'RE...
WEAR-ING IT.
WAIT, HOW CAN THEY BOTH BE LIGHT...?
Doom
WHY ARE YOU SELF-DESTRUCT-ING?
Gloom
DON'T DRAG MILE DOWN WITH YOU!!

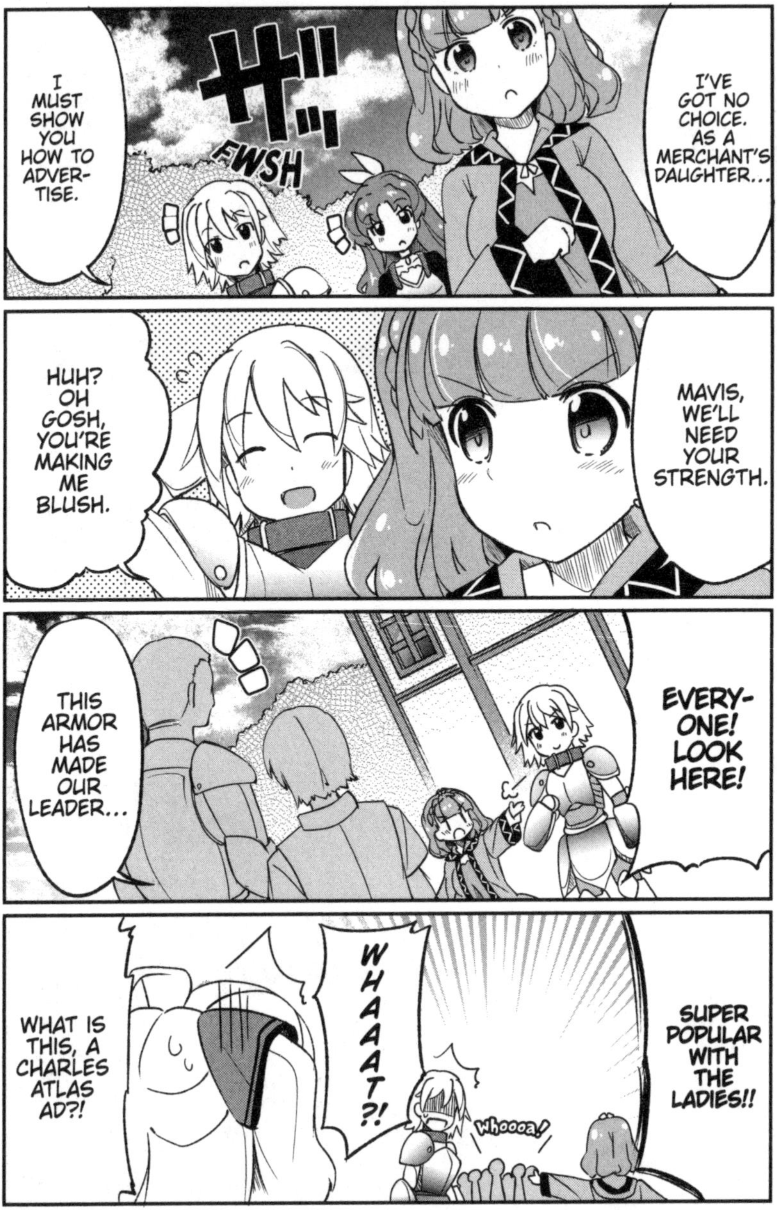
I'VE GOT NO CHOICE. AS A MERCHANT'S DAUGHTER...
FWSH
I MUST SHOW YOU HOW TO ADVERTISE.
MAVIS, WE'LL NEED YOUR STRENGTH.
HUH? OH GOSH, YOU'RE MAKING ME BLUSH.
EVERYONE! LOOK HERE!
THIS ARMOR HAS MADE OUR LEADER...
SUPER POPULAR WITH THE LADIES!!
Whoooa!
WHAAAAT?!
WHAT IS THIS, A CHARLES ATLAS AD?!

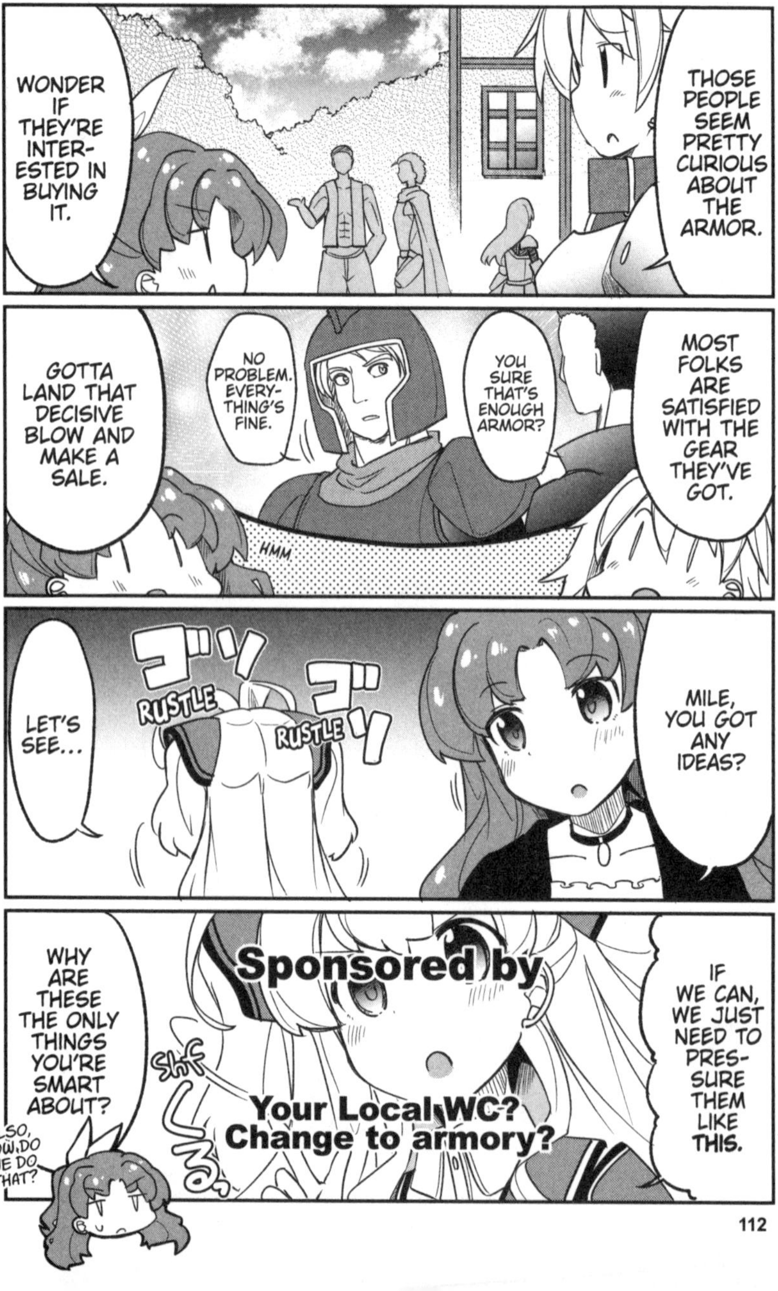

THOSE PEOPLE SEEM PRETTY CURIOUS ABOUT THE ARMOR.
WONDER IF THEY'RE INTER-ESTED IN BUYING IT.
MOST FOLKS ARE SATISFIED WITH THE GEAR THEY'VE GOT.
YOU SURE THAT'S ENOUGH ARMOR?
NO PROBLEM. EVERY-THING'S FINE.
HMM
GOTTA LAND THAT DECISIVE BLOW AND MAKE A SALE.
MILE, YOU GOT ANY IDEAS?
ゴソ RUSTLE
ゴソ RUSTLE
LET'S SEE...
IF WE CAN, WE JUST NEED TO PRES-SURE THEM LIKE THIS.
Sponsored by
Your Local WC? Change to armory?
Shf
WHY ARE THESE THE ONLY THINGS YOU'RE SMART ABOUT?
ALSO, HOW DO WE DO THAT?

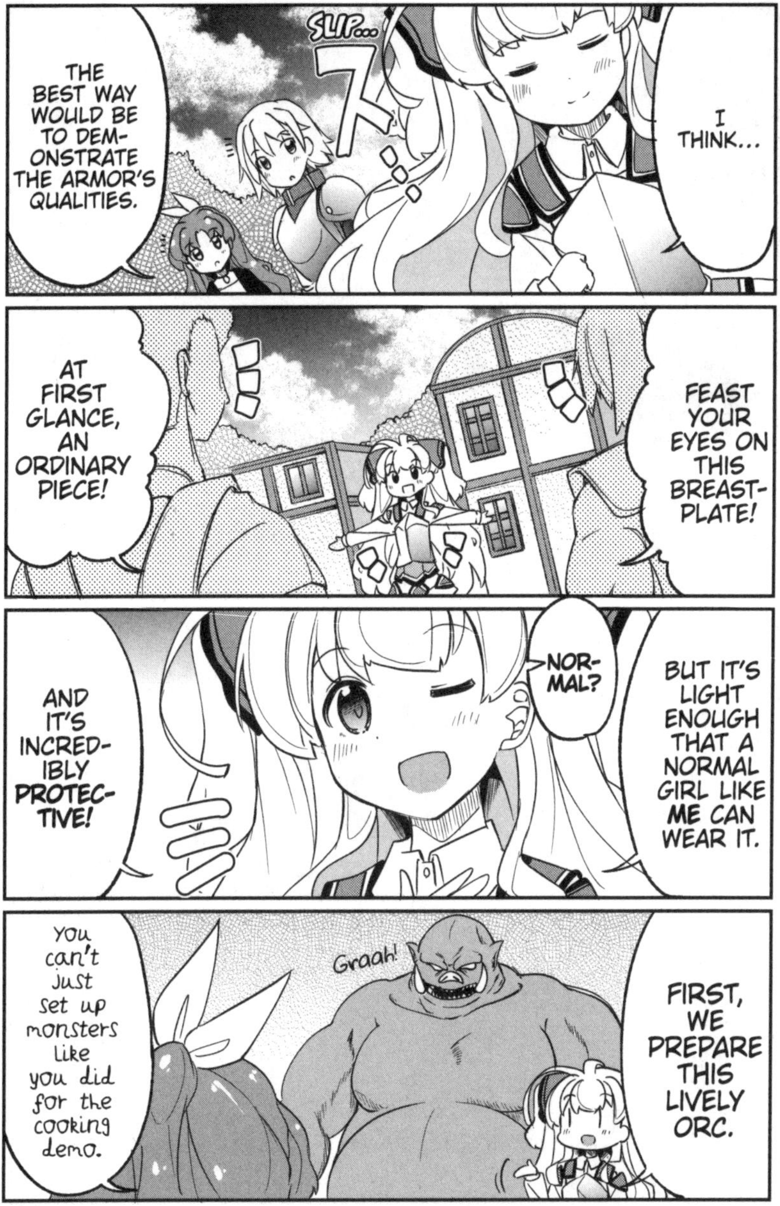
SLIP...
I THINK...
THE BEST WAY WOULD BE TO DEMONSTRATE THE ARMOR'S QUALITIES.
FEAST YOUR EYES ON THIS BREASTPLATE!
AT FIRST GLANCE, AN ORDINARY PIECE!
BUT IT'S LIGHT ENOUGH THAT A NORMAL GIRL LIKE ME CAN WEAR IT.
NORMAL?
AND IT'S INCREDIBLY PROTECTIVE!
FIRST, WE PREPARE THIS LIVELY ORC.
Graah!
You can't just set up monsters like you did for the cooking demo.

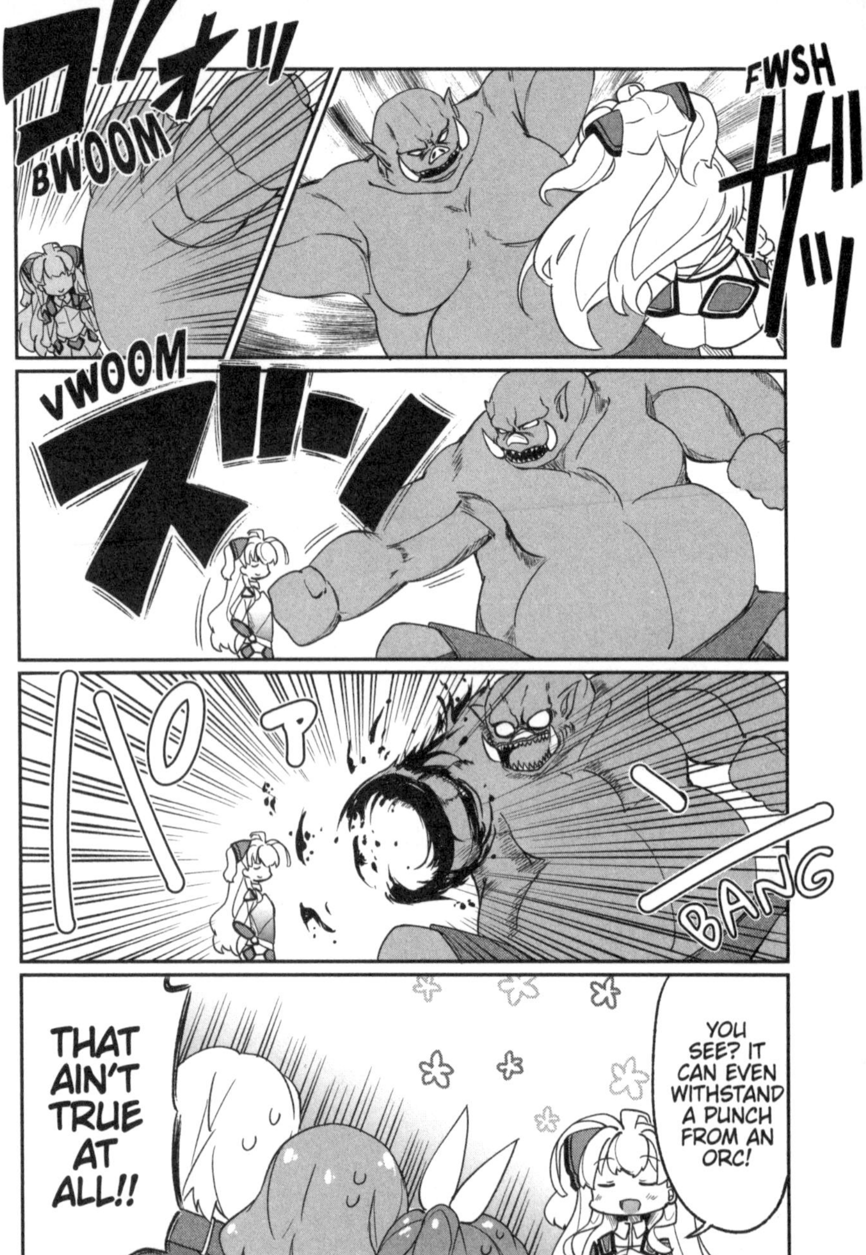
ゴオッ
BWOOM
FWSH
ザッ
VWOOM
ズーン
パァーン
BANG
YOU SEE? IT CAN EVEN WITHSTAND A PUNCH FROM AN ORC!
THAT AIN'T TRUE AT ALL!!

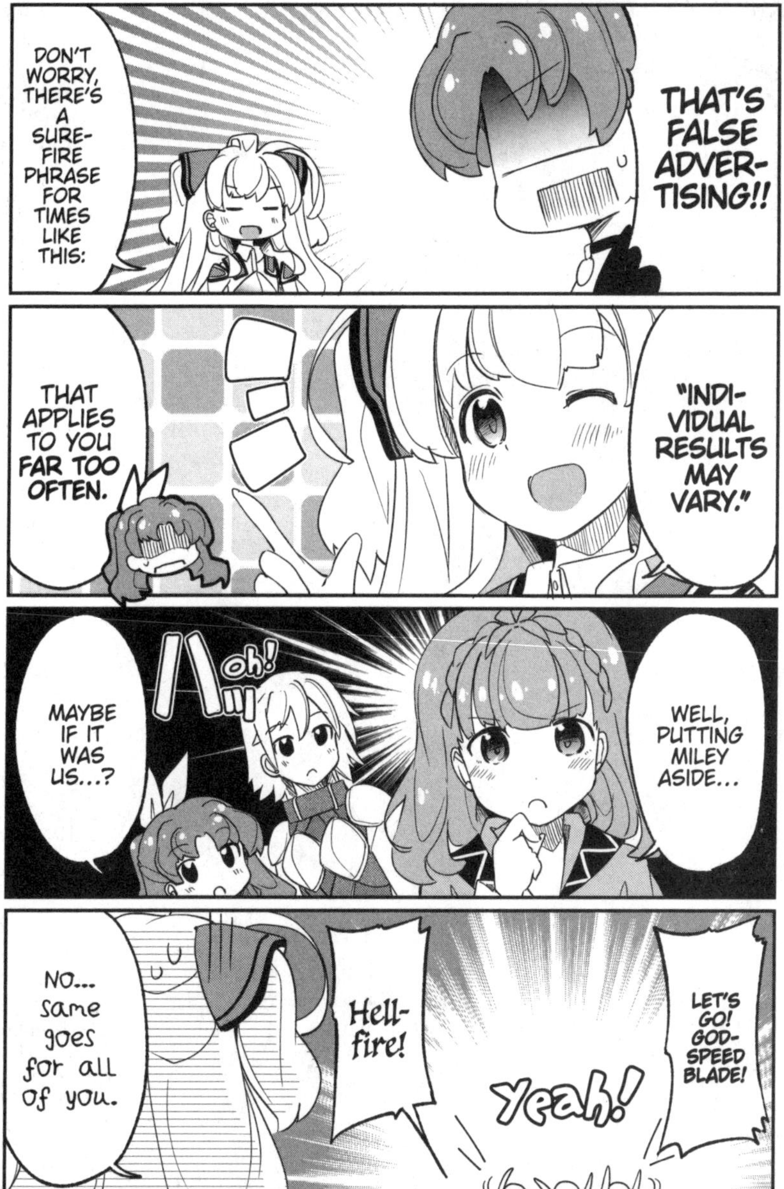
THAT'S FALSE ADVERTISING!!
DON'T WORRY, THERE'S A SURE-FIRE PHRASE FOR TIMES LIKE THIS:
"INDIVIDUAL RESULTS MAY VARY."
THAT APPLIES TO YOU FAR TOO OFTEN.
WELL, PUTTING MILEY ASIDE...
oh!
MAYBE IF IT WAS US...?
LET'S GO! GODSPEED BLADE!
Yeah!
Hell-fire!
NO... same goes for all of you.

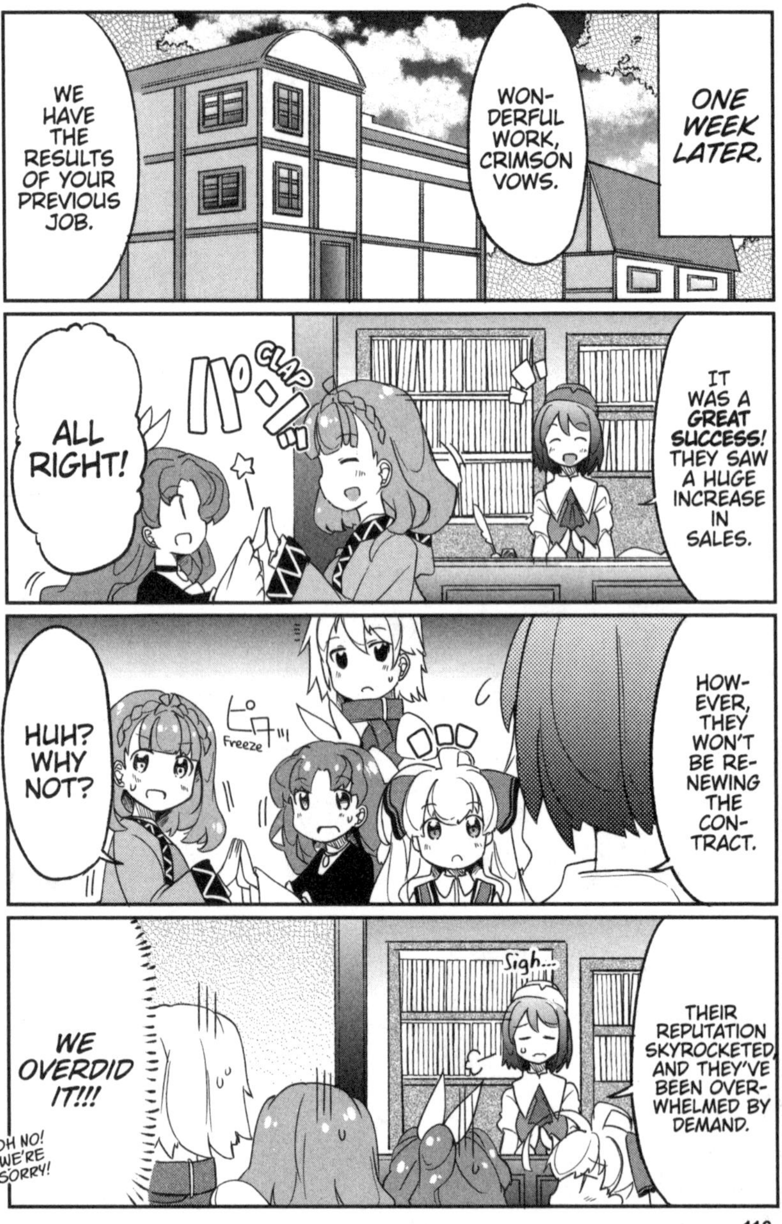

ONE WEEK LATER.
WON-DERFUL WORK, CRIMSON VOWS.
WE HAVE THE RESULTS OF YOUR PREVIOUS JOB.
IT WAS A GREAT SUCCESS! THEY SAW A HUGE INCREASE IN SALES.
CLAP
ALL RIGHT!
HOW-EVER, THEY WON'T BE RE-NEWING THE CON-TRACT.
Freeze
HUH? WHY NOT?
THEIR REPUTATION SKYROCKETED, AND THEY'VE BEEN OVER-WHELMED BY DEMAND.
Sigh...
WE OVERDID IT!!!
OH NO! WE'RE SORRY!

Didn't I Say to Make My Abilities Average in the Next Life?!

EVERYDAY MISADVENTURES!

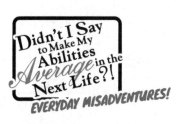

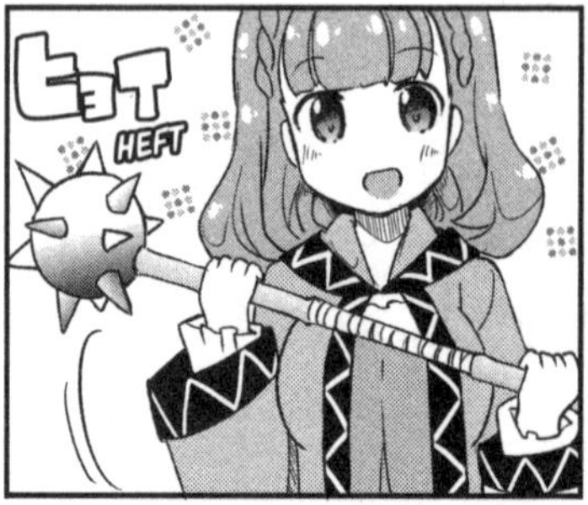
ヒョイ
HEFT

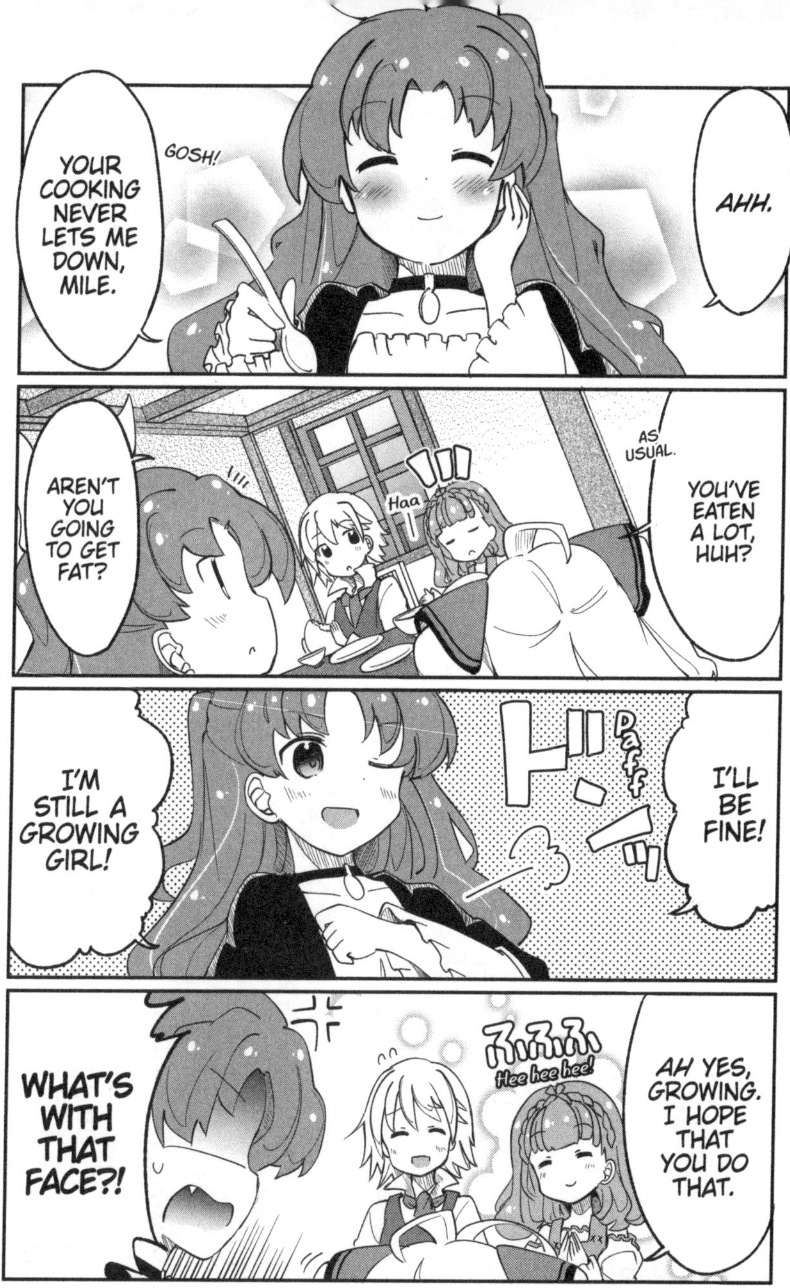
AHH.
GOSH!
YOUR COOKING NEVER LETS ME DOWN, MILE.
AS USUAL.
YOU'VE EATEN A LOT, HUH?
Haa
AREN'T YOU GOING TO GET FAT?
I'LL BE FINE!
Paff
I'M STILL A GROWING GIRL!
AH YES, GROWING. I HOPE THAT YOU DO THAT.
ふふふ
Hee hee hee!
WHAT'S WITH THAT FACE?!

Chapter 27

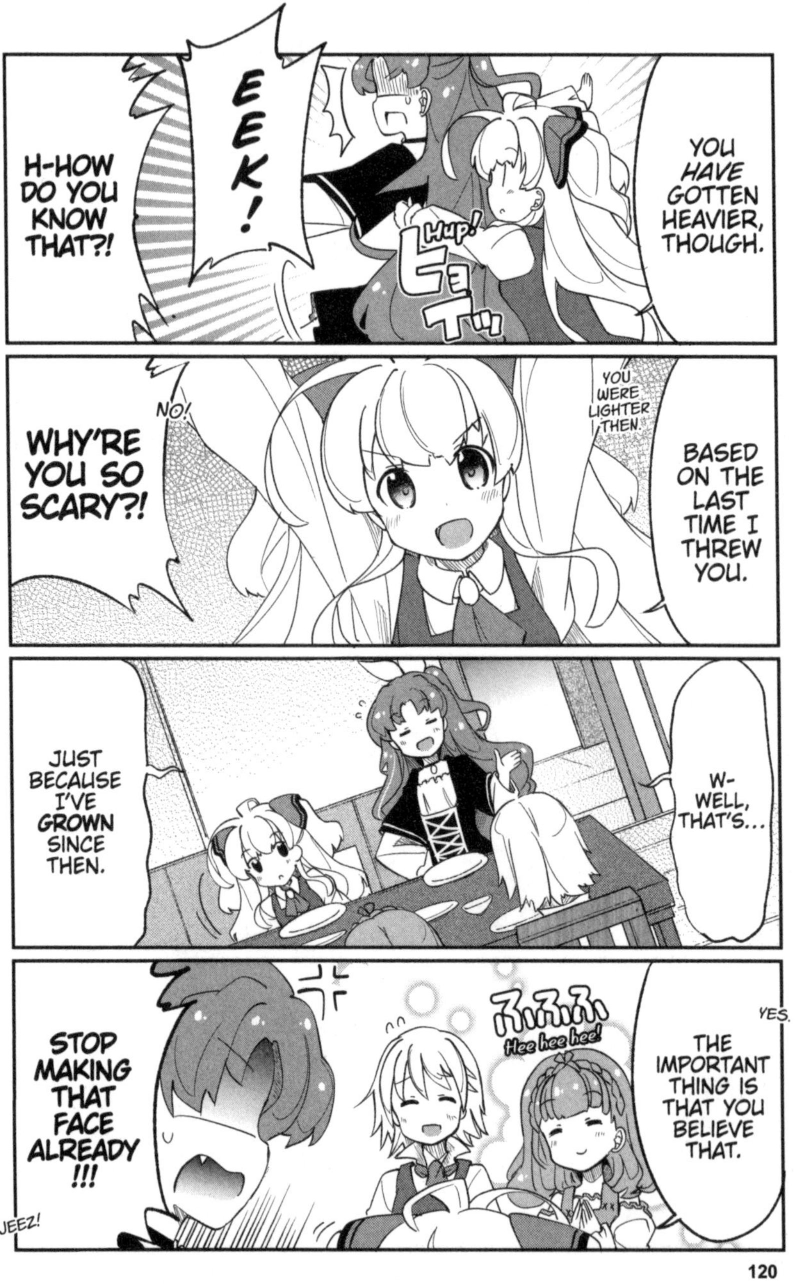
YOU HAVE GOTTEN HEAVIER, THOUGH.
Hup!
EEK!
H-HOW DO YOU KNOW THAT?!
BASED ON THE LAST TIME I THREW YOU.
YOU WERE LIGHTER THEN.
NO!
WHY'RE YOU SO SCARY?!
W-WELL, THAT'S...
JUST BECAUSE I'VE GROWN SINCE THEN.
YES.
THE IMPORTANT THING IS THAT YOU BELIEVE THAT.
ふふふ
Hee hee hee!
STOP MAKING THAT FACE ALREADY!!!
JEEZ!

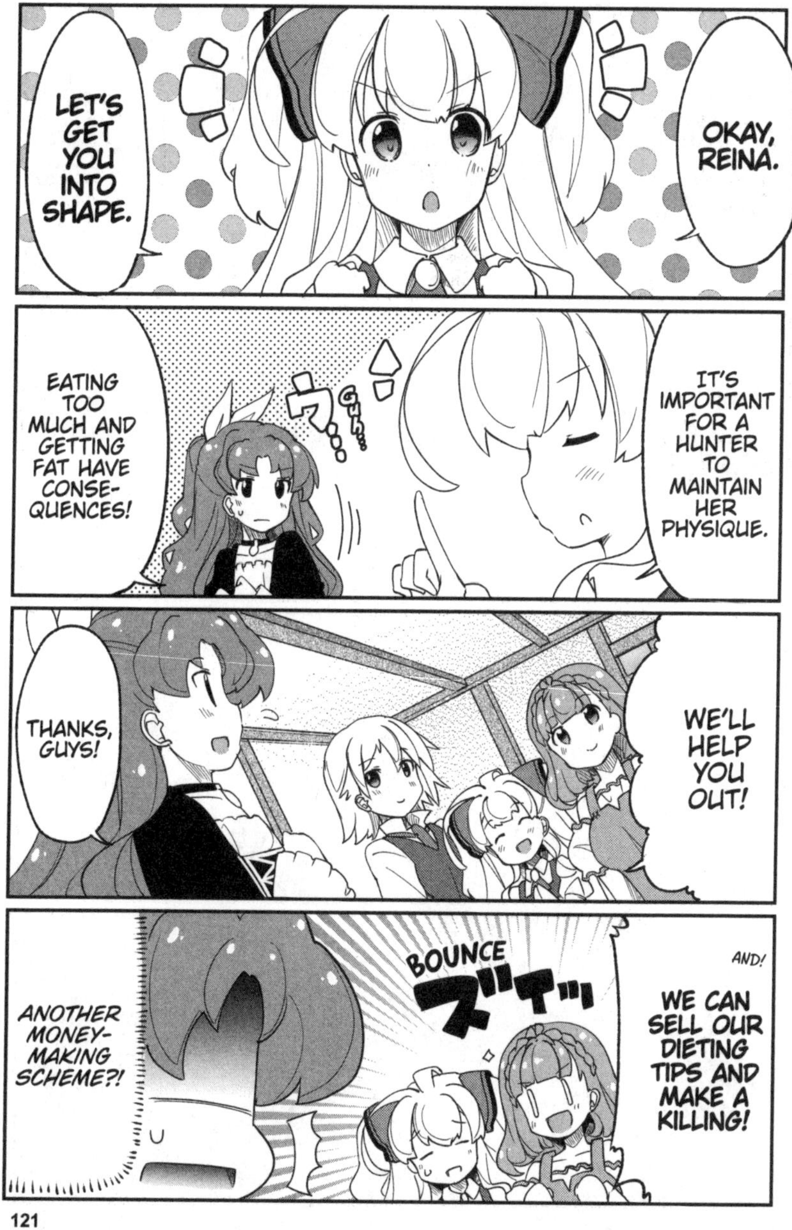
OKAY, REINA.
LET'S GET YOU INTO SHAPE.
IT'S IMPORTANT FOR A HUNTER TO MAINTAIN HER PHYSIQUE.
Guh...
EATING TOO MUCH AND GETTING FAT HAVE CONSE-QUENCES!
WE'LL HELP YOU OUT!
THANKS, GUYS!
AND!
WE CAN SELL OUR DIETING TIPS AND MAKE A KILLING!
BOUNCE
ANOTHER MONEY-MAKING SCHEME?!

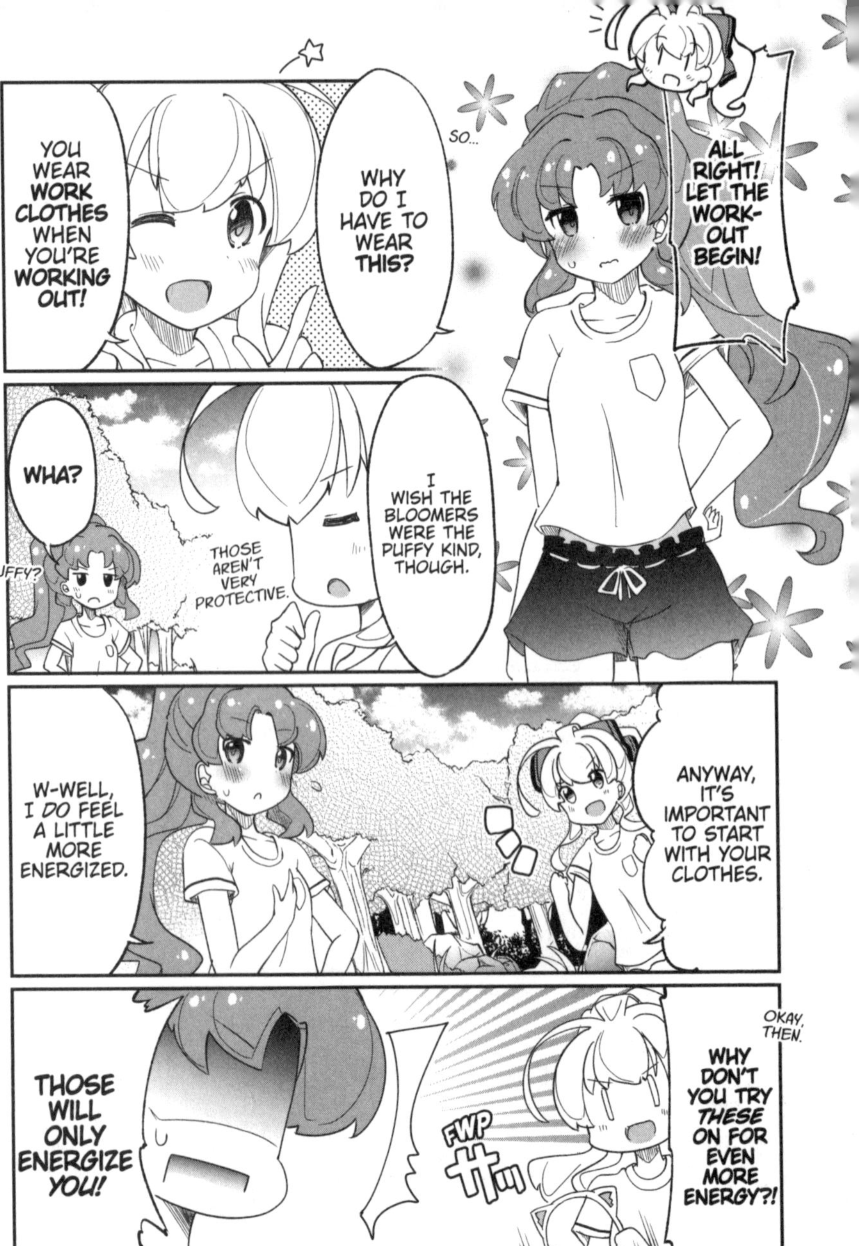
ALL RIGHT! LET THE WORK-OUT BEGIN!
SO...
WHY DO I HAVE TO WEAR THIS?
YOU WEAR WORK CLOTHES WHEN YOU'RE WORKING OUT!
I WISH THE BLOOMERS WERE THE PUFFY KIND, THOUGH.
THOSE AREN'T VERY PROTECTIVE.
WHA?
PUFFY?
ANYWAY, IT'S IMPORTANT TO START WITH YOUR CLOTHES.
W-WELL, I *DO* FEEL A LITTLE MORE ENERGIZED.
OKAY, THEN.
WHY DON'T YOU TRY *THESE* ON FOR EVEN MORE ENERGY?!
FWP
THOSE WILL ONLY ENERGIZE *YOU*!

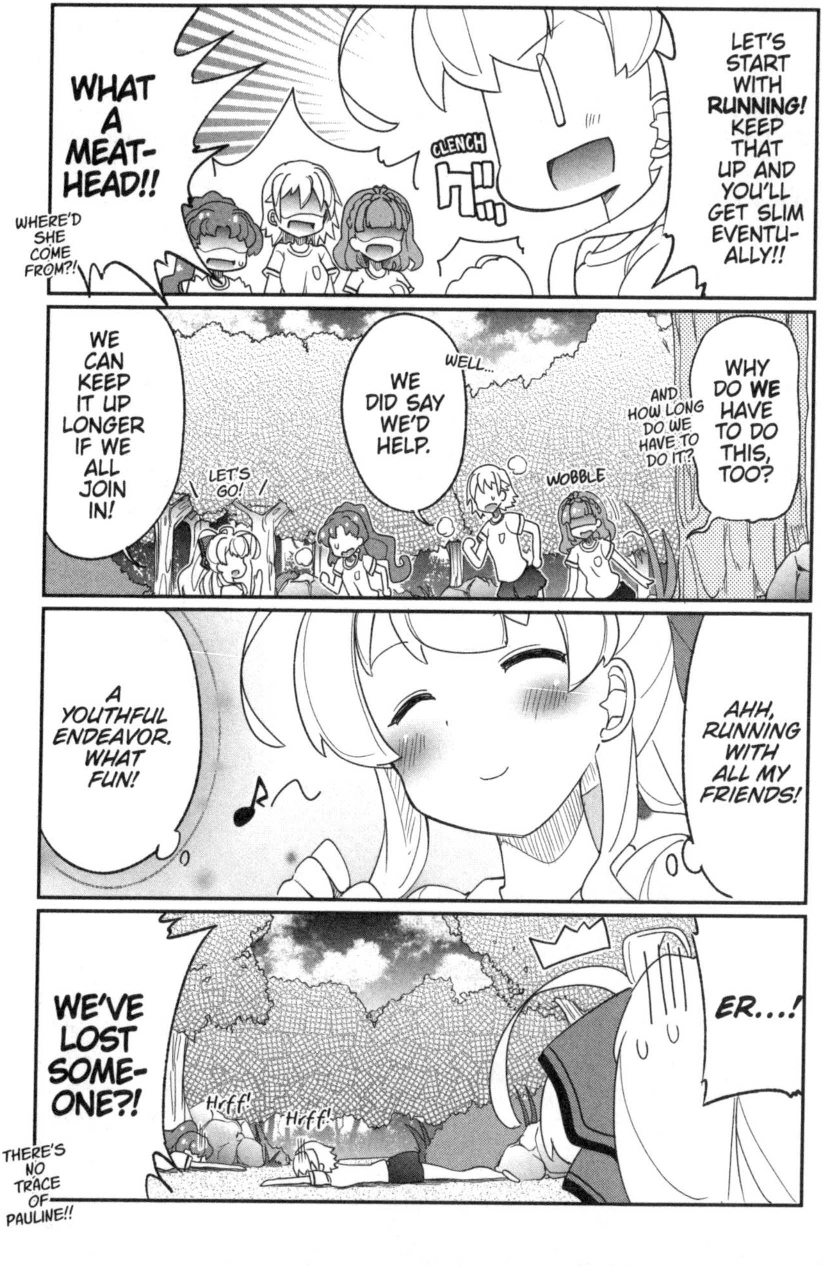

LET'S START WITH RUNNING! KEEP THAT UP AND YOU'LL GET SLIM EVENTUALLY!!
CLENCH
WHAT A MEAT-HEAD!!
WHERE'D SHE COME FROM?!
WHY DO WE HAVE TO DO THIS, TOO?
AND HOW LONG DO WE HAVE TO DO IT?
WOBBLE
WELL...
WE DID SAY WE'D HELP.
LET'S GO!
WE CAN KEEP IT UP LONGER IF WE ALL JOIN IN!
AHH, RUNNING WITH ALL MY FRIENDS!
A YOUTHFUL ENDEAVOR. WHAT FUN!
ER...!
WE'VE LOST SOMEONE?!
Hrff!
Hrff!
THERE'S NO TRACE OF PAULINE!!

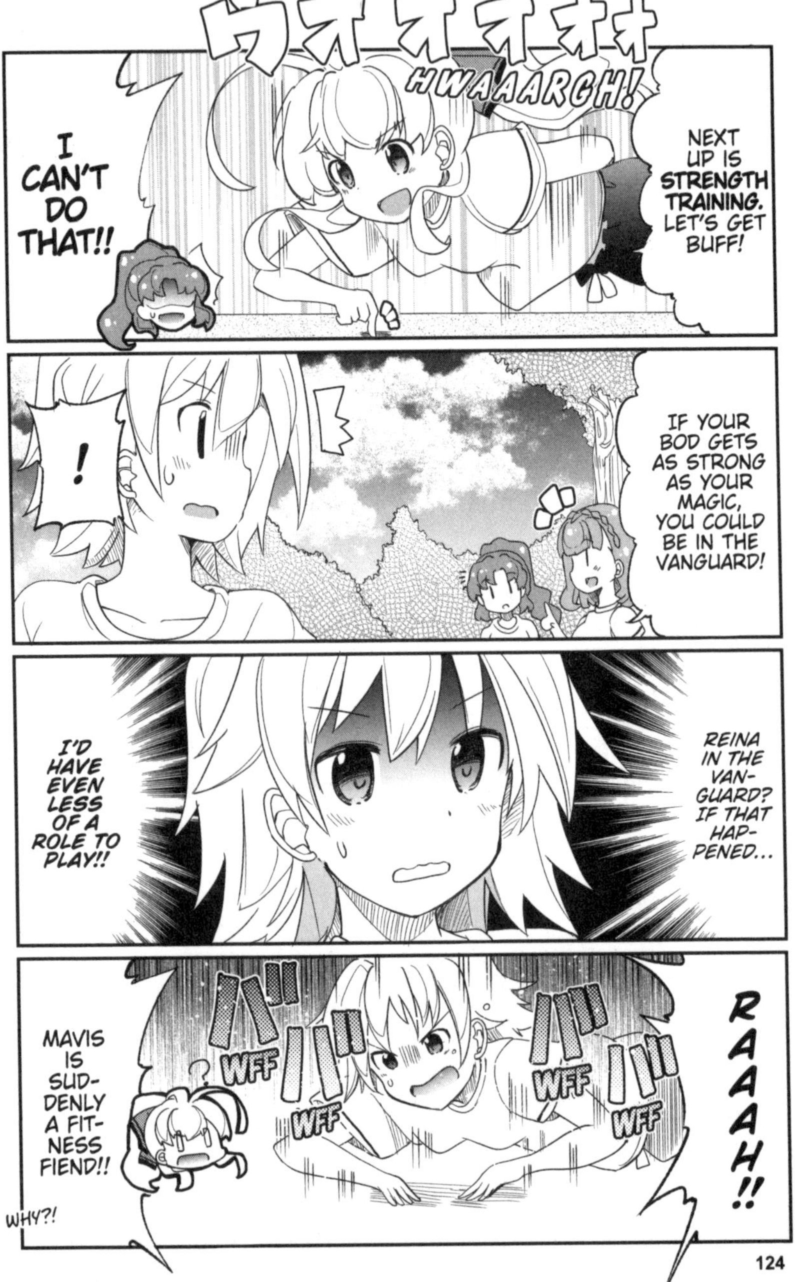
ウオオオオオ
HWAAARGH!
NEXT UP IS STRENGTH TRAINING. LET'S GET BUFF!
I CAN'T DO THAT!!
IF YOUR BOD GETS AS STRONG AS YOUR MAGIC, YOU COULD BE IN THE VANGUARD!
!
REINA IN THE VAN-GUARD? IF THAT HAP-PENED...
I'D HAVE EVEN LESS OF A ROLE TO PLAY!!
RAAAAH!!
バ バ バ バ
WFF WFF WFF WFF
MAVIS IS SUD-DENLY A FIT-NESS FIEND!!
WHY?!

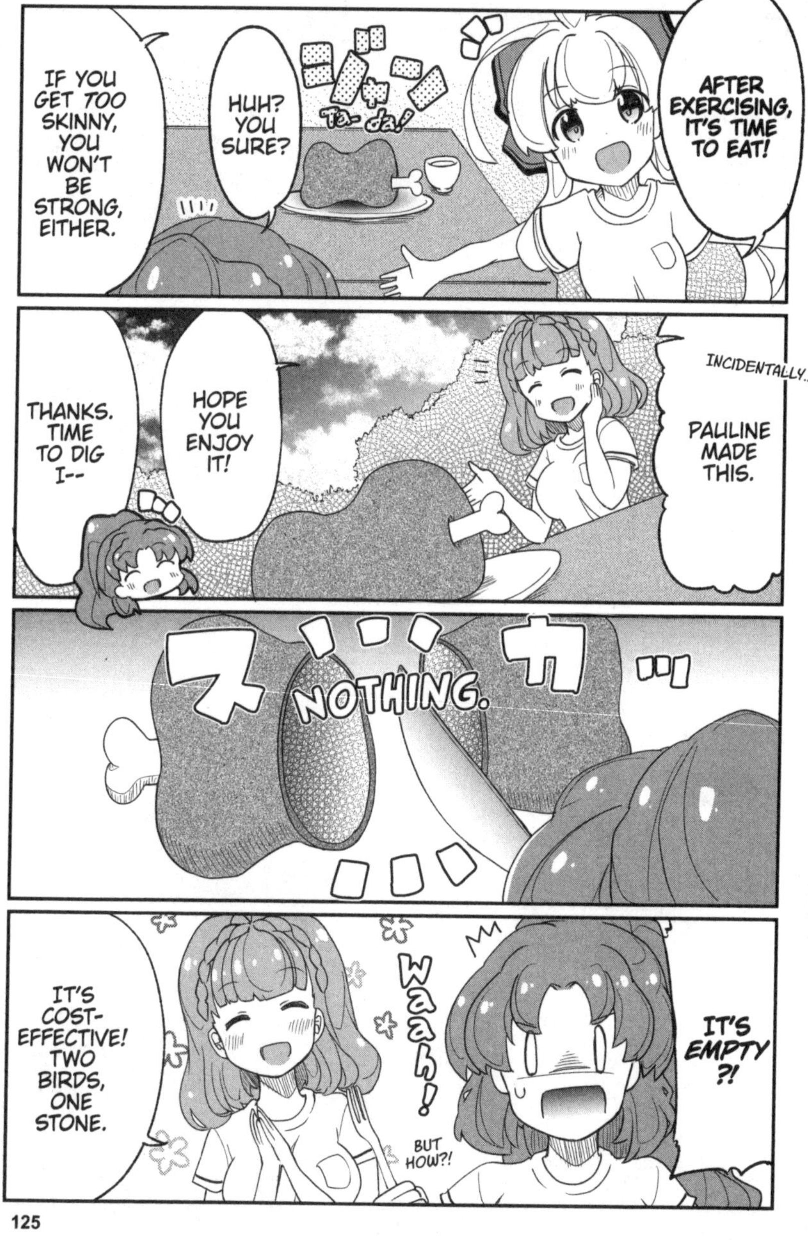
AFTER EXERCISING, IT'S TIME TO EAT!
TA-DA!
HUH? YOU SURE?
IF YOU GET TOO SKINNY, YOU WON'T BE STRONG, EITHER.
INCIDENTALLY...
PAULINE MADE THIS.
HOPE YOU ENJOY IT!
THANKS. TIME TO DIG I--
NOTHING.
IT'S EMPTY?!
Waah!
BUT HOW?!
IT'S COST-EFFECTIVE! TWO BIRDS, ONE STONE.

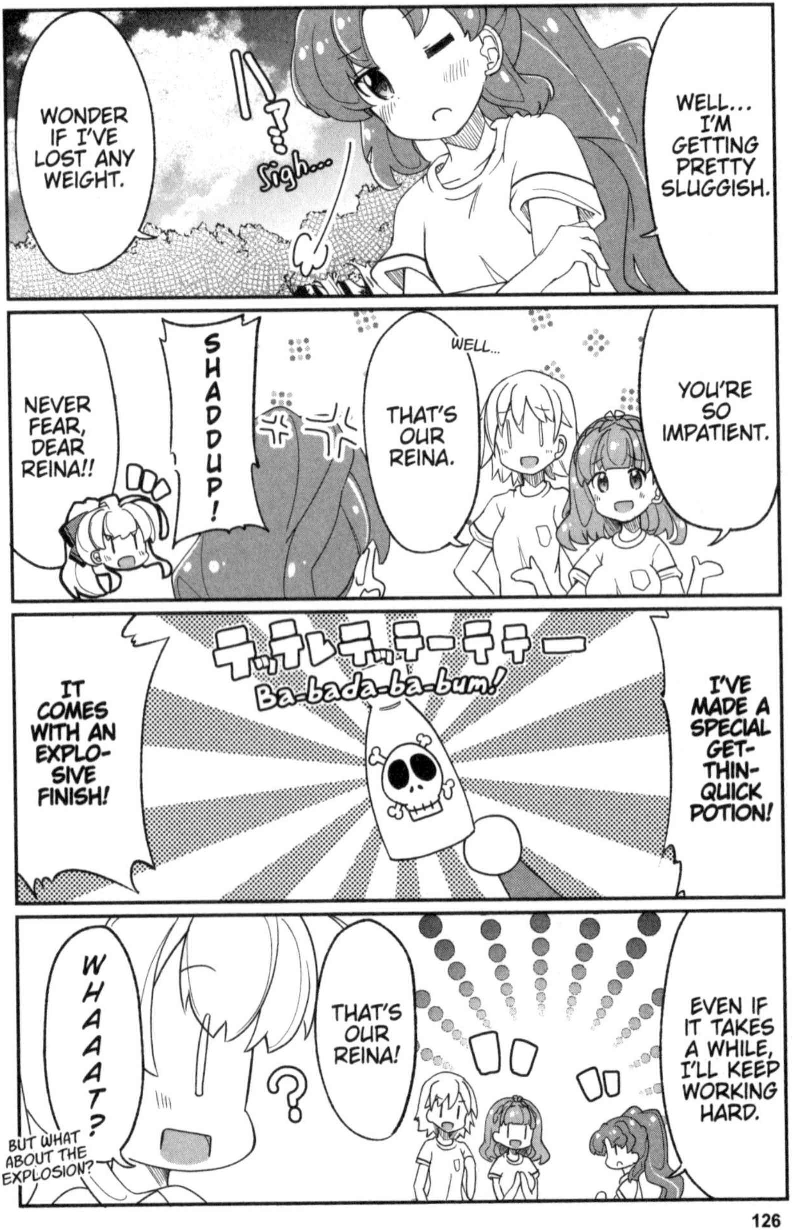
WELL... I'M GETTING PRETTY SLUGGISH.
ハァ…
Sigh...
WONDER IF I'VE LOST ANY WEIGHT.
YOU'RE SO IMPATIENT.
WELL...
THAT'S OUR REINA.
SHADDUP!
NEVER FEAR, DEAR REINA!!
I'VE MADE A SPECIAL GET-THIN-QUICK POTION!
テッテレテッテーテテー
Ba-bada-ba-bum!
IT COMES WITH AN EXPLOSIVE FINISH!
EVEN IF IT TAKES A WHILE, I'LL KEEP WORKING HARD.
THAT'S OUR REINA!
WHAAAAT?
BUT WHAT ABOUT THE EXPLOSION?

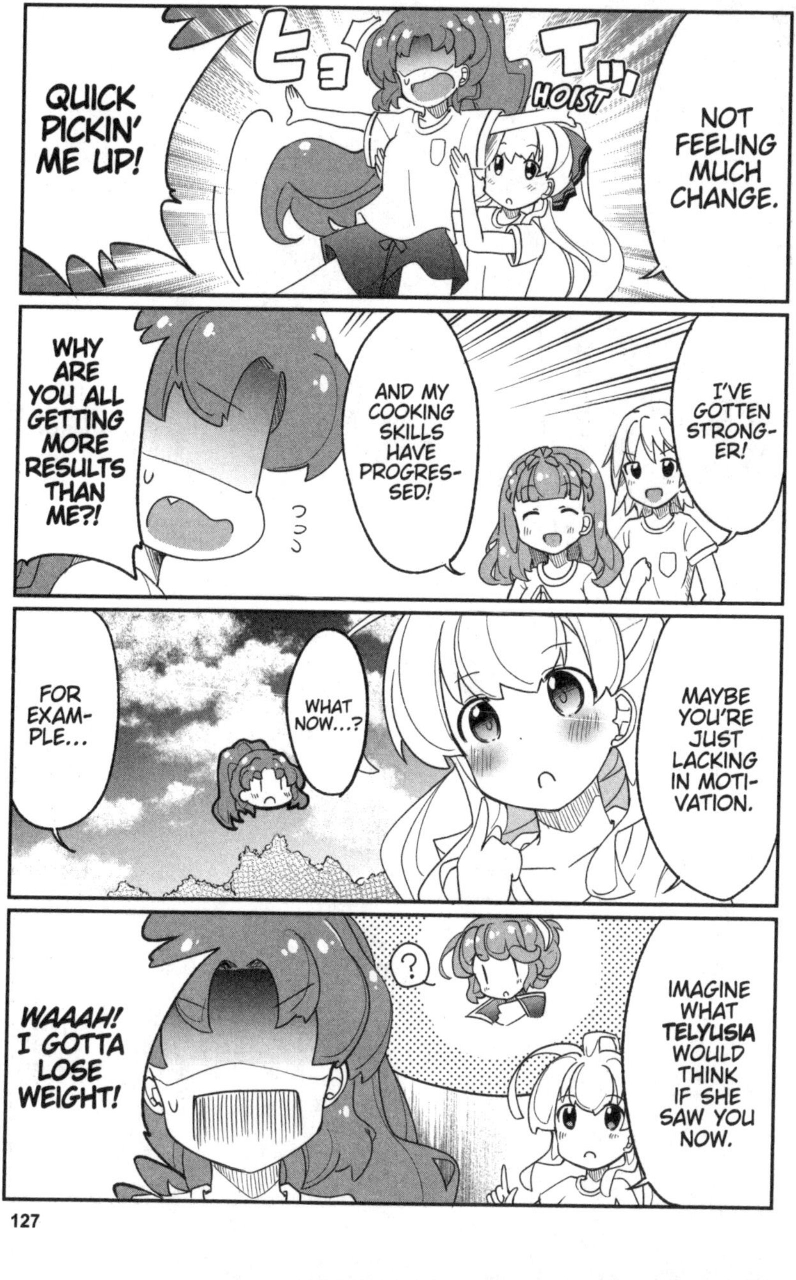

NOT FEELING MUCH CHANGE.
ヒョイッ
HOIST
QUICK PICKIN' ME UP!
I'VE GOTTEN STRONGER!
AND MY COOKING SKILLS HAVE PROGRESSED!
WHY ARE YOU ALL GETTING MORE RESULTS THAN ME?!
MAYBE YOU'RE JUST LACKING IN MOTIVATION.
WHAT NOW...?
FOR EXAMPLE...
IMAGINE WHAT TELYUSIA WOULD THINK IF SHE SAW YOU NOW.
?
WAAAH! I GOTTA LOSE WEIGHT!

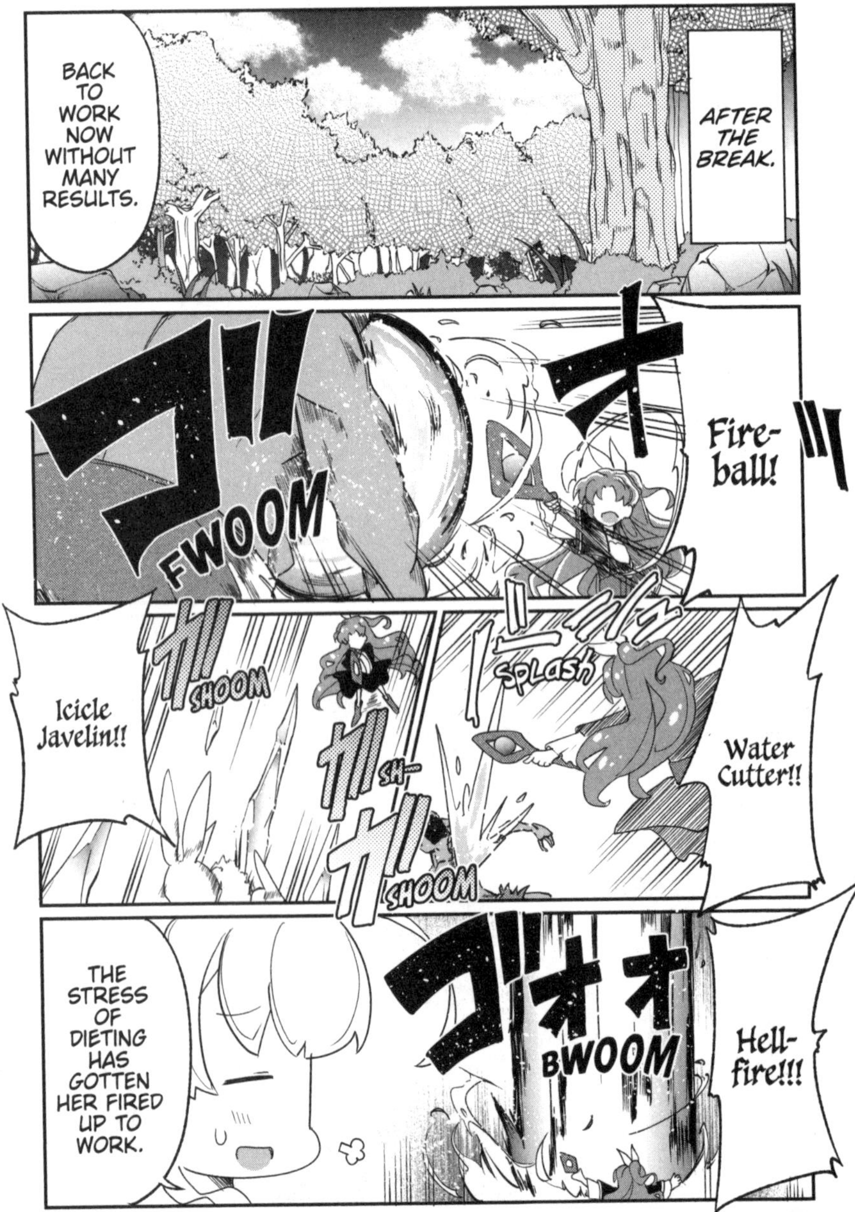

AFTER THE BREAK.
BACK TO WORK NOW WITHOUT MANY RESULTS.
Fire-ball!
FWOOM
Water Cutter!!
SPLASH
Icicle Javelin!!
SHOOM
SH—
SHOOM
Hell-fire!!!
BWOOM
THE STRESS OF DIETING HAS GOTTEN HER FIRED UP TO WORK.

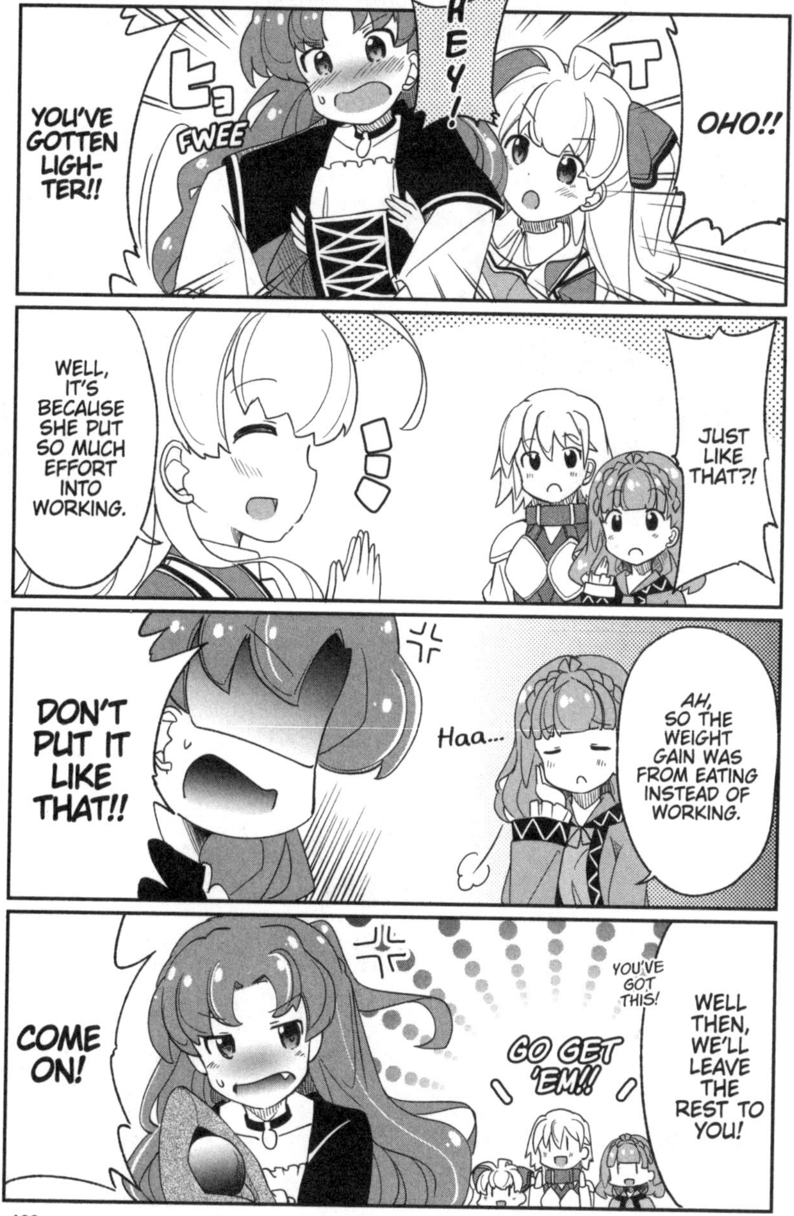
OHO!!
HEY!
ヒョ
FWEE
YOU'VE GOTTEN LIGHTER!!
JUST LIKE THAT?!
WELL, IT'S BECAUSE SHE PUT SO MUCH EFFORT INTO WORKING.
AH, SO THE WEIGHT GAIN WAS FROM EATING INSTEAD OF WORKING.
Haa...
DON'T PUT IT LIKE THAT!!
WELL THEN, WE'LL LEAVE THE REST TO YOU!
YOU'VE GOT THIS!
GO GET 'EM!!
COME ON!

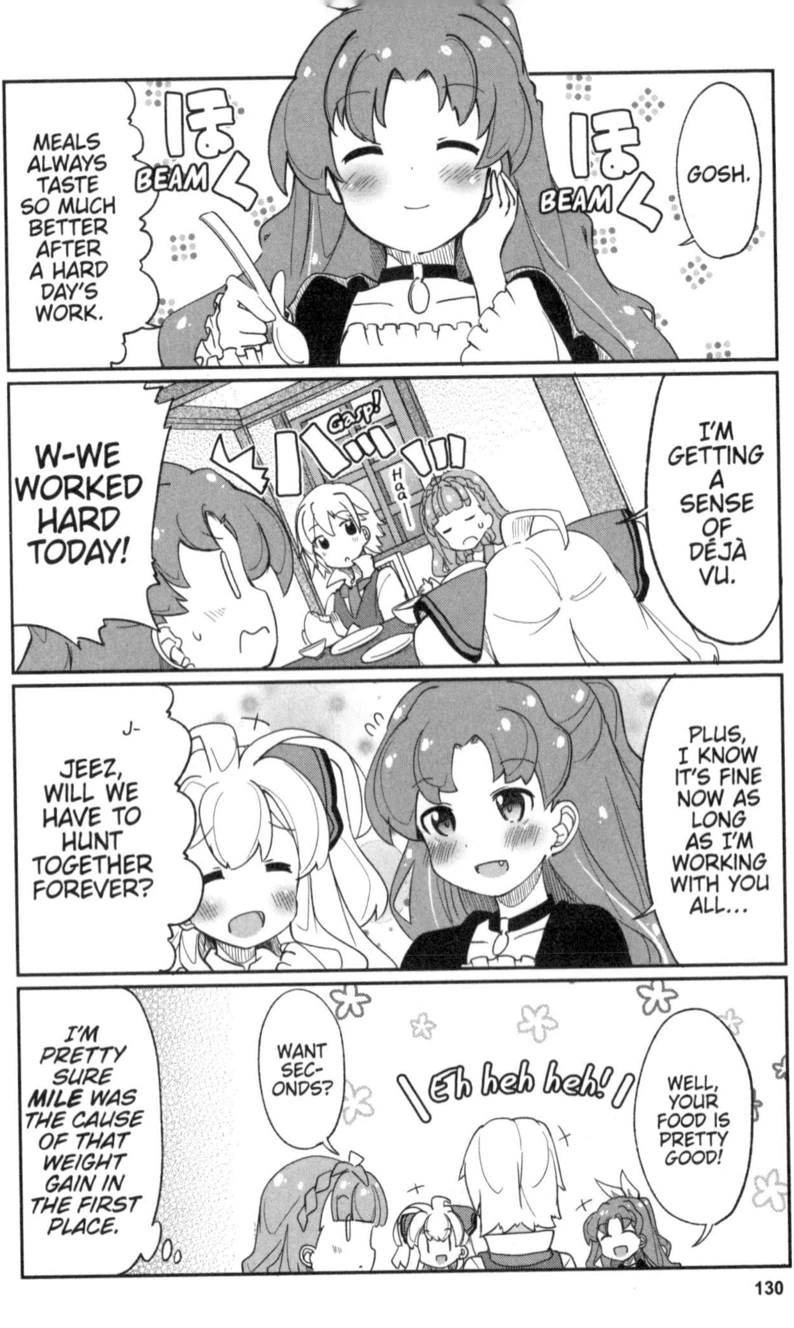
GOSH.
ほく BEAM
ほく BEAM
MEALS ALWAYS TASTE SO MUCH BETTER AFTER A HARD DAY'S WORK.
I'M GETTING A SENSE OF DÉJÀ VU.
Gasp!
Haa—
W-WE WORKED HARD TODAY!
PLUS, I KNOW IT'S FINE NOW AS LONG AS I'M WORKING WITH YOU ALL...
J-
JEEZ, WILL WE HAVE TO HUNT TOGETHER FOREVER?
WELL, YOUR FOOD IS PRETTY GOOD!
Eh heh heh!
WANT SEC-ONDS?
I'M PRETTY SURE MILE WAS THE CAUSE OF THAT WEIGHT GAIN IN THE FIRST PLACE.

Didn't I Say
to Make My
Abilities
Average in the
Next Life?!
EVERYDAY MISADVENTURES!

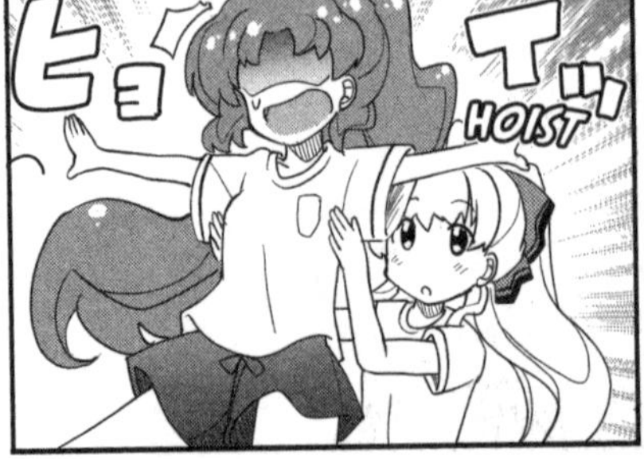
ヒョイッ
HOIST

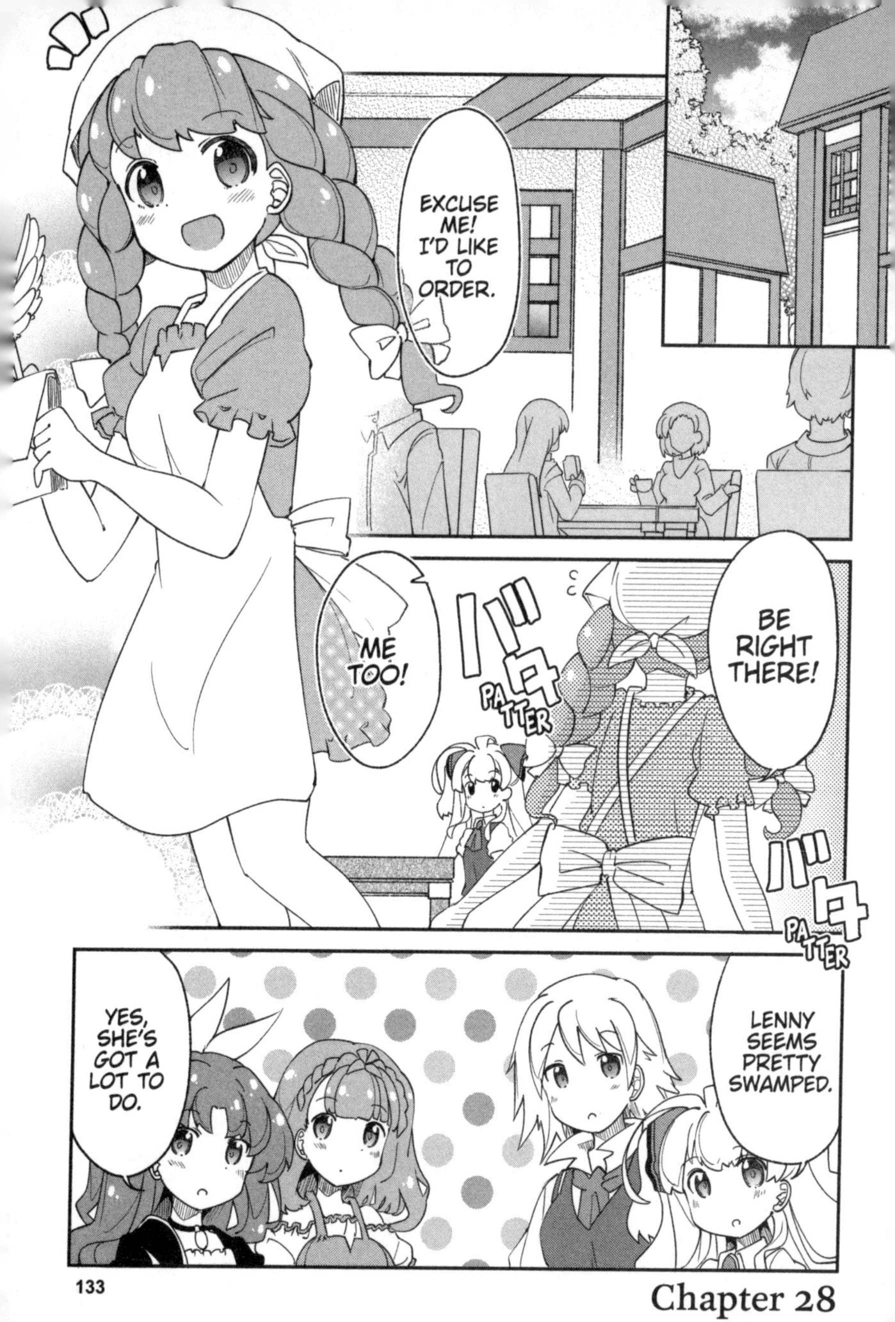
EXCUSE ME! I'D LIKE TO ORDER.
BE RIGHT THERE!
PATTER
ME TOO!
PATTER
LENNY SEEMS PRETTY SWAMPED.
YES, SHE'S GOT A LOT TO DO.

Chapter 28

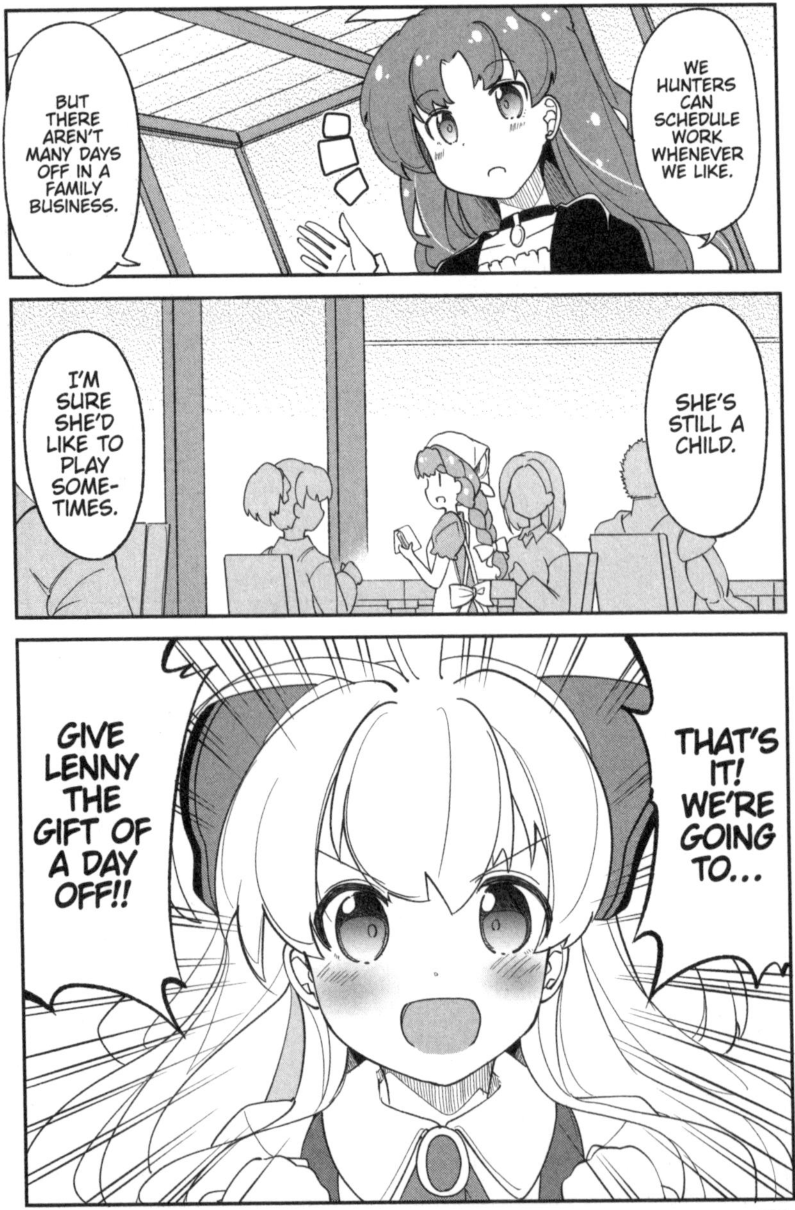
WE HUNTERS CAN SCHEDULE WORK WHENEVER WE LIKE.
BUT THERE AREN'T MANY DAYS OFF IN A FAMILY BUSINESS.
SHE'S STILL A CHILD.
I'M SURE SHE'D LIKE TO PLAY SOME-TIMES.
THAT'S IT! WE'RE GOING TO...
GIVE LENNY THE GIFT OF A DAY OFF!!

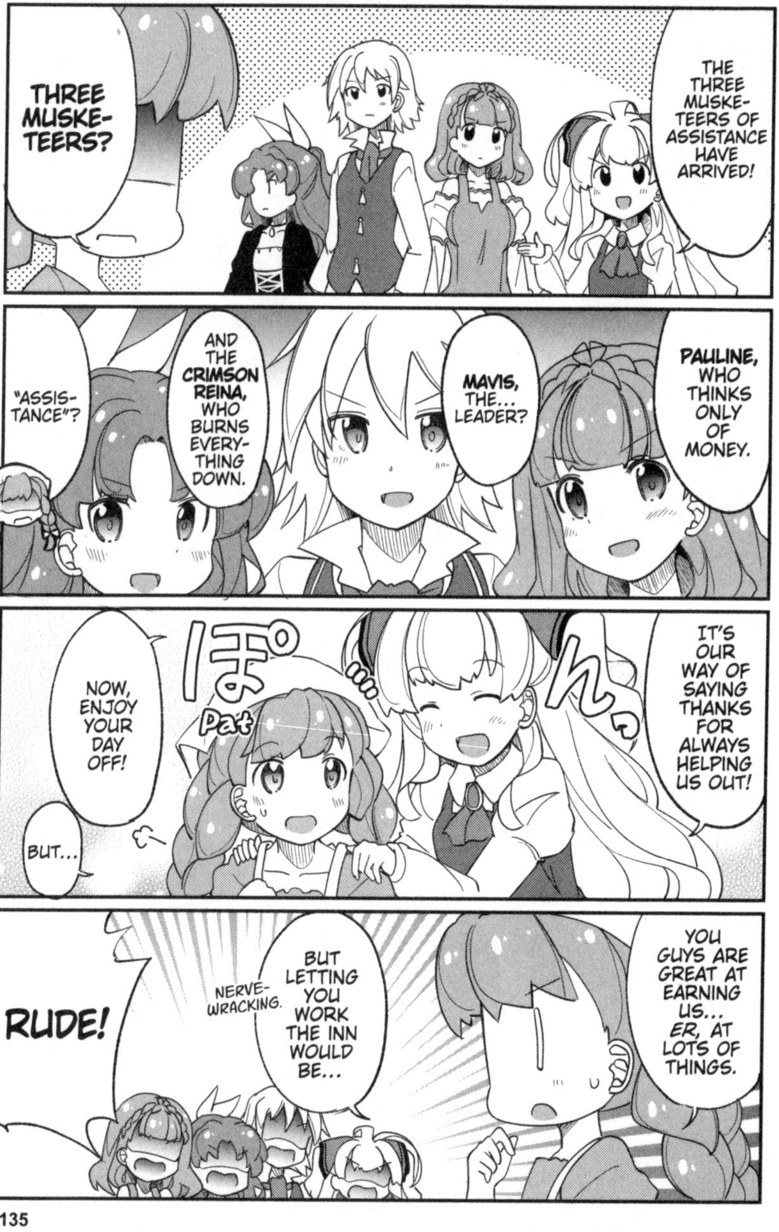
THE THREE MUSKETEERS OF ASSISTANCE HAVE ARRIVED!
THREE MUSKETEERS?
PAULINE, WHO THINKS ONLY OF MONEY.
MAVIS, THE... LEADER?
AND THE CRIMSON REINA, WHO BURNS EVERYTHING DOWN.
"ASSISTANCE"?
IT'S OUR WAY OF SAYING THANKS FOR ALWAYS HELPING US OUT!
ぽん
Pat
NOW, ENJOY YOUR DAY OFF!
BUT...
YOU GUYS ARE GREAT AT EARNING US... ER, AT LOTS OF THINGS.
BUT LETTING YOU WORK THE INN WOULD BE...
NERVE-WRACKING.
RUDE!

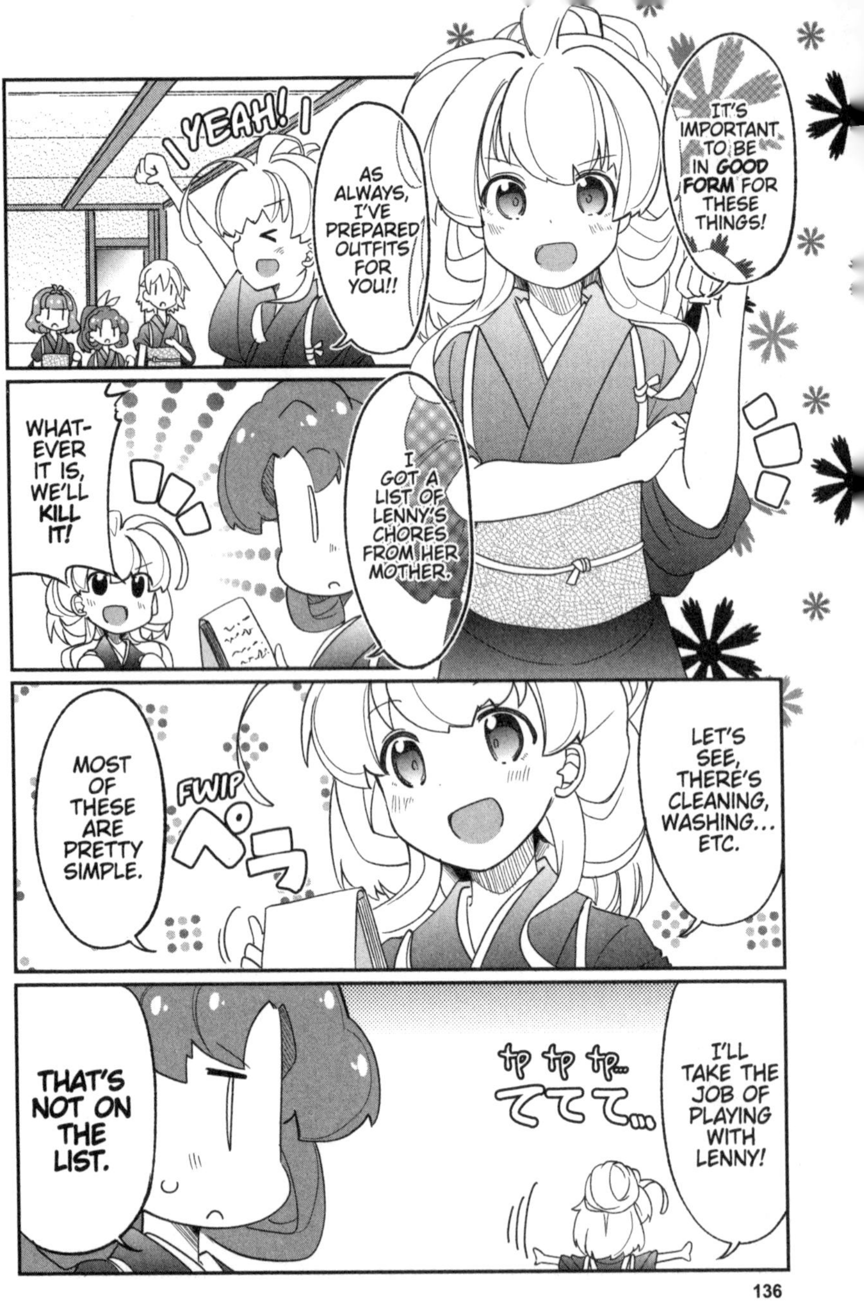
IT'S IMPORTANT TO BE IN GOOD FORM FOR THESE THINGS!
AS ALWAYS, I'VE PREPARED OUTFITS FOR YOU!!
YEAH!
I GOT A LIST OF LENNY'S CHORES FROM HER MOTHER.
WHAT-EVER IT IS, WE'LL KILL IT!
LET'S SEE, THERE'S CLEANING, WASHING... ETC.
FWIP
ペラ
MOST OF THESE ARE PRETTY SIMPLE.
I'LL TAKE THE JOB OF PLAYING WITH LENNY!
tp tp tp...
ててて...
THAT'S NOT ON THE LIST.

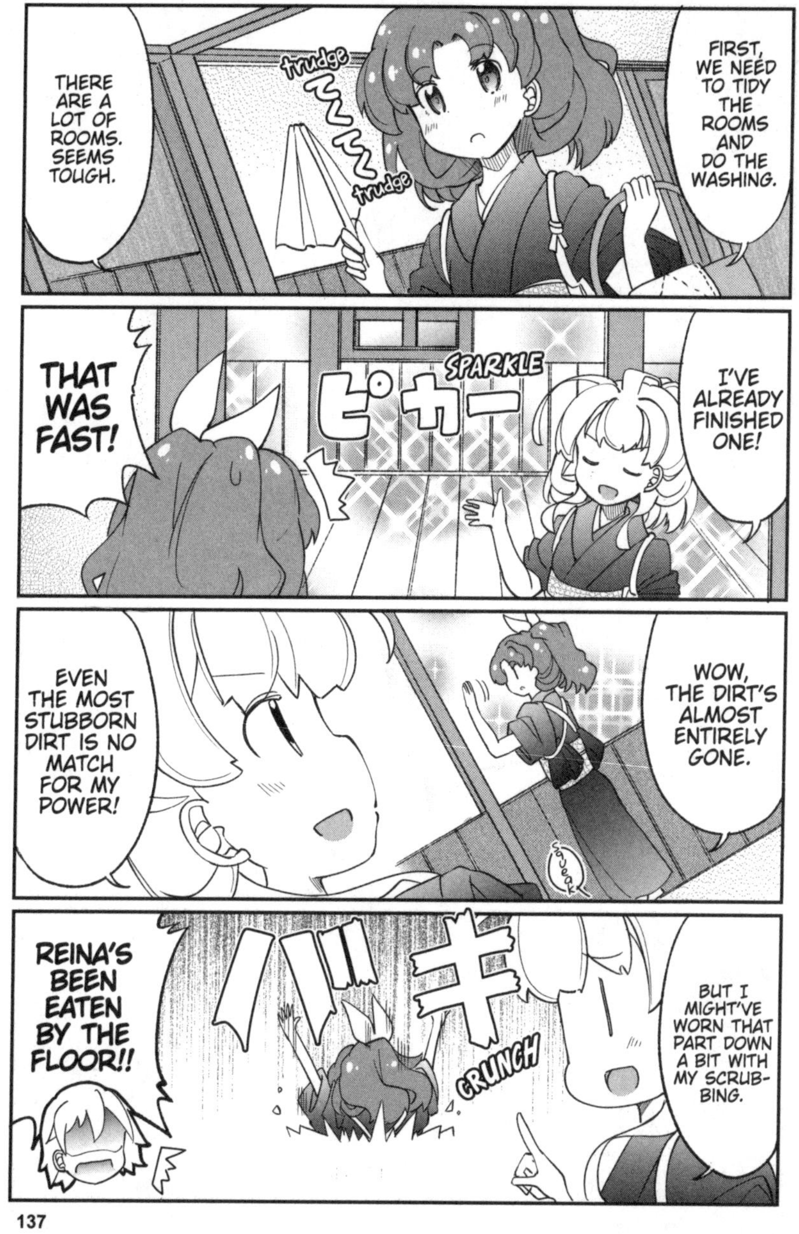
FIRST, WE NEED TO TIDY THE ROOMS AND DO THE WASHING.
trudge
trudge
THERE ARE A LOT OF ROOMS. SEEMS TOUGH.
I'VE ALREADY FINISHED ONE!
SPARKLE
THAT WAS FAST!
WOW, THE DIRT'S ALMOST ENTIRELY GONE.
squeak
EVEN THE MOST STUBBORN DIRT IS NO MATCH FOR MY POWER!
BUT I MIGHT'VE WORN THAT PART DOWN A BIT WITH MY SCRUB-BING.
CRUNCH
REINA'S BEEN EATEN BY THE FLOOR!!

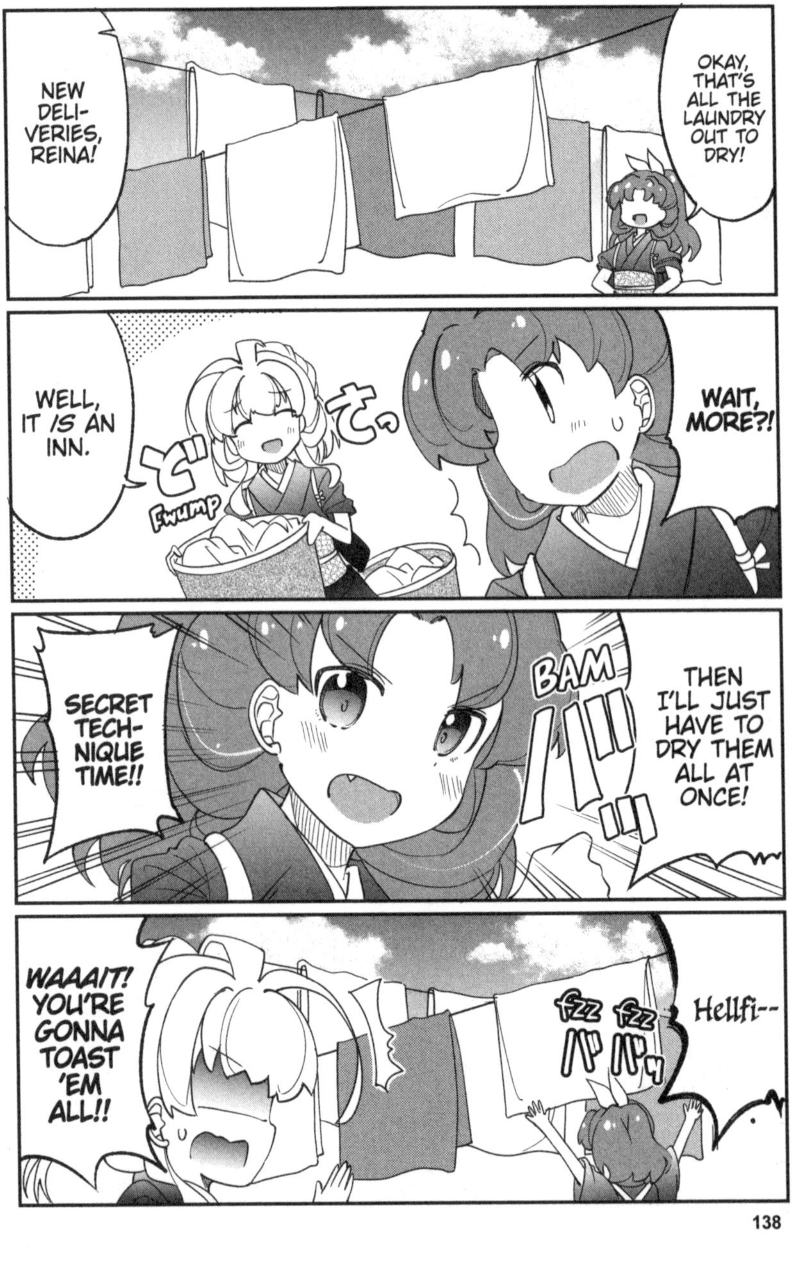
OKAY, THAT'S ALL THE LAUNDRY OUT TO DRY!
NEW DELI-VERIES, REINA!
WAIT, MORE?!
Fwump
WELL, IT *IS* AN INN.
THEN I'LL JUST HAVE TO DRY THEM ALL AT ONCE!
BAM
SECRET TECH-NIQUE TIME!!
Hellfi--
fzz fzz
WAAAIT! YOU'RE GONNA TOAST 'EM ALL!!

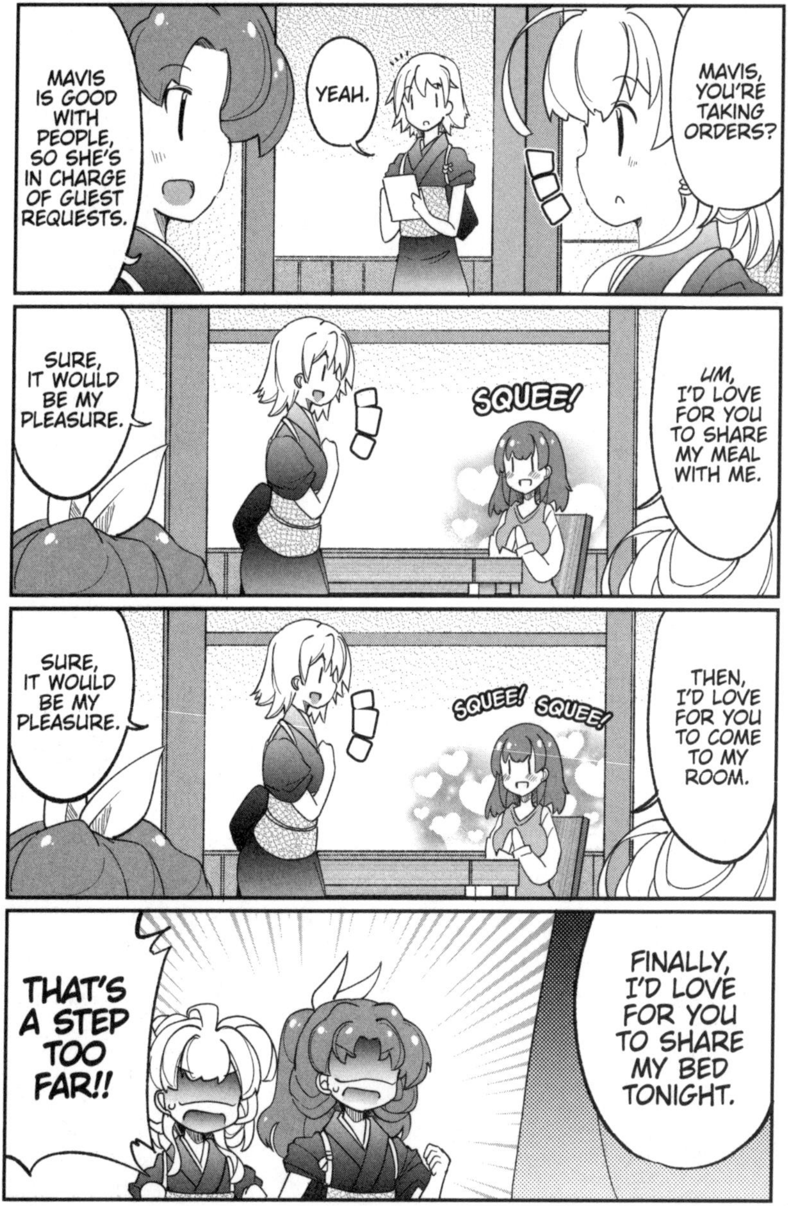
MAVIS, YOU'RE TAKING ORDERS?
YEAH.
MAVIS IS GOOD WITH PEOPLE, SO SHE'S IN CHARGE OF GUEST REQUESTS.
UM, I'D LOVE FOR YOU TO SHARE MY MEAL WITH ME.
SQUEE!
SURE, IT WOULD BE MY PLEASURE.
THEN, I'D LOVE FOR YOU TO COME TO MY ROOM.
SQUEE! SQUEE!
SURE, IT WOULD BE MY PLEASURE.
FINALLY, I'D LOVE FOR YOU TO SHARE MY BED TONIGHT.
THAT'S A STEP TOO FAR!!

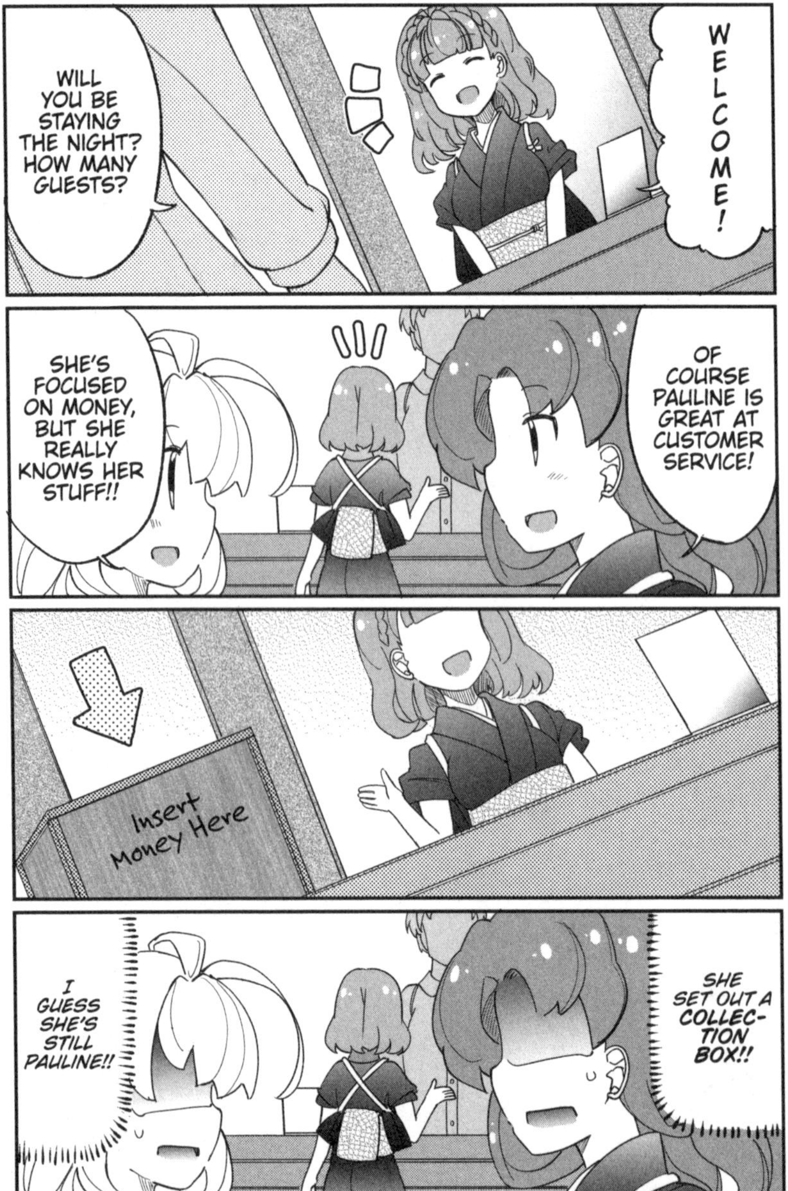
WELCOME!
WILL YOU BE STAYING THE NIGHT? HOW MANY GUESTS?
OF COURSE PAULINE IS GREAT AT CUSTOMER SERVICE!
SHE'S FOCUSED ON MONEY, BUT SHE REALLY KNOWS HER STUFF!!
Insert Money Here
SHE SET OUT A COLLEC-TION BOX!!
I GUESS SHE'S STILL PAULINE!!

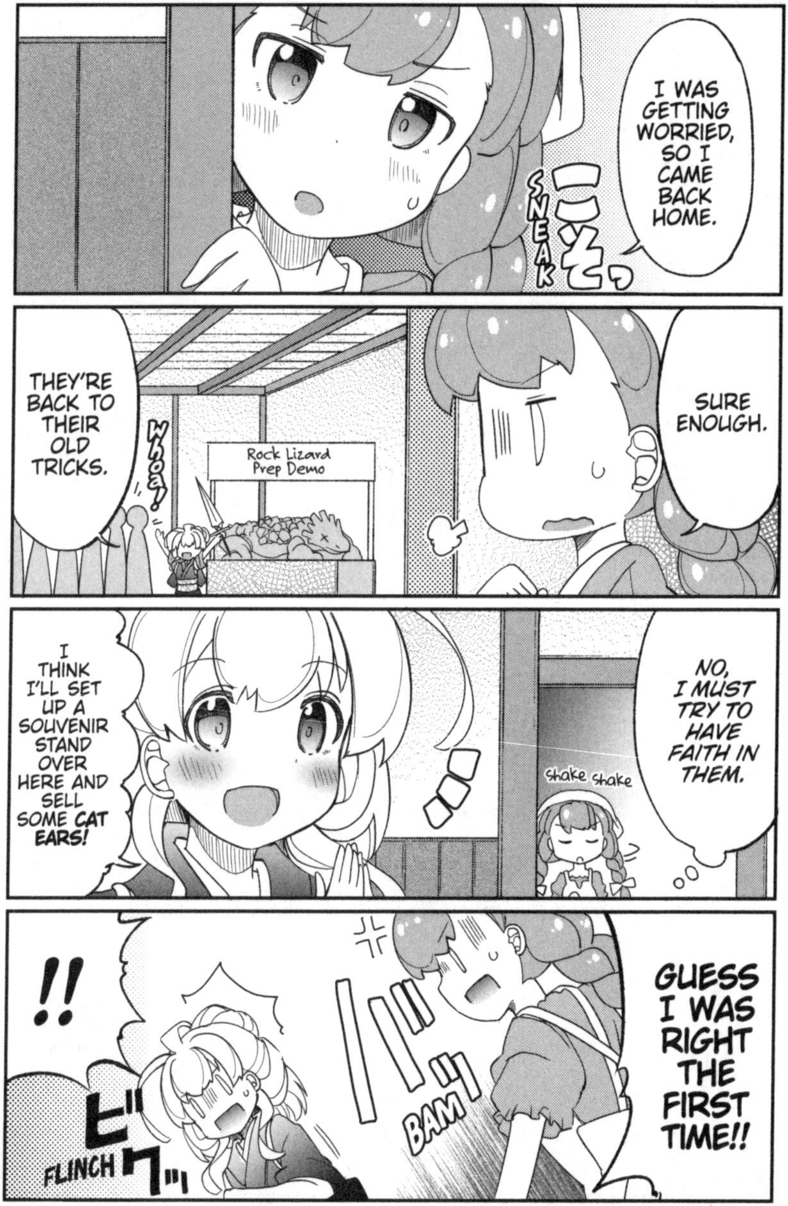

I WAS GETTING WORRIED, SO I CAME BACK HOME.
SNEAK
SURE ENOUGH.
THEY'RE BACK TO THEIR OLD TRICKS.
Rock Lizard Prep Demo
Whoa!
NO, I MUST TRY TO HAVE FAITH IN THEM.
Shake shake
I THINK I'LL SET UP A SOUVENIR STAND OVER HERE AND SELL SOME CAT EARS!
GUESS I WAS RIGHT THE FIRST TIME!!
BAM
!!
FLINCH

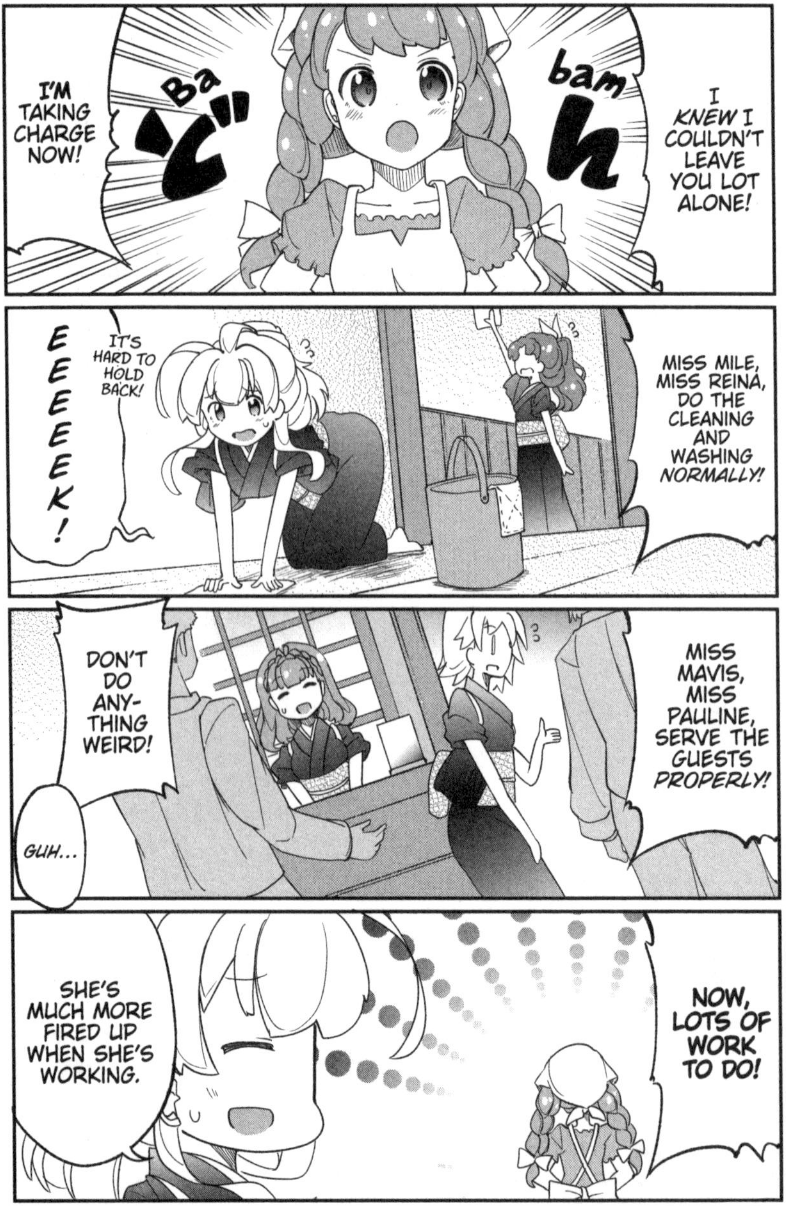

I KNEW I COULDN'T LEAVE YOU LOT ALONE!
Ba
bam
I'M TAKING CHARGE NOW!
MISS MILE, MISS REINA, DO THE CLEANING AND WASHING NORMALLY!
EEEEEEEK!
IT'S HARD TO HOLD BACK!
MISS MAVIS, MISS PAULINE, SERVE THE GUESTS PROPERLY!
DON'T DO ANYTHING WEIRD!
GUH...
NOW, LOTS OF WORK TO DO!
SHE'S MUCH MORE FIRED UP WHEN SHE'S WORKING.

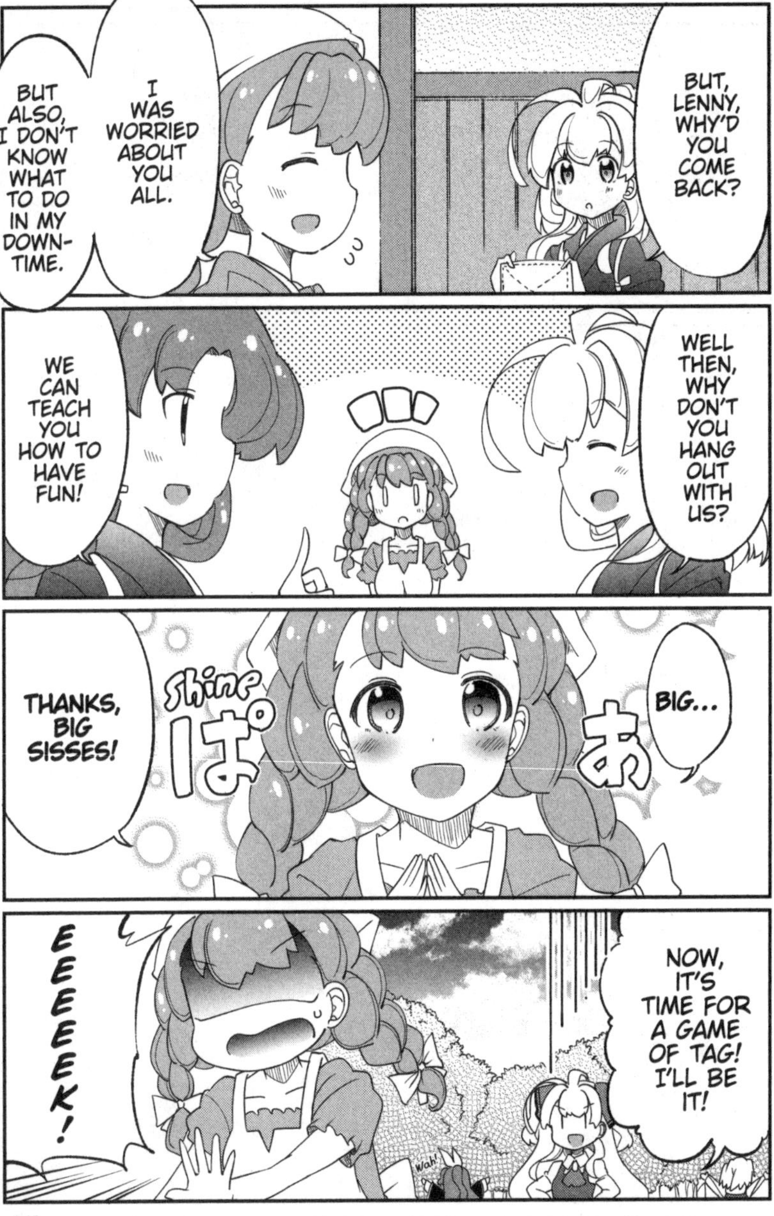
BUT, LENNY, WHY'D YOU COME BACK?
I WAS WORRIED ABOUT YOU ALL.
BUT ALSO, I DON'T KNOW WHAT TO DO IN MY DOWN-TIME.
WELL THEN, WHY DON'T YOU HANG OUT WITH US?
WE CAN TEACH YOU HOW TO HAVE FUN!
BIG...
あ
shine
ぱ
THANKS, BIG SISSES!
NOW, IT'S TIME FOR A GAME OF TAG! I'LL BE IT!
Wah!
EEEEEK!

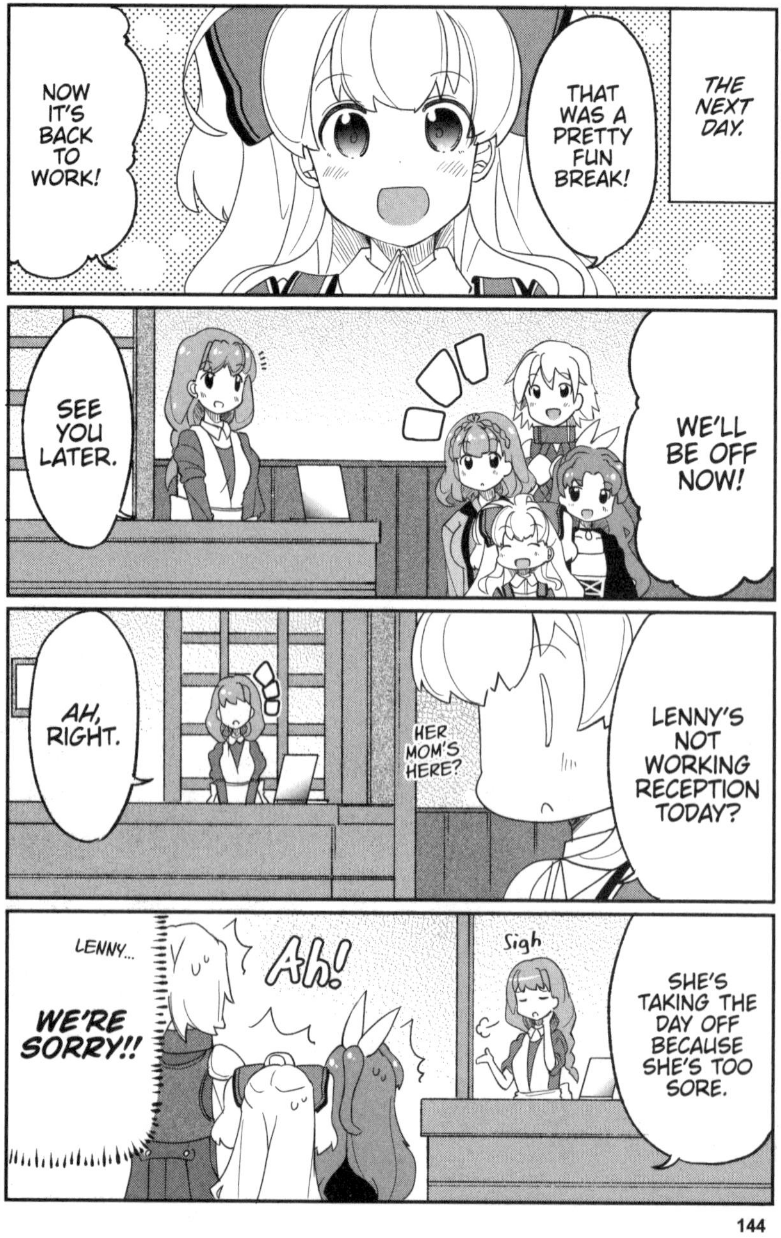
THE NEXT DAY.
THAT WAS A PRETTY FUN BREAK!
NOW IT'S BACK TO WORK!
WE'LL BE OFF NOW!
SEE YOU LATER.
LENNY'S NOT WORKING RECEPTION TODAY?
HER MOM'S HERE?
AH, RIGHT.
SHE'S TAKING THE DAY OFF BECAUSE SHE'S TOO SORE.
Sigh
Ah!
LENNY...
WE'RE SORRY!!

Didn't I Say to Make My Abilities Average in the Next Life?!

EVERYDAY MISADVENTURES!

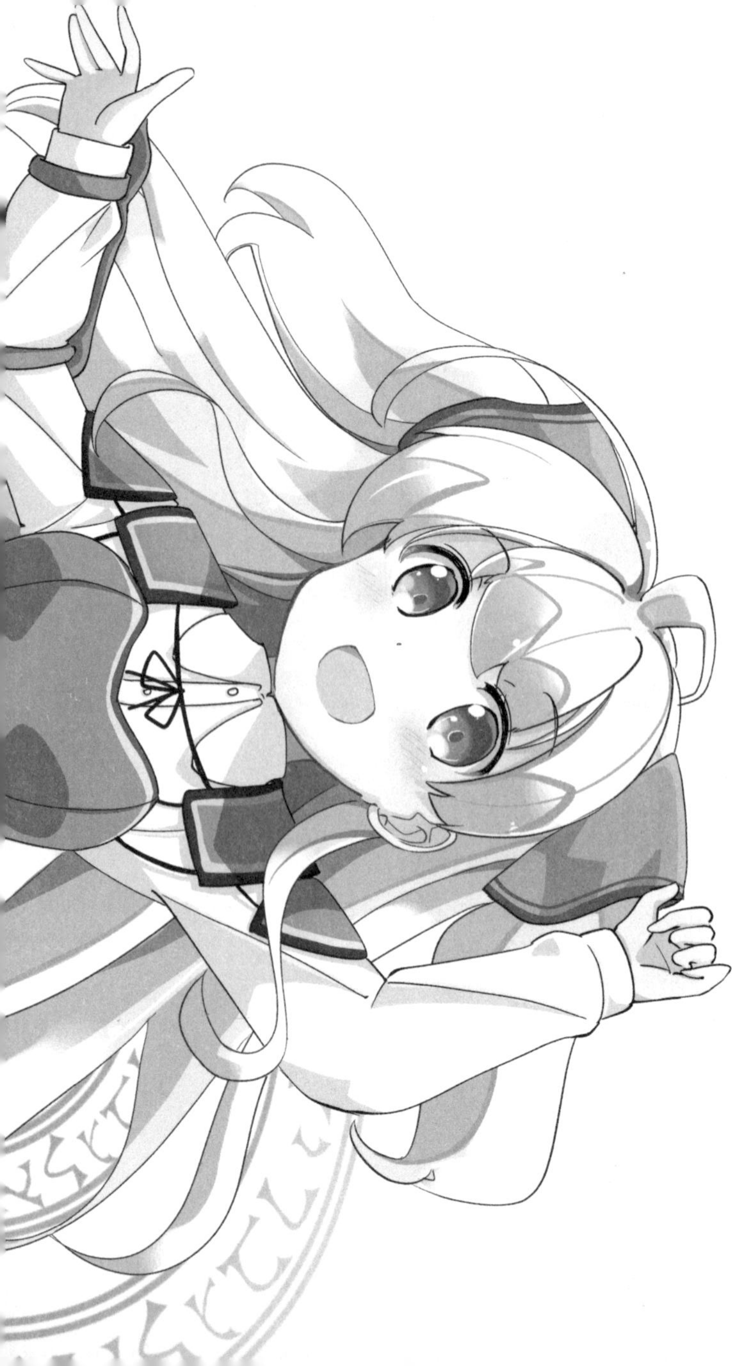

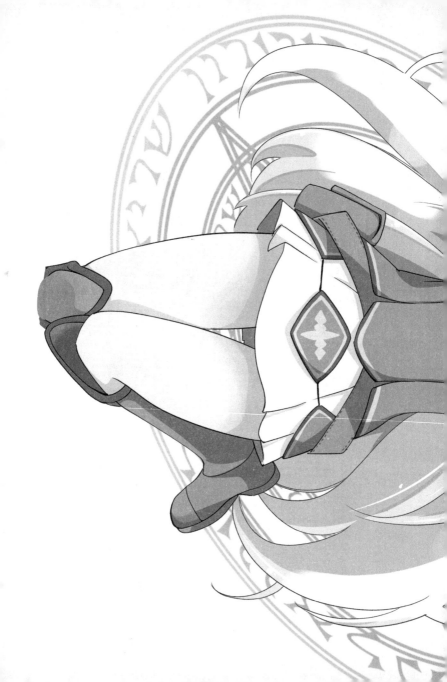

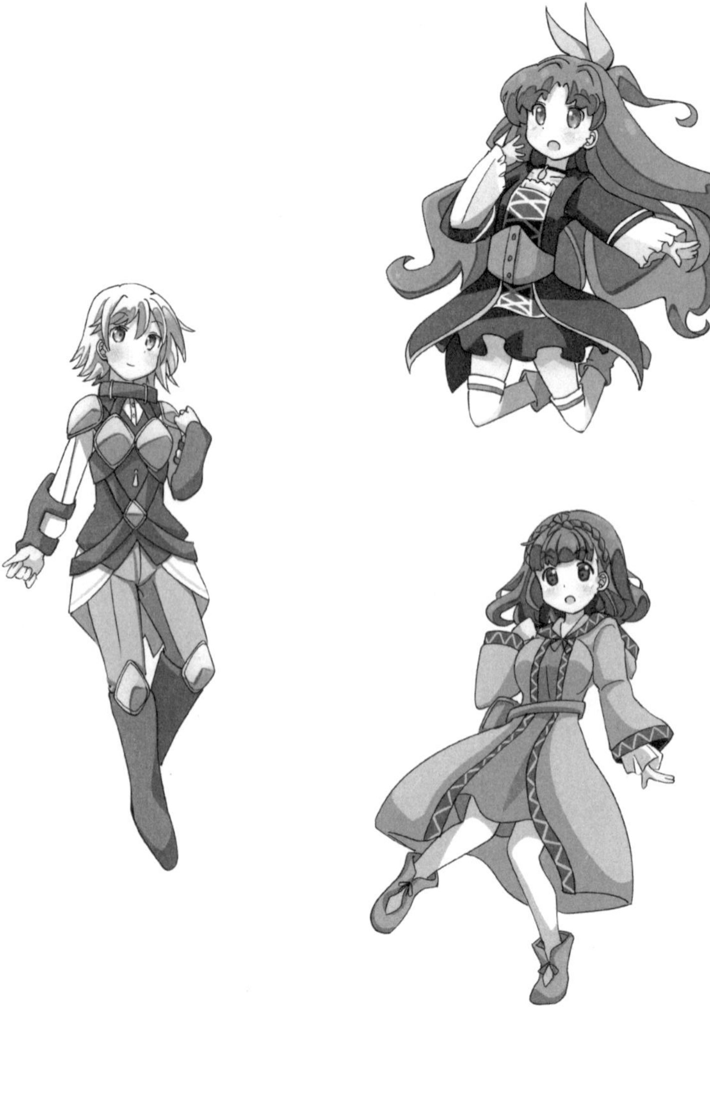

Didn't I Say
to Make My
Abilities
Average in the
Next Life?!
EVERYDAY MISADVENTURES!

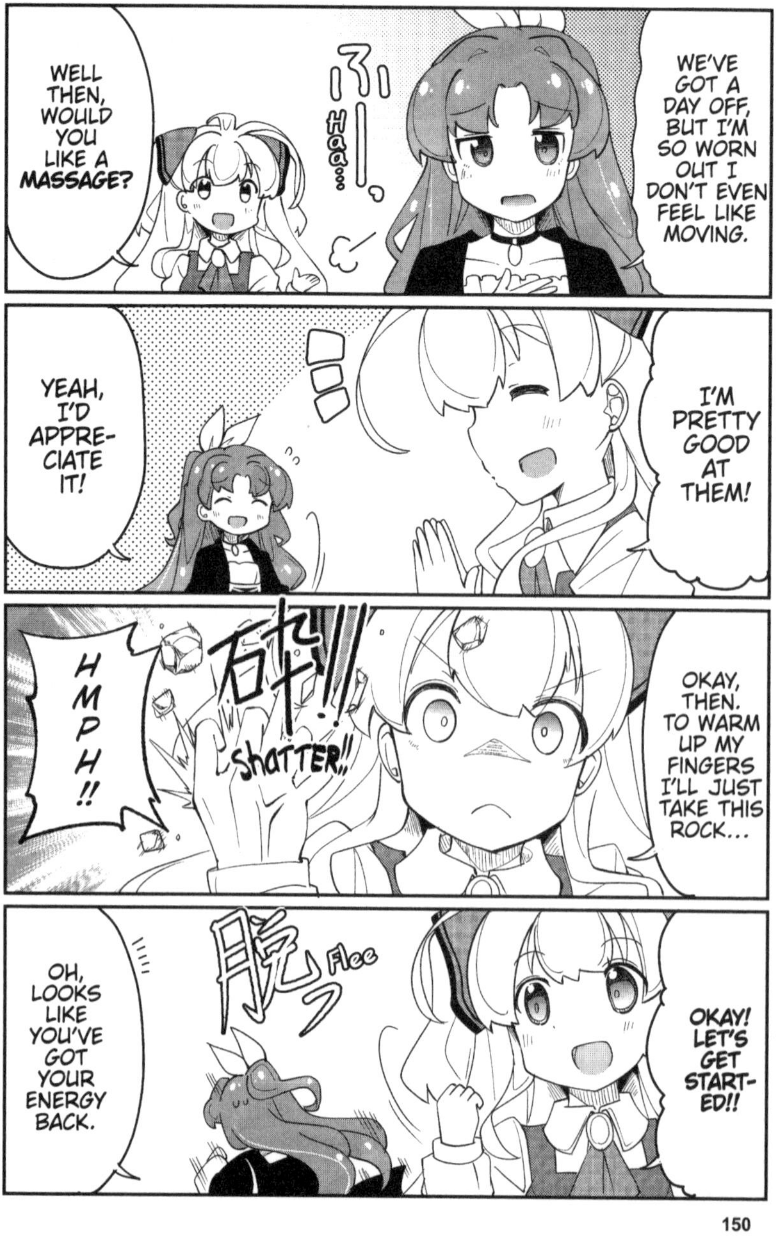
WE'VE GOT A DAY OFF, BUT I'M SO WORN OUT I DON'T EVEN FEEL LIKE MOVING.
ふー
Haa...
WELL THEN, WOULD YOU LIKE A MASSAGE?
I'M PRETTY GOOD AT THEM!
YEAH, I'D APPRECIATE IT!
OKAY, THEN. TO WARM UP MY FINGERS I'LL JUST TAKE THIS ROCK...
砕!!
SHATTER!!
HMPH!!
OKAY! LET'S GET STARTED!!
脱っ
Flee
OH, LOOKS LIKE YOU'VE GOT YOUR ENERGY BACK.

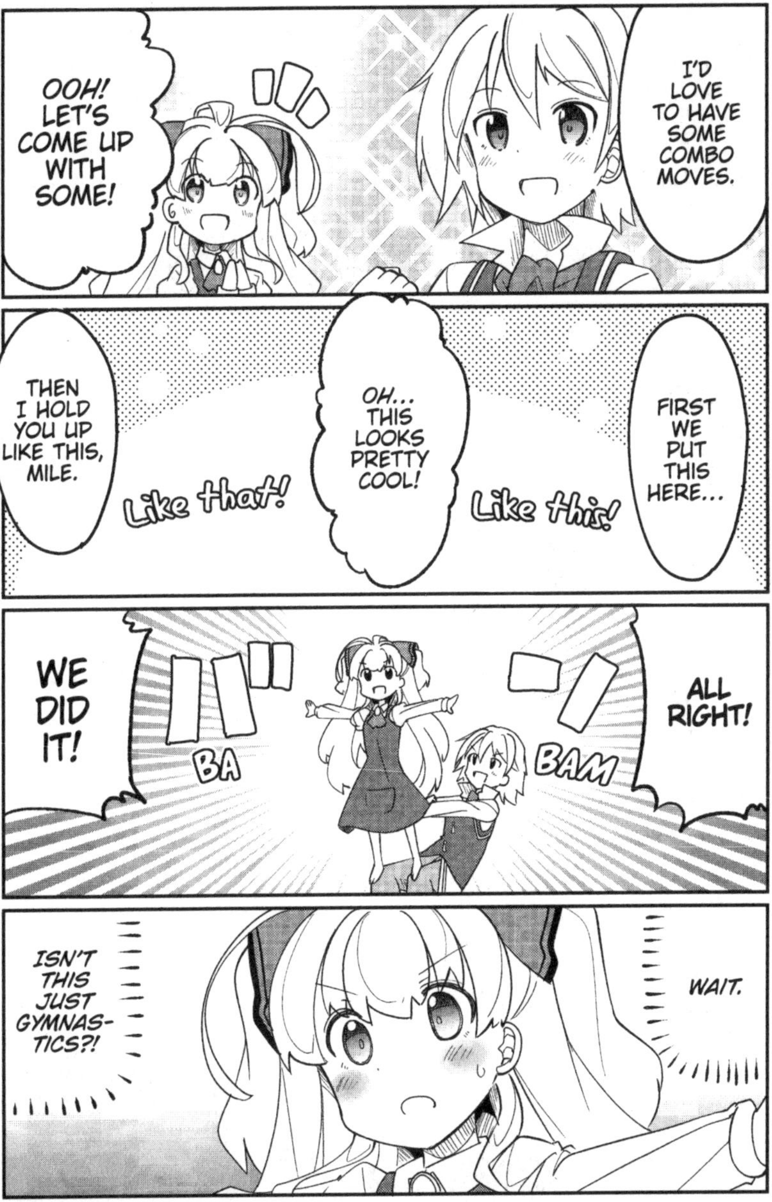
I'D LOVE TO HAVE SOME COMBO MOVES.
OOH! LET'S COME UP WITH SOME!
FIRST WE PUT THIS HERE...
Like this!
OH... THIS LOOKS PRETTY COOL!
Like that!
THEN I HOLD YOU UP LIKE THIS, MILE.
ALL RIGHT!
BA
BAM
WE DID IT!
WAIT.
ISN'T THIS JUST GYMNAS-TICS?!

Didn't I Say to Make My Abilities Average in the Next Life?!
EVERYDAY MISADVENTURES!